LAST CLASH
OF THE
TITANS

LAST CLASH OF THE TITANS

THE SECOND COMING OF HERCULES, LEVIATHAN, & THE PROPHESIED WAR BETWEEN JESUS CHRIST & THE GODS OF ANTIQUITY

DEREK P. GILBERT

DEFENDER

CRANE, MO

Last Clash of the Titans
Derek P. Gilbert

Defender Publishing
Crane, MO 65633 ©2018, this version by Thomas Horn

ISBN: 9781948014090

A CIP catalog record of this book is available from the Library of Congress.

Cover design by Jeffrey Mardis.

Unless otherwise noted, all Scripture from ESV.

CONTENTS

INTRODUCTION

As flies to wanton boys are we to th' gods;
they kill us for their sport.
—KING LEAR, ACT IV, SCENE I

The gods of Greek mythology are real. They're angry, and they're coming back.

Wait, you're thinking. *I thought this guy was a Christian.*

Exactly.

The Greek tales of their deities and demigods are bastardized versions of true history. Zeus is Satan. The Titans are the "sons of god [who] came in to the daughters of man." The heroes of the Golden Age were "the mighty men who were of old, the men of renown."

Now, let's be clear: We do not seek truth in the myths of Greece and Rome. We can, however, gain a deeper understanding of the Bible by viewing the world through the eyes of the prophets and apostles, and they knew very well what their pagan neighbors believed. Much of what they wrote was directed at the pagan gods.

If you were brought up in church, there's a good chance that, like me, you were taught that the idols of the pagans were lifeless blocks of wood and stone. That's true, to a point. The pagans didn't worship those carved images. An idol was like an antenna, a spiritual receiver that gave a god locality—a place to appear when the faithful called.

Those gods, though—they're real.

That's not the default teaching of most Christian churches. Sadly, most are out of step with the God they serve. *God* called the idols gods, so I'm on solid theological ground here. He's judged them, found them wanting, and proclaimed a sentence of death on these rebels.

But they're not dead yet. And just as you and I have free will to choose between right and wrong, so do they. God, who has seen the end from the beginning, has revealed enough about their plans through prophecy in the Bible to tell us that the ride on earth will get rough before Christ returns. Reading those prophecies with a better understanding of what the Hebrew prophets knew about the pagan gods reveals some startling insights about what lies ahead.

In this book, I will present evidence for a number of claims, most of which haven't been made before, to the best of my knowledge:

The Amorites of the ancient world are far more important to history than we've been taught.

The Titans, the old gods of the Greeks, are the biblical Watchers, the sons of God who took daughters of man as wives as described in Genesis 6:1–4.

Their offspring, the Nephilim (later called Rephaim), were the heroes and demigods of the Greeks.

The Amorites summoned the spirits of the Rephaim through necromancy rituals and believed they were the ancestors of their kings.

Balaam's prophecy over Israel foretold the final destruction of the Nephilim by the Messiah.

Ezekiel's prophecy of Gog and Magog tells us when and where they'll be destroyed.

Gog won't be human, and Magog is not Russia.

The spirit of primordial chaos, Leviathan, returns from the abyss as the Antichrist.

The Titans and their seed, the spirits of the Rephaim, return in the last days to fight at Armageddon.

As you may have noticed, this book focuses on the supernatural play-ers of the end times. We spend too much time debating whether Vladimir Putin is Gog and not enough trying to discern the principalities and pow-ers behind the scenes.

Now, I could be wrong about much of this. However, my analysis is backed by peer-reviewed, academic research. Most of it comes from secu-lar scholars with no dog in the eschatological hunt. They've found many of the pieces of the puzzle, but they don't see the whole picture because the missing pieces are in the Bible—and most of those scholars just won't look there.

Likewise, many learned students and scholars of the Bible don't look to secular academia for information. We Christians do see the big picture, but much of the background image is missing. There is no context for the crossing of the Red Sea, the march around the walls of Jericho, or the confrontation between Elijah and the priests of Baal. Why did God ask such things of His people? There are answers to those questions rooted in the history, culture, and religion of the people who lived in the lands of the Bible during the age of the prophets and apostles.

Is understanding that context essential to your eternal salvation? No. If you've accepted Jesus Christ as your Lord and Savior, your future is secure.

But understanding how the pagan gods of the ancient world have suc-cessfully rebranded themselves as action heroes for major motion pictures might be useful to reaching the lost. As Baudelaire wrote, "The finest trick of the devil is to persuade you that he does not exist." Recent research shows that nearly 60 percent of American Christians have fallen for that lie.[1] God's statement is as true today as it was 2,700 years ago: "My people are destroyed for lack of knowledge."[2] How do you resist an enemy you think is make-believe?

Zeus, Herakles, the Olympians, and the Titans are real. They hate us, they want to kill us, and they're coming back.

Get ready.

BACKGROUND

If you think the Bible is boring, you've probably been taught that most of the characters in it are imaginary.

Think about it. If you've been led to believe that the greatest enemy of God and His creation, the devil, is just a philosophical concept that represents the evil that men do, then what's the big deal about the Bible? Evil is on display every time we turn on cable news. What can the Bible tell us that we don't already know?

But what if the devil is real? And what if it's worse than that—what if he's got minions?

News flash: the truth is a *lot* worse than that. There isn't just one supernatural rebel; there are at least *hundreds* of the Fallen. They're very old, they're supernaturally intelligent, and they hate you. They *really* hate you. They want to kill you and everyone you love. And useful idiots in the media, Hollywood, and the education system have been doing PR for these foul creatures for generations.

Your children and grandchildren are soaking in a toxic bath of their sweet-smelling lies. Unless you've been talking with them about this since they were young, they don't realize they're being lied to. You may not realize it. The religion of the pagans that the prophets condemned more than two thousand years ago is now served up as wholesome family entertainment.

Fifty years ago, comic books were full of propaganda for the Fallen. The gods themselves were redrawn as characters for the comics, especially Thor and the Norse pantheon, although just about every one of the gods of the ancient world has appeared in Marvel or DC Comics at some point. Other superheroes are thinly veiled analogues for ancient deities. And since comic book heroes, like "babyface" professional wrestlers, play out soap-opera storylines while wearing Spandex costumes, fans get caught up in the drama and forget that their heroes are based on entities that God has judged and condemned to death—*because they want to destroy the human race.*

Take Herakles (or Hercules, if you prefer): He was worshiped from at least the time of Solomon until 200 B.C. or later, more than eight hundred years. The Phoenicians and Carthaginians called him Melqart, and he was the patron god of Tyre at the time that city's most famous daughter, Jezebel, was Ahab's queen in Israel. That means the Baal, which simply means "lord," of Jezebel was probably Herakles. And that means the 450 prophets of Baal slaughtered on Mount Carmel after their showdown with the Hebrew prophet Elijah were probably priests of Herakles.

If Herakles was a historic person and truly was the half-divine son of a god (Zeus, the Greek storm-god), then by definition he was one of the Nephilim. According to the Book of Enoch, Herakles would have died in the Flood of Noah, which means his spirit, like those of his demigod brothers and cousins, wanders the earth as a demon to this day.

But today, he's best known as a Disney cartoon.

Rebranding the Titans

The so-called imaginary characters of the ancient world have been repackaged and rebranded. An entire subculture of young adult fiction is mining ancient religion for characters and plots. In the spring of 2017, Disney's publishing division announced a new fiction imprint featuring the work of best-selling author Rick Riordan, who's created five series based on the old gods aimed at young readers: *Percy Jackson and the Olympians*, featuring the demigod son of Poseidon; *Magnus Chase and the Gods of Asgard*, featuring a homeless boy from Boston who meets the Norse gods and discovers his true identity; the *Kane Chronicles*, featuring two teenage siblings who discover that they're descended from powerful magicians, and only they have the power to set things right when the gods of ancient Egypt are accidentally let loose upon the world; the *Trials of Apollo*, in which the god is cast down from Olympus after angering his father, Zeus, to find himself a regular teenage boy in New York City; and now *The Heroes of Olympus*, which introduces a whole new generation of demigods.

For all of these series, Disney helpfully offers teacher guides to encourage kids to discuss how awesome life would be as a demigod. Seriously. One of the classroom activities is for kids to research which god or goddess they'd most like to be related to. So far, Riordan's series, aimed at middle-school readers, have been translated into forty-two languages and sold more than thirty million copies in the U.S. alone.

Now, I don't want to demonize Rick Riordan. He is not the problem. Nor is he the only manifestation of it.

The premise of the longest-running sci-fi series on television, *Stargate SG-1*, and the movie that spawned it, is the idea that the gods of the ancient world were aliens. The deities of the Norse, the Egyptians, and, to a lesser degree, the gods of the Celts and the ancient Near East were presented as alien races with technology so advanced it looked supernatural.

As my coauthor Josh Peck and I argued in *The Day the Earth Stands Still*, this concept comes right out of gnostic and New Age teachings from the likes of Helena Petrovna Blavatsky and Aleister Crowley, which were filtered through the horror fiction of authors like H. P. Lovecraft and then distilled by ancient alien evangelists like Erich von Däniken and Zecharia Sitchin. The deception is simple: If the old gods were just aliens with better gizmos, then we, too, can be as gods. That lie worked in Eden and it still works today.

How could this happen? In part, through education. Our schools taught us that the gods of ancient Greece and Rome were invented by our primitive distant ancestors to make sense of the world around them. Meanwhile, academia has decided that God was created as part of the national back story of a nomadic people who emerged in the Levant around the fourteenth century B.C. and set up a nation-state they called Israel.

So, since all those gods were imaginary, what's the harm of using Thor, Zeus, and Hercules as fodder for entertainment?

Well, none, unless the thought of eternity in the Lake of Fire bothers you.

Our churches have failed to teach us, or maybe we didn't take things seriously enough in Sunday school. Regardless of what our various denominations officially believe, surveys show that most American Christians don't think Satan and the Holy Spirit are real—much less Baal, Ishtar, Marduk, Chemosh, Dagon, Molech, and the rest. It's impossible to fight an enemy that you believe is imaginary.

Thank God we don't send our soldiers into battle with such bad intel.

Here's the truth: Since the Bible is the Word of God, we need to stop editing out the parts that make us uncomfortable, starting with the way we think about the old gods of the ancient world. *God Himself* called them gods. Who are we to say different?

Many key events in the Bible—the Red Sea crossing, the timing of the attack on Jericho, the confrontation on Mount Carmel, the Transfiguration on Mount Hermon, Jesus' practice of casting out demons, and more—were specifically directed at these supernatural rebels. He considered these fallen gods enough of a problem that He passed judgment on them in the divine council and sentenced them to death.[3]

If God takes them that seriously, why don't we?

Modern archaeology is literally digging up evidence of the reality behind the ancient myths of Greece and Rome. Those stories were based on history recorded in the Bible. And that ancient reality is tied to end-times Bible prophecy.

I thought the documented connection between the Titans, the old gods of the Greeks, and necromancy rituals of the Canaanites would be the big "wow" in my previous book. Maybe because I found Greek mythology so fascinating when I was younger, documenting the connection between the Titans and the Rephaim of the Bible was, to me, a bombshell.

You see, the old gods of Greece and Rome are not only real and plotting against God and man; they're coming back. The world is heading toward a prophesied final showdown between these entities and their Creator—the Last Clash of the Titans.

Literally.

Genesis 6

If you're already familiar with the teaching that the giants of Genesis 6 were really giants, then this will be old news. Please bear with me. For the benefit of readers new to the concept, we can't skip over this. While this may be repetitious to you, the majority of the Christian world still believes that the first four verses of Genesis chapter 6 can't possibly mean what they say.

To be fair, they are pretty hard to take at face value when you've been raised to believe that science is the only reliable tool for finding truth:

> When man began to multiply on the face of the land and daughters were born to them, the sons of God saw that the daughters of man were attractive. And they took as their wives any they chose. Then the LORD said, "My Spirit shall not abide in man forever, for he is flesh: his days shall be 120 years."
>
> The Nephilim were on the earth in those days, and also afterward, when the sons of God came in to the daughters of man and they bore children to them. These were the mighty men who were of old, the men of renown. (Genesis 6:1–4, ESV)

It's important to note that the phrase rendered "sons of God" in Genesis 6:1 (Hebrew: *bene ha elohim*) means angelic beings. It does not refer to godly men of the line of Seth, which is the traditional explanation for this passage. Somehow, the church has accepted the notion that the union of good men who descended from Seth and bad women from the line of Cain produced Nephilim.

The logic of that line of thinking is unclear. Why were all the Sethite boys good and all the Cainite girls bad? Why would good boys and bad girls produce Nephilim? What made the Nephilim mighty men of renown? Why did later Jews and early Christians think the Nephilim were giants? What happened when good Sethite girls had children with bad Cainite boys?

The two surviving sons of Adam and Eve are mentioned nowhere in Genesis 6, so reading Seth and Cain into an interpretation of the passage is going way outside the text to avoid weird, uncomfortable questions about how angels and humans could mate. It's understandable; Jesus said in Matthew 22:30, "For in the resurrection they neither marry nor are given in marriage, but are like angels in heaven." Doesn't that mean it's physically impossible for angels to procreate?

Yes, He did say that, and no, that's not exactly what it means. Note the key words, "in heaven." The sons of God in Genesis 6 weren't *in* Heaven. And we know from other stories in Scripture that angels have physical form and do human things—for example, when the three men, two of whom are clearly angels (the third was Yahweh Himself), visited Abraham and Sarah and ate a meal. (Besides, you're old enough to know that marriage isn't required for a couple to have children.)

Bottom line: Nothing in the Bible tells us that fathering children is beyond the power of angels—especially when the Bible plainly says they did.

Who or what, then, were the Nephilim? They're only mentioned twice in the Bible. The other reference is in Numbers, when Moses sends spies into Canaan to scout out the land that God had decreed for them.

So they brought to the people of Israel a bad report of the land that they had spied out, saying, "The land, through which we have gone to spy it out, is a land that devours its inhabitants, and all the people that we saw in it are of great height. And there we saw the Nephilim (the sons of Anak, who come from the Nephilim), and we seemed to ourselves like grasshoppers, and so we seemed to them." (Numbers 13:32–33, ESV)

It's clear from the context that the Nephilim were unusually large. The Anakim and their progenitor, Anak, are mentioned a handful of times in the Old Testament, and they are described as giants:

Hear, O Israel: you are to cross over the Jordan today, to go in to dispossess nations greater and mightier than yourselves, cities great and fortified up to heaven, a people great and tall, the sons of the Anakim, whom you know, and of whom you have heard it said, "Who can stand before the sons of Anak?" (Deuteronomy 9:1–2, ESV)

We'll deal with the Anakim in more detail in a later chapter when we analyze Joshua's military strategy for the conquest of Canaan. As you'll see, they were an important enough enemy that you can think of the campaign as Joshua's war against the giants.

And in keeping with the theme of this book—that archaeology backs up the Bible—we'll note here that the giants were enough of a nuisance to the Egyptians that they called on their gods to curse the Anakim:

The Ruler of Iy'anaq, Erum, and all the retainers who are with him; the Ruler of Iy'anaq, Abi-Yamimu and all the retainers who are with him; the Ruler of Iy'anaq 'Akirum and the retainers who are with him.[4]

Anaq is an Egyptian transliteration of Anak, the eponymous founder of the tribe that was the target of Joshua's campaign. The formulaic curse cited above is from the Execration Texts, which were sort of the ancient Egyptian equivalent of voodoo dolls. The names of enemies would be inscribed in clay, sometimes in the shape of a small person, but often just a pot or flat piece of clay, which would then be ritually cursed and smashed. (God bless the scholars who pieced those things back together for translation!)

We don't know who Erum, Abi-Yamimu, or 'Akirum were, or why the Egyptians wanted them cursed, but the text establishes that the Anakim lived somewhere in Canaan during the nineteenth or eighteenth century B.C., the time of Isaac and Jacob. We'll get into why God wanted these descendants of the Nephilim removed from the land as this story unfolds.

As for the Watchers, their fate was sealed. Although the Bible doesn't tell us much about what happened to them, what we do know doesn't sound pleasant:

> And the angels who did not stay within their own position of authority, but left their proper dwelling, he has kept in eternal chains under gloomy darkness until the judgment of the great day. (Jude 6, ESV)

> For if God did not spare angels when they sinned, but cast them into hell and committed them to chains of gloomy darkness to be kept until the judgment. (2 Peter 2:4, ESV)

These passages are critical to understanding the supernatural war because they identify the players. The Greek word Peter used to describe the punishment of the rebellious angels, the word translated into English as "cast them into hell," is *tartaróō*. More precisely, it means "cast them into Tartarus." This is key.

Tartarus is not the same place as Hell, which was Hades in Greek. Since he was guided by the Holy Spirit, we can assume Peter knew the difference. And because this is the only verse in the New Testament that uses the word *tartaróō*, it's significant.

To the Greeks, Hades was the realm of the dead, similar to the Jewish concept of Sheol. Tartarus was a level below Hades reserved for supernatural threats to the Olympian gods, "as far beneath Hades as heaven is above earth."[5] It's where the king of the Greek gods, Zeus, banished his father, Kronos, and most of the Titans after the Olympians successful rebellion. It's described as a dismal place, even more depressing than damp, moldy Hades:

[The hundred-handed Hekatonkheires] overshadowed the Titans with their missiles, and hurled them beneath the wide-pathed earth, and bound them in bitter chains when they had conquered them by their strength for all their great spirit, **as far beneath the earth as heaven is above earth; for so far is it from earth to Tartarus.** For a brazen anvil falling down from heaven nine nights and days would reach the earth upon the tenth: and again, a brazen anvil falling from earth nine nights and days would reach Tartarus upon the tenth. Round it runs a fence of bronze, and night spreads in triple line all about it like a neck-circlet, while above grow the roots of the earth and unfruitful sea.[6] (Emphasis added)

Note the parallels between the words of the Greek poet Hesiod and the epistles of Peter and Jude: A group of gods rebelled and suffered the consequences—imprisonment in a very dark place far below the earth.

Here's the point: Under the inspiration of the Holy Spirit, the Apostle Peter specifically linked the angels who sinned with the former gods of the Greeks, the Titans. We know Peter's angels are the Watchers, the sons of God from Genesis chapter 6, because they're clearly the same ones mentioned by Jude, who gave us an important clue to their identity:

And the angels who did not stay within their own position of authority, but left their proper dwelling, he has kept in eternal chains under gloomy darkness until the judgment of the great day—**just as Sodom and Gomorrah and the surrounding cities,**

which likewise indulged in sexual immorality and pursued unnatural desire, serve as an example by undergoing a punishment of eternal fire. (Jude 6–7, ESV; emphasis added)

The sin of the angels was like that of Sodom and Gomorrah—"sexual immorality" and "unnatural desire." The only place in the Bible where that happened was Genesis 6:1–4.

So, the Watchers of Genesis are the Titans of Greek myth. And those fallen angels still have a role to play in our future.

People in and around ancient Israel continued to worship those old gods into the classical period, the time of Jesus and the apostles. Some of them believed their kings descended from the old gods. They even summoned those gods and the spirits of their half-breed children in rituals.

In our modern world, we're liable to look at religions like this and pity the poor fools who trusted imaginary demons and deities to give them power. But God took them seriously. As we'll see, there are things we do in our churches and homes *to this day* in response to the rituals and practices of the pagan neighbors of ancient Israel.

You see, God saw all of this from the beginning of time. And He apparently enjoys reversing the rituals of the ancient pagans to demonstrate who truly is sovereign over all Creation.

Deuteronomy 32

The other bit of background we need to cover is the aftermath of the Tower of Babel incident. In my previous book, *The Great Inception*, I explained why Babel was not at Babylon and why God was compelled to stop its construction. In a nutshell, the tower was an artificial "mount of assembly" to serve as an "abode of the gods." The consequences of Nimrod's public works project have affected the earth to this day.

We all know that God confused the language of the workers, which made it impossible for things to continue. What isn't taught, because most English translations of the Bible hide it, is the *other* thing God did:

When the Most High gave to the nations their inheritance, when he divided mankind, **he fixed the borders of the peoples according to the number of the sons of God.** (Deuteronomy 32:8, ESV; emphasis added)

You've probably read that verse, "according to the number of the sons of Israel." This is not an example of the Mandela Effect; the English Standard Version and a couple of other modern translations render Deuteronomy 32:8 "sons of God." This is based on older manuscripts of Deuteronomy found among the Dead Sea scrolls, which were only discovered in 1947.

The Septuagint, which was translated into Greek from Hebrew in the third century B.C., makes it even more clear:

When the Most High divided the nations, when he separated the sons of Adam, he set the bounds of the nations according to the number of the angels of God. (Emphasis added)

In other words, God apparently decided that since humanity preferred to deal with small-G gods than Him, He'd give us what we wanted. This was punishment. God turned the nations over to the "sons of god" that Nimrod had tried to bring to his kingdom through the Tower of Babel.

And beware lest you raise your eyes to heaven, and when you see the **sun and the moon and the stars, all the host of heaven,** you be drawn away and bow down to them and serve them, **things that the** LORD **your God has allotted to all the peoples under the whole heaven.** (Deuteronomy 4:19, ESV; emphasis added)

The "host of heaven" means the angelic denizens of the heavenly realm. That's who God allotted to the nations. So mankind was divided into seventy nations, the number of people groups named in the Table of Nations in Genesis 10, and allotted them to the *bene ha elohim*, of which there were, presumably, seventy.

Not coincidentally, the Canaanites believed their creator god, El, lived on Mount Hermon[7] with his consort, Asherah, and his seventy sons—the *bn 'il.*[8] Apparently, the Canaanite neighbors of ancient Israel had heard the story, too, but from the wrong source.

The division of the nations and their allotment to the sons of God was the origin of the gods of the pagan world. Quite a few are named in the Bible: Zeus, Baal (who is one and the same with Zeus), Apollo, Marduk, Ashtoreth (Astarte/Ishtar), Molech, Dagon, Chemosh, and Hades are probably the best known. There are others not obvious from English translations—words like "plague" (Resheph), "pestilence" (Deber), "fortune" (Gad), "destiny" (Meni), "terror" (Pachad), and even "travelers" (Abarim) are the names of gods or demons. Yahweh assigned those entities to the nations as their gods, but He reserved Israel as "His allotted heritage."

So, where did this new generation of rebel gods come from? That's a good question. The Book of Enoch records that two hundred Watchers, a class of angel mentioned only once in the Bible (Nebuchadnezzar's dream, Daniel 4), descended to the summit of Mount Hermon, but Peter and Jude describe them as being confined until the Judgment. Were another seventy in the divine council of Yahweh just waiting for their turn to descend to Earth and exercise dominion? Why did they rebel? Why did God choose them? Didn't He know they'd rebel? (Rhetorical question. Of *course* He did.) Were they being tested by their Creator to see whether they would rule justly in His place?

Well, they didn't. Psalm 82 describes what seems to be a trial in Heaven:

> God has taken his place in the divine council; in the midst of the gods he holds judgment:
> "How long will you judge unjustly and show partiality to the wicked? *Selah*
> Give justice to the weak and the fatherless; maintain the right of the afflicted and the destitute.

Rescue the weak and the needy; deliver them from the hand of the wicked."

They have neither knowledge nor understanding,

they walk about in darkness; all the foundations of the earth are shaken.

I said, **"You are gods, sons of the Most High, all of you; nevertheless, like men you shall die, and fall like any prince."**

Arise, O God, judge the earth; for you shall inherit all the nations! (Psalm 82:1–8, ESV; emphasis added)

If it was a test, they failed. The gods of the pagan world set themselves up as deities in their own right, and they ruled unjustly. Judging by the things God told Moses and the Israelites *not* to do, the small-*G* gods ruled perversely. They're still with us, and based on the condition of the world today, their desperation is showing. They know their time is short. It's obvious they want to take as many of us with them as they can when they go.

GODS OF THE AMORITES

Bible teachers have been giving one particular group of people from the ancient world a free pass. When it comes to relations between the Israelites and their neighbors, we hear about the evil Canaanites, Babylonians, Egyptians, Arameans, and Assyrians; a little about the Amalekites and Midianites; and of course, there were the hostile cousins across the Jordan in Ammon, Moab, and Edom. But there's another group that's far more important and it barely gets a mention. It's time to correct the record.

This group is in the Bible, but only rarely after the Book of Joshua. Not only did these people occupy the land God had allotted to Israel; they *were* the Canaanites, Babylonians, and Egyptians (at the time of the sojourn). They were the ancestors of the Arameans and the Phoenicians (the people of Jezebel). Their culture dominated the ancient Near East for nearly two thousand years. And their occult practices were so evil that they became the symbol for the spiritual wickedness of the end times—Babylon the Great, mother of prostitutes.

Yet they're usually lumped in with the seven nations the Israelites encountered in Canaan: the Hittites, Girgashites, Amorites, Canaanites, Perizzites, Hivites, and the Jebusites.

We're talking about the Amorites.

They first emerged on the world stage in the middle of the third millennium B.C. The oldest known reference to an Amorite comes from the twenty-sixth century B.C. in the ancient city of Shuruppak,[9] now a ruin on the banks of the Euphrates about 160 miles southeast of modern Baghdad. A hundred years later, texts from the kingdom of Ebla in what is now northern Syria, about thirty-five miles southwest of Aleppo, mention a nearby city or cult center called MAR.TU[ki10] that was ruled by a king named Amuti.[11] From the Ebla texts, it appears to have been centered on the middle Euphrates, roughly between the low mountain called Jebel Bishri, on the west bank of the river just north of the modern city of Deir ez-Zor, and the ancient city of Tuttul, near modern Raqqa.

The Amorites were tribal people, like the later Israelites. There were two main divisions, the Binu Sim'al and the Binu Yamina. Translated, those names mean "sons of the left" and "sons of the right," respectively— or, more simply, "northerners" and "southerners," based on the directions of your hands as you face the rising sun. This seems to have been based on where the tribes pastured their flocks.

Scholars note that Binu Yamina can also be rendered "Benjaminites," since the Semitic *Y* is anglicized into a *J*. Some have tried to connect the Amorite Benjaminites with the Israelite tribe of Benjamin, but you can only reach that conclusion if you dismiss the biblical accounts of Abraham, Isaac, and Jacob altogether and ignore the fact that the Binu Yamina was a confederation of five separate tribes. All it shows is that Benjamin was not an uncommon name in that place and time.

The Amorites were very different from their Sumerian neighbors. Sumer was a collection of city-states located fairly close together in what is now southeastern Iraq. The Sumerians were city-dwellers with a sophisticated society that included literature, music, and a complex pantheon of gods and goddesses. The Amorites, on the other hand, were pastoral nomads or semi-nomads roaming the steppes of Syria and Iraq with their herds and flocks. Prior to about 1900 B.C., they left no written records; in fact, all we know of the Amorite language is what scholars can learn from their names, and all of those are found in records written in Akkadian or Sumerian.

From surviving Mesopotamian texts, it appears that most Sumerians felt about Amorites the same way a Millennial in, say, Los Angeles or New York would feel about people from the mountains of West Virginia.

Do I exaggerate?

> The MAR.TU (i.e., the Amorites) who know no grain.… The MAR.TU who know no house nor town, the boors of the mountains.… The MAR.TU who digs up truffles…who does not bend his knees (to cultivate the land), who eats raw meat, who has no house during his lifetime, who is not buried after death.[12]

The typical Sumerian wandering into the open spaces of northern Mesopotamia apparently felt as out of place as somebody from Chicago traveling the back roads of east Tennessee. *Hey, where's the Starbucks?*

This, by the way, is one of the reasons I'm convinced that Abraham was not born and raised in Sumerian Ur, an important city that was at the heart of Mesopotamian politics for centuries. The nomadic lifestyle of the patriarchs was so similar to that of the Amorite tribes that some scholars speculate that Abraham, Isaac, and Jacob were Amorites themselves. I disagree, but it's far more likely that Abraham came out of the nomadic Amorite culture of northern Mesopotamia than from the settled, urban civilization of Sumer.[13]

One of the peaks in the Jebel Bishri range is called Jebel Diddi, which may recall the name of one of the ancient Amorite tribes, the *Didanūm* (also rendered Ditanu, Tidanu, or Tidnum).[14] The name, which appears in the Bible as the proper name Dedan and Dathan, may come from the Akkadian *ditānu* or *didānu*, meaning "aurochs" or "bison."[15] The aurochs was a species of cattle, huge by modern standards, that roamed Europe and Asia until it was finally hunted to extinction in the seventeenth century.

Whatever its origin, the Ditanu tribe was considered the ancestors of the royal houses of Babylon, Upper Mesopotamia (a short-lived Amorite kingdom that covered roughly the same area as the later Assyrian kingdom), and Ugarit, a small but wealthy kingdom on the Mediterranean shore just south of the modern border with Turkey.

In other words, the Ditanu/Tidanu/Tidnum were important enough to the shared history of the Amorites that their kings made a point of claiming descent from them for at least five hundred years. File a mental bookmark here, because we'll explain why that's significant in the next chapter.

The Sumerians, who were on their last legs as the calendar approached 2000 B.C., were genuinely afraid of the Tidanu. The last Sumerian kings to rule Mesopotamia, the Third Dynasty of Ur, launched a huge building project to try to keep the Tidanu out of their homeland—a wall about 175 miles long north of modern Baghdad that may have stretched from the Euphrates across the Tigris to the area of the Diyala River.[16]

The wall was ordered by king Šu-Sîn, who probably reigned between 2037 and 2029 B.C.[17] Šu-Sîn's high commissioner, a man named Šarrum-bāni, sent the king this report on his progress:

> You commissioned me to carry out construction on the great fortifications [bàd gal] of Muriq-Tidnim and presented your views to me as follows: "The Amorites have repeatedly raided the frontier territory." You commanded me to rebuild the fortifications, to cut off their access, and thus to prevent them from repeatedly overwhelming the fields through a breach (in the defenses) between the Tigris and Euphrates... When I had been working on the fortifications that then measured 26 dana [about 167 miles] after having reached (the areas) between the two mountain ranges, the Amorite camped in the mountains turned his attention to my building activities.[18]

We know this wall was directed specifically at the Tidanu because the Sumerians literally named it bàd martu muriq tidnim,[19] the "Amorite Wall Which Keeps the Tidnum at a Distance."[20]

The fatal flaw in this cunning plan was that the wall *didn't* keep the Tidnum at a distance.

It's not certain that the Amorites in general or the Tidnum/Tidanu specifically caused the collapse of the last Sumerian kingdom. Invaders from Elam (modern Iran) sacked Ur and carried away its last king, Ibbi-Sîn. However, it appears that Amorites had already made it so dangerous to travel that it was impossible for the cities of Sumer to communicate or trade with one another, weakening them so they were easy pickings for the Elamites. Some scholars have even speculated that the reason the powerful kingdom of Ur collapsed so quickly—it only lasted about a century—was that it had grown powerful by depending on Amorite mercenaries.[21]

The fall of Ur around 2004 B.C. led to a Mesopotamian dark age that lasted about a hundred years. Apparently, the power vacuum that followed the violent end of the Ur III dynasty led to a decades-long period of chaos. When the fog lifted, Amorite kings ruled nearly every everywhere from the Persian Gulf to the Mediterranean Sea—all of what today is Iraq, Syria, Jordan, Lebanon, and Israel, with some of southern Turkey and western Iran to boot. Even part of Egypt came under Amorite control for a couple hundred years, from about the time of Isaac until about a hundred years before the Exodus, a period that roughly coincides with the Israelite sojourn. That means, curiously enough, that the gods of Egypt during the sojourn weren't Egyptian.

A number of powerful Amorite kingdoms emerged, such as Mari, on the Euphrates River near the modern border between Iraq and Syria, Yamkhad (Aleppo) to the northwest, and the one that became synonymous with licentious behavior and the occult down to the present day—Babylon.

Nimrod and Babylon

Nimrod gets a bad rap. Many of us were taught that because the Tower of Babel was at Babylon, Nimrod is the villain responsible for the evil associated with that city. That sounds right; the names are close enough that it seems like a no-brainer to connect the two. However, history is a harsh mistress. Getting it right means digging a little deeper than finding two names that sound alike.

The Bible tells us that the kingdom of Nimrod had its beginnings at "Babel, Erech, Accad, and Calneh, in the land of Shinar."[22] Shinar, of course, was Sumer, home of the first civilization on earth to produce writing and the first advanced civilization to emerge on the earth. However, as I argue in *The Great Inception* (based on the work of Egyptologist David Rohl), the Tower of Babel was the temple of Enki at the ancient city of Eridu. That city was remembered by Sumerians as the first one ever built, and evidence suggests it may even be the city built by Cain.[23]

Erech is Uruk, in what is now southeastern Iraq. Accad was the city from which Sargon the Great conquered all of Mesopotamia around 2334 B.C., making him the first Semitic ruler of the ancient Near East. That city hasn't been found, but it's believed to have been on the Tigris River somewhere near modern Baghdad and may even be beneath Baghdad itself.[24]

Sargon is also credited with being the world's first empire-builder, but that's only because historians generally don't believe Nimrod was a historic character. (Sargon is one of the candidates put forward as the basis of the Nimrod "legend.")

Calneh likewise hasn't been found, but the name may be a misreading of a Hebrew phrase that simply meant "all of them." So, the original sentence might have read, "the beginning of his kingdom was Babel, Erech, and Accad, and *all of them* were in the land of Shinar."[25] From there, we're told Nimrod went to Assyria, or northern Mesopotamia, and built Nineveh, Rehoboth-Ir, Calah, and Resen.[26] In other words, those two verses in Genesis 10 are a condensed history of a man who's cast a shadow across five thousand years of history.

Because you're paying attention, you noticed that the modern state of Iraq bears the name of Nimrod's kingdom, Uruk. In short, sometime after the Flood but before the first written records in Sumer, a king from the city of Uruk extended his reach north and west in the Fertile Crescent at least as far as what is now the Kurdish regions of northern Iraq and northeastern Syria.

Secular scholars and historians know that the city-state of Uruk dominated the ancient Near East during most of the fourth millennium B.C., roughly between 3900 and 3100 B.C. They call this period the Uruk Expansion. Pottery from Uruk has been found as far away as the ancient city of Hamoukar in northern Syria, nearly 450 miles to the northwest. In 2005, archaeologists digging at Hamoukar discovered that the city had been destroyed during a violent attack by an army from Uruk around 3500 B.C.[27]

Bear in mind that an army on foot had to march about thirty days straight to cover that distance, assuming there were no interruptions along the way to forage for food or fight other people who objected to their passage. In other words, it was a powerful leader with a disciplined army who pulled off that mission. This battle wasn't a raid on the next town over; it was an organized military campaign. Nimrod's Uruk, not Sargon's Akkad, was the world's first empire.

Of course, this doesn't prove that Nimrod lived in the fourth millennium B.C., but it's the most logical time period for his career, and it fits the Bible's account. That's why he had nothing to do with Babylon.

You see, Babylon didn't exist until the time of Sargon, around 2300 B.C., but even then, it was an unimportant village on the Euphrates for another four hundred years. Finally, around 1894 B.C., an ambitious Amorite chieftain named Sumu-Abum started Babylon on its path to greatness by expanding his influence at the expense of a neighboring city-state. Still, Babylon was little more than an independent city for the first century or so of its existence. The first four rulers of Babylon didn't even call themselves kings. It wasn't until about 1800 B.C., the reign of Hammurabi's father Sîn-Muballit, that Babylon began to expand.

Not that Nimrod was a good guy, you understand. You have to transgress pretty seriously for God to descend from Heaven for a personal intervention.

Hammurabi, Enlil, and Marduk

Hammurabi the Great, who reigned from 1792 to 1750 B.C., is mostly remembered for his law code, one of the oldest discovered. It was carved into a basalt pillar shaped like a giant index finger, and covered a variety of legal issues from family matters to penalties for medical malpractice and shoddy home construction.[28] However, his ability to assemble an empire from a city without any natural strategic advantages was probably his most remarkable attribute. During his forty-two-year career, Hammurabi managed to subdue the Amorite kings ruling the former Sumerian homeland to the south, the Akkadian homeland of which he was a part, and the lands along the Euphrates River as far as Mari, near the border of modern-day Iraq and Syria. And he wasn't above turning on allies to do it, as when he destroyed Mari, a sour turn of events for Hammurabi's ex-friend, the Mariote king Zimri-Lim.

The rise of Hammurabi's Babylon completed a transition from the Sumerian-style city-states of the third millennium B.C. to what we think of as kingdoms. One of the aspects of Sumerian culture that also changed with the rise of Babylon was the power structure of the gods. You see, the cities of Sumer and Akkad each had a patron god or goddess. Oddly, the most important religious cities didn't always carry the most political clout. Case in point: The chief god of the Sumerian pantheon, Enlil.

Enlil was the patron god of Nippur, which never ruled Sumer but was, along with Eridu, one of the two most important religious sites in the region. Nobody knows why Nippur, about a hundred miles southeast of modern Baghdad, was founded where it was. It began as a collection of reed huts in a marsh alongside the Euphrates River. Over time, garbage, debris, and earth were piled up to lift the town above the surrounding marsh. You'd think the "king of heaven and earth" and "father of the gods" could find a better piece of real estate.

But while Nippur never dominated the politics of Mesopotamia, control of the city was important. Enlil was subject only to Anu, the sky-god, and he was the only god who could even reach Anu. Enlil was sort of

Anu's agent, and, most important, only Enlil could convey "kingship" to human rulers. So, as the old saying goes, possession of Nippur was nine-tenths of the law. You can imagine the temptation for an ambitious ruler in ancient Sumer; grabbing control of Nippur would be proof that Enlil *wanted* him to be king.

The temple of Enlil was the *E-kur* ("House of the Mountain"), a curious title for a temple in the middle of a marsh. Enlil himself was called "Great Mountain." This is even more interesting when we remember that mountains have always been considered the home of gods and that there aren't any mountains in southeast Iraq. That's why Nimrod tried to build Babel as "the abode of gods"—it was an artificial "mount of assembly."[29] Even in flat, marshy Sumer, gods lived on mountains, even when they had to be made out of stacked mud bricks.

However, Enlil's days at the top of the virtual mountain were numbered when the Amorite dynasty of Hammurabi transformed Babylon from a third-rate village into a political force. Like an aging movie star relegated to character parts when a talented young newcomer arrives in Hollywood, Enlil was gradually replaced at the king of Mesopotamian deities by the city-god of Babylon, Marduk.

We don't know much about Marduk before his rise to the top. Most of the texts about him come from the Neo-Babylonian period, during the Chaldean empire that arose in the seventh century B.C. That was the Babylon of Nebuchadnezzar, which is what most of us think of when we hear the name. We do know that a ritual sacred to Marduk, the *akitu* festival, was performed at his temple in Babylon on the spring equinox, the 1st of Nisan. It was a new year's festival, during which the creation myth would be reenacted to remind all of the glory of Marduk, who defeated the evil chaos dragon, Tiamat. Then it was believed the god and his consort, Sarpanitu, would descend to a cultic bed inside the temple, where they performed ritual lovemaking to bless the land for the coming year.

It's a fertility thing that's lost something in translation over the last 2,600 years.

But even though Marduk was officially the top dog in Babylon, the symbol of occult wickedness that's been applied to the prophesied one-world religion of the Antichrist, other gods in the pantheon were just as important as Marduk to the Amorites, if not more so.

They're also important to you and me—and to our future.

The Gods

The Amorite pantheon in the time of Hammurabi, who was probably a contemporary of the patriarchs Abraham (arrived in Canaan 1876 B.C., died 1776 B.C.), Isaac (born 1851 B.C., died 1671 B.C.), and Jacob (born 1791 B.C.), was complex, and the gods in charge differed depending on where one lived in Mesopotamia. Although Marduk was the king of the gods in eastern Mesopotamia because of Babylon's importance, and Enlil was still given lip service as the kingmaker, they weren't mentioned in the texts from western Mesopotamia—modern-day Syria, Lebanon, and Israel.

To try to make sense of a complicated situation, we'll focus on the most prominent gods across the ancient Near East (excluding Egypt, but the Egyptians during the time of the sojourn and Exodus were Amorites, anyway). We'll follow the chart below with a brief synopsis of the gods named:

	East (Babylonia)	Central (Euphrates River valley)	West (Canaan)
"Old" god	Enlil	Dagan	El
King of the gods	Marduk	Addu (storm-god)	Hadad/Baal (storm-god)
Moon-god	Sîn	Sîn	Yarikh
Sun-god/dess	Shamash (male)	Shamash (male)	Shapash (female)
God/dess of war/sex	Ishtar	Ishtar	Astarte

First, a note on geography: When we use the terms "Babylonian" and "Canaanite," we normally think of them as ethnicities. They are not. They are terms that indicate the people who lived in certain areas of the ancient

Near East, and by the time of Abraham, all of those areas were under the control of Amorites. Babylonians were eastern Amorites and Canaanites were western Amorites.

The middle Euphrates, the region along the river in modern-day Syria, was a sort of buffer zone between the more densely populated areas to the southeast (Babylonia and Sumer) and west (Syria and Canaan). North and northwest of the mid-Euphrates region were areas that would eventually form the Hurrian kingdom of Mitanni and the Hittite empire, but we're going to stay focused on the Amorites for this study.

And just as the various Amorite kingdoms were ruled independently of one another, their pantheons were slightly different. Since we've already discussed Enlil, chief god of the Sumerian pantheon, we'll begin with his counterparts in central and western Mesopotamia.

Dagan

Dagan, the chief god of the middle Euphrates region, is still a mystery after two hundred years of digging in the Syrian sand. Because you paid attention in Sunday school, you've noticed the similarity between the name of this god and Dagon, chief god of the Philistines in the time of the judges. Good catch. It's the same god, the one whose idol bowed before the Ark of the Covenant. (To be precise, he fell on his face, losing his head and hands in the process—a rather important bit of symbolism.[30]) Scholars believe the way his name was pronounced changed over the centuries, which is why the last *a* became an *o* in English.

Contrary to popular belief, Dagan was not a fish-god. An Internet search for pictures of Dagan/Dagon usually turns up images of a guy in a fish costume who's identified as Dagon or a priest of the god. This is an error that was made popular about 150 years ago by Alexander Hislop's book *The Two Babylons*. While Hislop meant well, he was wrong.

The guy in the weird fish cloak was actually a supernatural being the Mesopotamians called an *apkallu*, which roughly means "big water man" in Akkadian. They were, in fact, the Watchers we met in chapter 6 of Genesis and the Book of 1 Enoch.[31] More about the *apkallu* and the Watchers in a later chapter.

The notion that Dagan was a god of fish may have started with a bit of folk etymology. *Dāg* is Hebrew for fish, and since the Philistines lived on the coastal plain between Israel and Egypt, the worship of a fish-god seems logical. However, Dagan first appeared in the middle Euphrates region more than a thousand years before Samson started whacking Philistines with a donkey jawbone. Since the Amorite kingdoms along the Euphrates River were never based on fishing, the notion of a fish-god at the top of their pantheon just doesn't fit.

Some scholars believe that Dagan was a grain-god. That's a better fit with the evidence. The Semitic root for "grain" is *dgn*, and Dagan was equated with the Hurrian god Kumarbi, who in turn was identified with the Greek god Kronos, king of the Titans.[32] According to myth, Kronos used a sickle to castrate his father, Ouranos, which—since sickles were used during the harvest—is further evidence that Dagan was likewise a grain-god.

One thing we do know: Dagan was very important in the ancient Near East, even if we don't know much about his character. His cult may have been spread across the region in the twenty-fourth century B.C. by the great conquerer Sargon of Akkad, who led his troops from near modern Baghdad all the way to the Mediterranean. On the way, Sargon stopped to pay homage at the temple of Dagan in Tuttul, a city on the Euphrates southeast of Mari. Sargon's grandson, Narām-Sîn, likewise credited Dagan with his military triumphs.

We know that Dagan/Dagon was still worshiped by the Philistines more than a thousand years after Sargon, although how the god moved from the middle Euphrates to the Gaza Strip is still a mystery. Recently, scholars have identified an ancient kingdom north of Aleppo called Palistin that was ruled from Kinalua, a city located at Tell Ta'yinat about fifteen miles southeast of Antakya (ancient Antioch) in Turkey. Because you're observant, you noticed the similarity of the names of this kingdom, Palistin, and the main enemy of the Israelites from the time of the judges through the time of David, the Philistines.

Interestingly, Palistin seems to have flourished briefly at about the same time as David.[33] It appears that the branch of the Sea Peoples we call the Philistines, or a subset thereof, migrated from somewhere in the Aegean and set up a kingdom in what is now the border between Syria and Turkey. It lasted a short while at the beginning of the Iron Age, leaving behind only a place name to its successor state, Patin or Patina.[34]

The best-known king of Palistin was one Taita, who left impressive statues of himself and Tarhunz (the Hittite name for the storm-god Hadad, or Baal) at the Temple of the Storm-God in Aleppo. The inscription on the statue of the king describes him as "King Taita, the Hero, the King of Palistin." Given the cultural and religious cross-pollination between the historically Amorite lands of Lebanon and Syria to the south and southeast and the Hurrian and Hittite lands to the north and northwest, it's possible that this short-lived kingdom, located at the gateway from Mesopotamia to Anatolia, is where the Philistines first encountered Dagan/Dagon.

Palistin probably emerged from the rubble of the Bronze Age collapse around 1200 B.C. That's the term scholars use to describe a period of chaos in which the aforementioned Sea Peoples roared out of the Aegean, overran the Hittites, and destroyed most of the kingdoms in the eastern Mediterranean. One of those was Ugarit, which reached its peak around the time of the Exodus. Ugarit, being just twenty miles south of Mount Zaphon, may have been part of the territory absorbed by the new state of Palistin. Oddly, though, while Dagan was named among the chief deities of Ugarit, he doesn't appear at all in their myths. Dagan is mentioned only as the father of the king of the gods, Baal.

The puzzle is that Baal is also the son of Dagan's counterpart in the Canaanite pantheon, the creator-god El. A number of theories have been floated to explain Baal's dual parentage: El and Dagan were brothers, or El and Dagan played the roles of Ouranos and Kronos in an earlier version of the Greek myths, with Baal, a storm-god like Zeus, emerging as king of the pantheon.

Or, maybe the answer is simpler: Dagan and El were one and the same.

This view is supported by the fact that KTU 1.118 and 1.47 have both El and Dagan sharing the same epithet, "father god" (*'ilib*). Additionally, inscriptions at what most scholars consider the temple of Dagan at Ugarit make an identification very likely, the Mesopotamian pantheon identified both Dagan and El with the supreme god (Anu/Enlil), and at Ebla Dagan is the high god, also called "lord of Canaan." Combining Wyatt's reasonable conclusion that Dagan was a weather god with the shared epithet and this comparative material persuades this writer that, in the words of del Olmo Lete, "there can be no doubt that the equation of Ilu and Daganu expresses the process of cultural and cultic identification of two (Canaanite/Amorite) pantheons." This fusion explains the dual reference to Baal's parentage alongside the clear descriptions of his kinship with the other sons of El.[35]

El

El was the creator-god of the Canaanite pantheon and supreme among the gods, at least in name. While he played an active role in Canaanite religion, he appeared to be rather disinterested in running the show. It seems that the chief deity would have taken a more active role in settling the question of who would rule as king of the gods. Instead, El did little to settle the question. The Baal Cycle describes the storm-god's violent struggle for kingship with the god of death, Mot, and the chaos-god of the sea, Yamm, both of whom were described in Ugaritic texts as "beloved of El."[36]

By the way, it's not a coincidence that the conflict between the Baal, Yamm, and Mot is echoed by the tension between the Greek gods of storm, sea, and underworld, Zeus, Poseidon, and Hades. It's more evidence that confirms that the religions of Greece and Rome borrowed heavily from the Semitic people of the Near East.

El is mentioned more than five hundred times in the Ugaritic texts,[37] portrayed as an old god, with the gray hair of his beard a sign of wisdom as well as age. He's depicted as the father of the gods and the creator of humanity.[38] A common epithet of the god, *Ṯôr 'Il*, "Bull El," is thought to refer to El's power and dignity.[39]

We can't miss the fact that the name of El was also a noun, the generic word meaning "god" in Ugaritic and Hebrew, the root behind *elohim*. For that reason, many scholars conclude that El and Yahweh were the same deity. And to be fair, God did call Himself El for a long time:

> God spoke to Moses and said to him, "I am [Yahweh]. I appeared to Abraham, to Isaac, and to Jacob, as [El Shaddai], but by my name [Yahweh] I did not make myself known to them." (Exodus 6:2–3, ESV, content in brackets added)

But there are too many differences between El and Yahweh to confuse the two. Yahweh, the God of the Bible, is an active warrior god, remembered for defeating Leviathan, riding on the clouds (a descriptor of the storm-god repurposed from *The Baal Cycle*), and fighting for Israel against its enemies.

El, on the other hand…

> El summoned his drinking-companions;
> El took his seat in his feasting house.
> He drank wine to satiety,
> new wine until intoxication.
> El went off to his house;
> he stumbled off towards his dwelling;
> Thukamun and Shanim supported him.
> A creeping monster approached him,
> with horns and tail!

> He floundered in his (own) faeces and urine:
> El fell down as though dead;
> El was like those who go down into the underworld.[40]

That is *not* the God of the Bible.

We should note that El's home is described as a tent, which is similar to the Tabernacle of the Israelites, Yahweh's home for more than four hundred years until the construction of Solomon's Temple. The location of El's tent was "the source of the rivers, at the midst of the springs of the two deeps."[41] This is reflected in a psalm that takes on new meaning in this context:

> My soul is cast down within me;
> therefore I remember you
> from the land of Jordan and of Hermon,
> from Mount Mizar.[42]

> Deep calls to deep
> at the roar of your waterfalls;
> all your breakers and your waves
> have gone over me. (Psalm 42:6–7, ESV)

The word translated "deep" is *tehom*, which means the abyss, the deepest parts of the earth. As we noted earlier, Mount Hermon was believed to be El's mount of assembly. Apparently, there was a belief in the Near East that the two deeps of the world—a fountain that emerged from Banias, which is the Grotto of Pan at the base of Hermon, and the celestial ocean that produced the rain—met at the region of the upper Jordan River and the great mountain.[43]

Because you don't miss a thing, you've already figured out why that's significant. It's another clue that we're unraveling the identity of this old god. In fact, we may have figured out why the so-called supreme god of the Canaanites turned over his kingship to the storm-god, Baal: El was Dagan, a god linked to the underworld; Dagan was the Hurrian god Kumarbi, who was banished to the netherworld by the storm-god, Teshub; and Kumarbi was Kronos, king of the Titans, who was likewise sentenced by the storm-god to eternity in the "deep"—the abyss.

In other words, El was portrayed as semi-retired not because he was bored with being king, but because he's chained up in a very dark place, waiting and plotting for one last shot at dethroning the true King.

Sun, Moon, and Venus

The other principal gods across the Near East were pretty much the same except for name. The moon-god was called Sîn in the east and Yarikh in the west. Contrary to what many of us have thought, the moon-god was far more important in the ancient Near East than the sun-god, especially in Babylon. The moon-god was believed to be the father of the sun-god and Venus (Ishtar), and it appears that there were times during the third and second millennia B.C. when the moon-god presided over the Mesopotamian divine council.[44]

The eastern sun-god Shamash was transformed into the sun-goddess Shapash by the western Amorites, and in the west, the goddess was believed to be the child of El and his consort, Asherah, rather than the moon-god. The common thread was the sun's role as judge among the gods and of the dead, which makes a kind of sense. After all, the sun appears to spend about half its time in the underworld to people who believe the earth is flat, as they did four thousand years ago.

Along with the sun-god/dess and the moon-god, the god/dess of sex and war, known across the Near East as Inanna, Ishtar, and Astarte (Ashtoreth in the Bible), comprised a cosmic triad—moon, sun, and the planet Venus. Many ancient inscriptions feature symbols of the three deities across the top.

The goddess was depicted in ancient texts as selfish, impulsive, headstrong, and bloodthirsty. In the *Epic of Gilgamesh*, when she's rejected by the hero, she storms off to demand that the sky-god, Anu, release the Bull of Heaven to trample Gilgamesh. Other hymns to the goddess paint a portrait of possibly the first gender-fluid entity on the earth, praised for her ability to "to turn a man into a woman and a woman into a man."[45] Ishtar was an androgynous deity followed by eunuchs and transvestites whose cult involved homosexual prostitution from the

Sumerian period at least through the last days of the kingdom of Judah. Around 620 B.C., King Josiah "broke down the houses of the male cult prostitutes who were in the house of the LORD,"[46] almost certainly servants of Astarte/Ishtar.

In Ugarit, around the time of the judges, the goddess had been separated into male and female—the war-god Athtar as Venus the morning star, and the goddess of carnal sex, Astarte, as Venus the evening star.

One can make a good case that Ishtar/Astarte is the spirit of the present-day Western world—self-absorbed, fixated on sex and violence, and denying the pattern God established in Eden, where "he who created them from the beginning made them male and female."[47] Today, progressives in academia tell us the concept of binary gender is archaic and harmful; a relic from the days of Moses, whose patriarchal moral code simply reflected the primitive culture of the world around him.

Sadly, some Christians today are beginning to buy into that idea. It's especially tragic because the notion is based on fake history. The fact is that the Law given to Moses by God on Sinai was progressive, a rejection of the perverse sexual teachings of an androgynous goddess that were more than a thousand years old when Moses came down from the mountain. But as the song goes, "Everything old is new again."

One final point as we near the end of this chapter: Across the ancient Near East, and among the nearby nations to the north (the Hurrians and Hittites) and, later, to the west (the Greeks and Romans), a pattern was repeated among the gods: Older generations were pushed out of the way for younger gods, sometimes violently. In Sumer, the sky-god Anu was replaced at the top of the pantheon by Enlil, who was replaced in turn by Marduk. In the middle Euphrates region, it was Anu, then Dagan, then Addu (the storm-god Baal), while out west in Canaan, it was perhaps El (or El-who-was-Dagan) to Hadad (Baal). The Greeks eventually got the story as Ouranos to Kronos to Zeus.

The names changed, but the pattern remained the same: Old gods were deposed and replaced by younger deities, and the former gods were demoted or banished to the netherworld.

Now, this brief summary of the chief gods of the Amorites covers a period from about the time of Abraham, around 2000 B.C., until the end of the Old Testament, a few hundred years before the birth of Jesus. It is in no way a scholarly treatment of the subject. A study like that would fill a lot of books and still not get to the point of this one, which is: The pagan gods of the ancient world were real, they're coming back, and the Bible gives us a good idea of who, where, and when.

And the surprising thing about the old gods is that even though they no longer ruled the pantheon, the Amorites and their descendants never stopped calling on them or sacrificing to them—and to their giant, half-human children.

AMORITES AND
THEIR ANCESTORS

Being an Amorite meant depending on your descendants for the quality of your afterlife. That's a lousy way to live. It was bad enough knowing that the netherworld was a dim and musty place, but if your descendants didn't perform their responsibilities in preparing food and drink offerings for you, you faced an eternity of eating dust and clay.

For the living, this meant a monthly, ritual meal for dead ancestors (twice monthly for dead kings) called *kispum*.[48] The offerings included provisions like cold water, bread, hot broth, beer, or wine.[49] It was usually performed on the last day of the month, the day of "no moon," as opposed to the first day of the month, the new moon.[50] Apparently it was believed that the darkest nights gave the spirits the most access to the living. That night was characterized in one ancient text as "the 30th day, the day of the new moon, dangerous day, the evil day, the day of the *kispum*."[51]

This was more than just setting out food and water the way children set out cookies and milk for Santa Claus on Christmas Eve. The *kispum* literally summoned the spirits of the dead to eat with the living. It was a necromancy rite that involved a care-of-the-dead ritual, a libation (drink offering), and an invocation of the names of the deceased.[52]

The *kispum* ritual was performed at home. This may explain a practice common in Mesopotamia that seems morbid and unhealthy to us today: the burial of dead relatives beneath the floor of the house. While there may have been community cemeteries in Mesopotamia during the second millennium B.C., there is little evidence for them. Home burials were the rule and not the exception.[53]

From the perspective of the families, it made sense. The *kispum* kept the ancestral spirits content so they wouldn't haunt the living and cause unnecessary trouble. It must have been easier for the dead to find the *kispum* if the distance between their final resting place and the monthly meal in their honor was only six feet, give or take.

Mourning the dead was an important part of this ritual. For prominent people, the mourning period could last seven days.[54] We see an echo of this in the Bible, where Jesus delayed visiting his sick friend Lazarus until four days after he died. This was the Bible verse guaranteed to make kids in Sunday school classes giggle: "Lord, by this time he stinketh" (John 11:39). The point is that four days after death, "many Jews" were still with Mary and Martha to console them, and they followed Mary to the tomb "supposing that she was going to the tomb to weep there."[55]

The takeaway: In Old Testament days, especially early in the time of the patriarchs, people in the lands of the Bible believed their existence after death was literally in the hands of their descendants. If the kids didn't perform the rituals and prepare the meals, they were doomed to a long, miserable existence in the netherworld. (Of course, they got to haunt the family, so at least there were opportunities for payback.)

This puts Abraham's desire for an heir in a whole new light, doesn't it?

> But Abram said, "O Lord GOD, what will you give me, for I continue [or, "I shall die"] childless, and the heir of my house is Eliezer of Damascus?" (Genesis 15:2, ESV)

If God appeared to most of us today and said, "Fear not, I am your shield; your reward shall be very great," how many of us would immediately ask for children? (In our society, not enough of us, frankly.) Abraham came from an area dominated by Amorite culture and religion, and he was getting up in years. At that point in his life, he was probably thinking, "I'm going to have to depend on a servant to take care of me after I die!"

But that was a worry for those living in that time and place. Somebody had to perform the *kispum* and the ritual mourning if you were going to have a decent quality of afterlife:

> That such rites were important for the well-being of the deceased in the hereafter may readily be seen from the fact that when childless persons made arrangements for adopted heirs to care for them, they stipulated mourning as well as burial among the adoptee's obligations. It was not a comforting thought to imagine that one's mourning rites would end prematurely... Professional mourners, both male and female, were available to swell the numbers of the grieving or to lead the laments; prostitutes seem occasionally to have been similarly pressed into this service.[56]

As you can see, this was serious business. Legal texts from the time of the judges in the Amorite city of Emar, which was on the great bend of the Euphrates in northern Syria, spelled out the requirements for a family's main heir to care for a family's dead (*mētu*) and the family gods (*ilāni*).[57] But if an heir didn't live up to expectations, legal documents from the ancient Near East show that a son could also be disinherited not only from real property, but from access to the ghosts and gods.[58]

Of course, if you're reading this and have a Christian worldview, you understand what's going on here. The Bible only gives one example of an actual ghost visiting the living: when Samuel was allowed to return to deliver a message from God to Saul.[59] However, the *belief* that spirits could "cross over" was widely held in ancient times. Even the apostles thought

Jesus was a ghost when He came to them by walking across the surface of the Sea of Galilee.[60]

In fact, the pagan belief in spirits who travel from the netherworld to the land of the living is one of the reasons this book was written. It was a fundamental part of the religion and worldview of the pagan neighbors of ancient Israel, and it's a key element of an important end-times prophecy—one that hasn't been explored before, to the best of my knowledge.

Lord of the Corpse

What may be surprising to modern readers is learning that there are places in the world today where people live under similar obligation to what they believe are the spirits of their ancestors. For example, Rev. Dr. Robert H. Bennett documented the animist religion of the people of Madagascar in his excellent, highly recommended book, *I Am Not Afraid: Demon Possession and Spiritual Warfare.*[61] His description of the obligations people there feel toward their dead is very much like what archaeologists have discovered about ancient Near Eastern beliefs: Either people provide for their ancestors in a manner they deserve or they face supernatural consequences.

Some scholars have suggested that the *kispum* rite, the ritual meal for the dead, originated with the Amorites. The custom seems to have become standard practice in Mesopotamia at about the time the Amorites emerged as the dominant people group in the Near East, around 2000 B.C., and because of the Amorite habit of calling tribal leaders *abu*, "father."[62] As you'll see shortly, the Amorites put a lot of importance on dead royalty—the "mighty men who were of old," if you catch my drift.

This is one of the reasons the Amorite god Dagan is an intriguing character. Even after two hundred years of digging up ancient cities in Syria where this god topped the pantheon, the character of Dagan is still a mystery.

As we mentioned previously, the worship of Dagan continued for at least 1,500 years, mainly along the Euphrates River in what is today Syria. One of Dagan's epithets was *bēl pagrê*, which has been translated "lord of corpse offerings, lord of corpses (a netherworld god), lord of funerary offerings, and lord of human sacrifices."[63] The great Amorite king of northern Mesopotamia in the days of Hammurabi, Shamshi-Adad, arrived once at Terqa, a city known as a center for the Dagan cult, on the day of the *kispum*, and while there the king dedicated a *bīt kispim* ("house of the *kispum*") to Dagan.[64]

But scholars can't seem to agree on Dagan's relationship to the netherworld or how he was honored. The Semitic root *pgr* behind the Akkadian *pagrê* is a cognate (same word, different language) for the Hebrew *peger*, which means "corpse" or "carcass." Did the Amorites of Abraham's day literally sacrifice humans to Dagan? It seems unlikely that something so outrageous would have slipped past the prophets without a mention. Still, there was a connection between Dagan and the dead,[65] and that's the point. The dead required offerings and sacrifices from the living, and in central Mesopotamia, Dagan played a role in the process.

As we get deeper into this book and show the links between Dagan, the Canaanite creator-god El, the king of the Greek Titans, Kronos, and the chief god of the Phoenicians, Baal Hammon, and possibly other Amorite and Canaanite gods of the netherworld, the relevance of this hazy connection between Dagan and the spirits of the dead in Amorite religion should become clearer.

Molech

If anything, the Ammonite god Molech (sometimes spelled Molek or Moloch) is even more mysterious than Dagan. Since Semitic languages such as Akkadian, Ugaritic, and Hebrew had no vowels, it's difficult to tell when *mlk* means "king" and when it's the proper name, Molech. Isaiah 57, a condemnation of idolatry, is a case in point:

> You journeyed to the king [*mlk*] with oil
> and multiplied your perfumes;
> you sent your envoys far off,
> and sent down even to Sheol. (Isaiah 57:9, ESV)

In context with the reference to the Hebrew underworld, Sheol, "the king," could just as easily read "Molech," a god linked almost exclusively to the netherworld. Obviously, that changes the entire sense of the verse.

Molech first appears in the Bible in Leviticus 18, where God told the Israelites that they were forbidden to give their children as an offering to the dark god. Molech's cult, however, appears to extend back at least a thousand years before Moses.

A god called Malik is known from texts found at Ebla, a powerful kingdom in what is now northern Syria between about 3000 and 2400 B.C. (For reference, Abraham probably arrived in Canaan around 1876 B.C.) Of the approximately five hundred deities identified from texts found at Ebla, one of most common theophoric elements in personal names—like *el* in Daniel ("God is my judge") or *yahu* in Hezekiah ("YHWH strengthens")—was *ma-lik*.[66]

Getting a handle on the character of Malik is difficult. It appears that by the time of Abraham, Isaac, and Jacob, he was still worshiped in the Amorite kingdom of Mari, which was based at a city on the Euphrates River near the modern border between Syria and Iraq. Further, it appears that Malik was served by a group of underworld deities called *maliku*. And five hundred years later, during the time of the judges, Malik and the *maliku* (called *mlkm* by then) were still venerated at Ugarit.[67]

What's more, the Ugaritic texts link Malik with a god called Rapi'u, the "King of Eternity." Now, we have to point out a couple things about Rapi'u: First, his name is the singular form of "Rephaim." In other words, just as Malik had his band of netherworld followers, the *maliku* or *mlkm*, Rapi'u was apparently lord of the Rephaim. Second, the Ugaritic texts connect both Malik and Rapi'u to Ashtaroth, a city in Bashan near Mount Hermon.[68] In fact, Rapi'u is described as "the god enthroned at Ashtaroth, the god who rules in Edrei."[69] Those two cities are the same two from which Og, last of the Rephaim kings, ruled over Bashan.[70] In other words, to the pagan Amorites, the kingdom of Og *was literally the entrance to the underworld.*

To be clear, archaeologists haven't found evidence of child sacrifice at Ugarit, Mari, or Ebla. Nor has any turned up near Jerusalem, despite references in the Bible to the ritual practice outside the walls of the city. If children were being slaughtered for Molech/Malik in the Levant before the Israelites arrived, scholars haven't found the physical evidence yet.

Still, the Bible mentions it in Moses' day, around 1400 B.C.; Solomon built a high place for Molech around 950 B.C.;[71] and about 325 years later, King Josiah defiled the Topheth in the Valley of the Son of Hinnom, which was used to burn children as offerings to Molech.[72]

Baal Hammon

The Phoenicians, however, are a different story. Descendants of the Canaanites who spread out from the city of Tyre to establish colonies all around the Mediterranean, they continued this horrific practice into the Roman era. Diodorus Siculus, a Greek historian of the first century, wrote:

> In former times they (the Carthaginians) had been accustomed to sacrifice to this god the noblest of their sons, but more recently, secretly buying and nurturing children, they had sent these to the sacrifice.[73]

Diodorus identified the god of Carthage as Kronos, king of the Titans. The Romans knew him as Saturn, but the Carthaginians called him Baal Hammon. You've already met this god—their Canaanite ancestors called him El.

> There is now overwhelming evidence identifying *B'l Hmn* of Zincirli and *B'l Hmn* of the western Punic colonies with Canaanite 'El. As a matter of fact, both the epithets *B'l Hmn* and *Tnt* (his consort) survived only on the peripheries of the spread of Canaanite culture, a mark of archaism comparable to the survival of linguistic archaism at the frontiers of the spread of a family of languages.

Philo Byblius, and other classical sources, and inscriptions in Greek and Latin all establish the formula that *B'l Hmn* on the one hand, and *'El* on the other, are Greek *Kronos*, Latin *Saturnus*. These equations have long been known, and all new data confirm the ancient. Moreover, we now perceive the significance of the epithets *gerontis* used of the Kronos of Gadir (Cadiz), *senex* used of Saturnus of New Carthage, and, indeed, of the epithet *saeculo [frugifero]* used of the African Saturnus. They reproduce 'El's appellation *'ôlām*, "the Ancient One."[74]

It's no coincidence that this epithet of El is similar to one you've heard for Yahweh, Ancient of Days. As we noted above, scholars take this as evidence that Yahweh was El before the Hebrews changed his cult. Entire books have been written on this topic, so we won't veer off course here. We disagree; Yahweh and El are separate and distinct. It's our view that the similarities were intended by the Fallen to deceive the people of God.

How many faces has this entity worn over the millennia? Working our way backward in roughly chronological order:

1. Baal Hammon: Chief god of Carthage and its colonies in the Mediterranean
2. Kronos (Saturn): King of the Titans in Greece and Rome, overthrown by storm-god Zeus (Jupiter)
3. El: Creator-god of the western Amorites (i.e., the Canaanites), succeeded as king of the gods by storm-god Hadad (i.e., Baal)
4. Dagan: Chief god of the middle Euphrates region; Dagon to later Philistines
5. Kumarbi: Grain-god of Hurrians and Hittites, overthrown by storm-god Teshub/Tarhunz
6. Enlil: Former chief god of Babylonia and Sumer, replaced by Marduk
7. And to this list we can add Shemihazah: Leader of the two hundred Watchers who descended on Mount Hermon

This list is somewhat speculative, you understand. While the evidence fits our theory, we must remember that we're seeing "through a glass, darkly"—and besides, these entities lie.

El's epithet "the Ancient One" may lead to another connection:

> [A] mine inscription, owing to a poor facsimile, had been misread and hence remained undeciphered." It reads *'ld'lm, 'if ḏū 'ôlami*, "El, the Ancient One" or "'El, lord of Eternity.'"[75]

Now, is this enough evidence to link El (and thus Kronos, Baal Hammon, and his other manifestations) to Rapi'u, the underworld god who reigned at Ashtaroth and Edrei? Some scholars think so. The renowned Frank Moore Cross, for example, translated the phrase *Rapi'u malk 'ôlami* from Ugaritic text KTU 1.108 as an epithet of El ("the Hale One, eternal king") rather than "Rapi'u, King of Eternity." If that's correct, then we've also connected El to Molech. But other well-respected scholars disagree with Cross, so the jury is still out on that.

It is probable, however, that Baal Hammon means "Lord of the Amanus,"[76] which refers to a mountain range in southern Turkey. The Amanus, today called the Nur Mountains (from the Turkish *Nur Dağları*, "Mountains of Holy Light"), run alongside the Gulf of Iskenderun at the northeastern corner of the Mediterranean Sea, just north of ancient Antioch (modern Antakya) and northeast of Mount Zaphon. Zincirli, mentioned in the citation above, is in Turkey about seventy miles north of Antakya. It controlled the northern pass through the Amanus mountains while Kinalua, capital city of the kingdom of Palistin, located about fifteen miles southeast of Antakya, guarded the southern pass.

By the way, I know the names of these pagan gods are coming at you fast and furious. Check the appendices to get a handle on which deity was god of what, where, and when. I'll try to make it clearer there. In the meanwhile, we'll take a quick detour here to sort out the Baals.

Baal Hammon is not the Baal of the Bible. That was the storm-god,

Hadad. "Baal" simply means "lord," and it was used by the Canaanites and Phoenicians the same way we Christians call our God "Lord" instead of Yahweh. But you noticed, no doubt, that Baal Hammon's mountains, the Amanus, are only about seventy miles north of Mount Zaphon, home of Baal Hadad's palace (and only about ninety miles east is Aleppo, which in the days of Abraham was known as the City of Hadad).

The worship of Baal Hammon continued until rather late in history. The Phoenicians, descendants of the Canaanites, built a maritime trading empire unrivaled in the ancient world that lasted from about the time of Ahab and Jezebel in the ninth century B.C. until the end of the Third Punic War in 146 B.C. when Carthage was finally destroyed by Rome. Carthage was a colony founded by Tyre in what is modern-day Tunisia. As the Phoenicians extended their influence across the Mediterranean through settlements and trading outposts on the North African coast, southern Spain, and islands like Sicily and Sardinia, the worship of Baal Hammon spread as well. It appears the god and his consort, Tanit, became the supernatural power couple of Carthage around 480 B.C., when a disastrous military defeat on the island of Sicily led to a break with Tyre.[77]

Tanit, sometimes rendered Tannit or Tinnit, was the Carthaginian version of the goddess Asherah,[78] although some scholars connect Tanit to the other great goddesses of the Canaanite pantheon, Astarte and Anat.[79] However, identifying Tanit as Asherah seems most likely if, as most scholars agree, equating Baal Hammon to El is correct.

The etymology of her name is interesting, to say the least. Tanit is a feminine form of the Canaanite/Phoenician *tannin*, which means "serpent." Thus, the goddess is literally the "Serpent Lady," or possibly, "Dragon Lady."[80] This parallels epithets of Asherah, *rabbat 'atiratu yammi*: "The Lady Who Treads on the Sea(-dragon),"[81] and, *dt bṯn*, which likewise means "Serpent Lady."[82] Tanit/Asherah was sometimes called Qudšu ("the Holy One"),[83] and she was known by this name in Egypt as well as the Levant from about the time of Jacob through the time of the Judges, about 1700–1200 B.C. In Egyptian art, she's usually shown holding snakes in one or both hands.[84]

Not coincidentally, *bṯn* is the Ugaritic form of "Bashan," the land at the foot of Mount Hermon ruled by Og in the days of Moses, so the epithet *ḏt bṯn* could be read, "Lady of Bashan." (In the same way, Bashan means "Place of the Serpent.") As you'll see in the next chapter, there are angelic beings who, based on clues in the Bible, may well be serpentine in appearance.

While scholars don't completely agree on the identities and origins of Baal Hammon and Tanit, it is clear that the two required a most precious sacrifice from worshipers—their children. In recent years, some scholars have tried to downplay biblical accounts of child sacrifice, suggesting that they were fabrications by the prophets to justify the conquest of Canaan and rationalize the destruction of Jerusalem and the Temple by Babylon.

You shall not give any of your children to offer them [literally, "to make them pass through (the fire)"] to Molech, and so profane the name of your God: I am the LORD. [...]

Do not make yourselves unclean by any of these things, for by all these the nations I am driving out before you have become unclean, and the land became unclean, so that I punished its iniquity, and the land vomited out its inhabitants. (Leviticus 18:21, 24–25, ESV; emphasis added)

[Manasseh] **burned his son as an offering** and used fortune-telling and omens and dealt with mediums and with necromancers. He did much evil in the sight of the LORD, provoking him to anger. [...] And the LORD said by his servants the prophets, **"Because Manasseh king of Judah has committed these abominations and has done things more evil than all that the Amorites did,** who were before him, and has made Judah also to sin with his idols, therefore thus says the LORD, the God of Israel: Behold, I am bringing upon Jerusalem and Judah such disaster that the ears of everyone who hears of it will tingle." (2 Kings 21:6, 10–12, ESV; emphasis added)

For the sons of Judah have done evil in my sight, declares the LORD. They have set their detestable things in the house that is called by my name, to defile it. And **they have built the high places of Topheth, which is in the Valley of the Son of Hinnom, to burn their sons and their daughters in the fire, which I did not command, nor did it come into my mind.** Therefore, behold, the days are coming, declares the LORD, when it will no more be called Topheth, or the Valley of the Son of Hinnom, but the Valley of Slaughter; for they will bury in Topheth, because there is no room elsewhere. (Jeremiah 7:30–32, ESV; emphasis added)

But the prophets weren't alone in their condemnation of the Amorite-Canaanite-Phoenician practice of child sacrifice. Greeks and Romans were appalled by it as well. According to Diodorus Siculus, in the year 310 B.C., the citizens of Carthage responded to a disastrous military defeat to Agathocles, ruler of the Sicilian city-state of Syracuse, by slaughtering hundreds of their children:

Therefore the Carthaginians, believing that the misfortune had come to them from the gods, betook themselves to every manner of supplication of the divine powers.... They also alleged that Cronus [Baal Hammon] had turned against them inasmuch as in former times they had been accustomed to sacrifice to this god the noblest of their sons, but more recently, secretly buying and nurturing children, they had sent these to the sacrifice; and when an investigation was made, some of those who had been sacrificed were discovered to have been supposititious (i.e., substitutions).... **In their zeal to make amends for their omission, they selected two hundred of the noblest children and sacrificed them publicly; and others who were under suspicion sacrificed themselves voluntarily, in number not less than three hundred.**[85] (Emphasis added)

Diodorus also provides the most graphic description of how this sacrifice was performed:

There was in their city a bronze image of Cronus, extending its hands, palms up and sloping toward the ground, so that each of the children when placed thereon rolled down and fell into a sort of gaping pit filled with fire. [86]

Plutarch, a Greek author of the second half of the first century A.D., adds this disturbing detail:

[W]ith full knowledge and understanding they themselves offered up their own children, and those who had no children would buy little ones from poor people and cut their throats as if they were so many lambs or young birds; meanwhile the mother stood by without a tear or moan; but should she utter a single moan or let fall a single tear, she had to forfeit the money, and her child was sacrificed nevertheless; and the whole area before the statue was filled with a loud noise of flutes and drums so that the cries of wailing should not reach the ears of the people. [87]

Now, if we've learned only one thing from the political situation in the United States over the last ten years, it's that the media promotes a narrative, and stories are often shaped to fit that narrative. The same was true two thousand years ago. So, some modern archaeologists prefer to believe that the Hebrew, Greek, and Roman commentators who offered their opinions of Canaanite and Punic religion were simply biased. Besides, they say, the high rate of infant mortality in the ancient world would have made regular child sacrifices impossible. Any society engaging in such a practice, it's argued, would collapse by artificially elevating its death rate above the birth rate. [88] They argue that children found buried at Phoenician settlements around the Mediterranean simply died of natural causes, and that for some as yet undiscovered reason, the Phoenicians set aside special burial grounds for deceased children. Archaeologists have borrowed the biblical term, tophet, to describe these sites.

It's an imprecise use of the term. The Hebrew word *topheth* literally means "place of fire," a reference to the practice of burning children as offerings to Molech. The horror of the Topheth led Jews to use the Valley of the Son of Hinnom, where these sacrifices took place, as a symbol to represent the place of eternal torment for the wicked. The name in shortened form, *gei hinnom* ("Valley of Hinnom"), became *Gehenna* in Greek, and is usually translated "hell" in the New Testament.

However, the arguments of these revisionists just don't hold up. Analysis shows that the Phoenicians could, in fact, have sacrificed as many as all their firstborn children, or up to one-third of their baby girls, without affecting their society in a significant way.[89]

The physical evidence that has so far escaped archaeologists in Israel has turned up in numerous places around the Mediterranean. Tophets similar to the one described in the Bible have been found at Carthage and nearby Phoenician sites in modern Tunisia and Algeria, at Motya on Sicily, and at Monte Sirai, Nora, Tharros, and Sulcis on Sardinia.[90] One of the most disturbing pieces of evidence comes from a Phoenician site in Spain, a stone relief on a funerary monument constructed around 500 B.C:

> The relief depicts a banquet prepared for a monster that sits, facing the left part of the image. The monster has a human body and two heads, one above the other. The heads have open mouths with lolling tongues. In its left hand it holds the rear leg of a supine pig lying on a banquet table in front of it. In its right hand, it holds a bowl. Just over the rim of the bowl can be seen the head and feet of a small person. In the background, a figure in a long garment raises a bowl in a gesture of offering. Opposite the monster is the mutilated image of a third figure. It is standing and raising in its right hand a sword with a curved blade. Its

head is in the shape of a bull or horse. Its left hand is touching the head of a second small person in a bowl on a second table or a tripod near the banquet table. The funerary tower on which this relief is carved comes from an area that, in the period of its construction, was clearly subject to Punic or Phoenician influence and resembles monuments from Achaemenid western Asia. The relief itself resembles eastern Mediterranean depictions of offerings or sacrifices, and the sword with the curved blade, associated with sacrifice, supports the resemblance. It appears that the small figures, most likely children, are being offered in bowls to the two-headed monster. Accordingly, it is reasonable to believe that the relief, however imaginatively, represents Northwest Semitic child sacrifice.[91]

Still, the debate continues up to the time of this writing. Some scholars see nothing unusual in the special burial sites the Phoenicians set aside for infants and young children.[92] However, a recent analysis of teeth retrieved from 342 burial urns at Carthage, where the largest tophet contains more than twenty thousand such urns,[93] found that infants under the age of three months were significantly over-represented, suggesting—putting this nicely—that they died of something other than natural causes.[94]

So, the question is not whether the Phoenicians who colonized the Mediterranean world sacrificed their children, or even if they could have done it the way the prophets, Greeks, and Romans said they did. The question is simply why they did it.

Generally speaking, Phoenician parents couldn't have been heartless, unfeeling monsters. Even an unfriendly witness like Plutarch noted that poor mothers who sold their children as substitute offerings for the children of the wealthy were compelled to keep from showing grief during the sacrifice by the threat of losing their fee. No, there was something more at work here—something spiritual.

As Diodorus noted, the Carthaginians believed their loss to the tyrant of Syracuse, Agathocles, was punishment for failing to provide the required sacrifices to their chief god, Baal Hammon. To atone, the city slaughtered some five hundred of its children.

Why children?

By now, you're wondering how this connects to Molech. Here's how: Although the worship of Molech faded from history after Josiah's reforms in the late seventh century B.C., it was just about that time tophets like the one described in the Bible began to be established at Phoenician colonies in north Africa, Sicily, and Sardinia. Apparently, the sacrifices demanded by Molech were also required by Baal Hammon—who, as we noted above, may have been the same entity. And if you remember your Greek mythology, you've already connected this gruesome practice to the myth of Kronos, who ate his own children to prevent the fulfillment of a prophecy that a son would rise up to destroy him someday.

Now, why would this Watcher-class fallen angel demand child sacrifice from his human followers anyway? There are a couple of possible reasons, but because the Bible doesn't tell us specifically, they are both speculative.

First, we know from Genesis 9 that "the blood is the life." God forbade consuming blood, and further, He declared that for the shedding of human blood—even by animals—a reckoning would be required. It's possible that the shedding of blood produces something the Fallen can use for supernatural power.

Second, this may be as simple as revenge. The Watchers witnessed the deaths of their children, the Nephilim, in the Flood of Noah. Maybe convincing humans that sacrificing our children brings supernatural blessing from the gods was an act of retribution. Imagine how God the Father feels as He watches His children willingly slaughtering the most vulnerable and helpless among us, those He placed in *our* care, so we can win the favor of our older siblings, the angelic children of God who rebelled against Him.

Actually, we don't have to imagine. God told us *exactly* how He feels about it 2,600 years ago in His condemnation of the pagan of the kingdom of Judah:

> And you took your sons and your daughters, whom you had borne to me, and these you sacrificed to [the gods] to be devoured. Were your whorings so small a matter that you slaughtered my children and delivered them up as an offering by fire to them? (Ezekiel 16:20–21, ESV)

In short, because Israel and Judah worshiped other gods, which Yahweh compared to a faithless wife sleeping around on her husband, He declared through Ezekiel that judgment was coming in the form of conquest by foreign invaders, both natural and supernatural. In this context, the pronouns "they" and "them" are just as likely to refer to the gods allotted to the nations as to the people of the pagan nations God was going to bring against Jerusalem.

Let's put this together: The references in 2 Peter and Jude suggest that the Watchers were the Titans, the angels who were banished to Tartarus for their sin, a sexual transgression that produced unholy children, the Nephilim. Thus, Shemihazah, leader of the rebellious Watchers named in the Book of Enoch, would have been Kronos, king of the Titans, who was called Baal Hammon by the Phoenicians. According to Enoch, the Watchers were condemned by God to "see the destruction of their beloved ones" before being bound in the depths of the earth until the Judgment.[95]

So, is it possible that vengeful Watchers and/or the demon spirits of their dead children, the Rephaim/Nephilim,[96] lured the pagan nations of the ancient world into burning *their* sons and daughters as sacrificial offerings to gods of the dead?

Now, consider this: How did God buy our freedom from the wages of sin, which is death? That's right. By sacrificing *His* Son for *us*—the ultimate reversal of the evil introduced to the world at Hermon.[97]

Enter the Rephaim

While the Amorites of the ancient world believed the spirits of their ancestors had some power to affect their lives, there was another group of spirits who received special attention—the Rephaim.

That's not exactly what the Amorites called them. The Semitic root from which we get the biblical name Rephaim (or Rephaite, in older translations) is probably *rp'*, but scholars aren't in complete agreement on that point. The discovery of the texts at Ras Shamra in Syria, site of the ancient Canaanite kingdom of Ugarit, has shed a lot of light on the nature of the Rephaim. However, there still is no consensus among secular scholars about what the name means, where the Rephaim originated, or even who they were to the people outside of Israel.

For example, the majority of scholars believe the underlying meaning of *rapha* is "healer." And, to be fair, there are verses in the Bible where the root word behind "Rephaim" is used that way:

> If you will diligently listen to the voice of the LORD your God, and do that which is right in his eyes, and give ear to his commandments and keep all his statutes, I will put none of the diseases on you that I put on the Egyptians, for I am the LORD, your healer. (Exodus 15:26, ESV)

The root of the word rendered "healer" is *rp'*, the same one behind the name Rephaim, but it's a pretty safe bet that God wasn't telling Moses, "I am Yahweh, your Rapha." However, scholars admit that there isn't a single text outside the Bible where the same root is used in any context that implies health or healing.

So, who were the Rephaim? One thing is sure: There was a special link between them and the Amorites:

> According to Healey, the *rp'um* "were an early Amorite tribe related to Ditānu, whose eponymous ancestor was regarded as the

god Rapi'u. In Ugarit they are looked back to with awe and reverence as ancestors of legendary glory. They may have persisted as part of the royal family.[98]

Talk about divine right to rule! As we make our way through the rest of that chapter, you'll see how important that citation is. Remember the names Ditanu and Rapi'u, because you will see them again.

War with the Rephaim

In the Bible, the Rephaim usually refer to the dead, and specifically to dead royalty. You might not get that impression from your English translation, but that's because the name also applied to tribes that occupied the Transjordan, the area east of the Jordan River from Mount Hermon and Bashan (the modern Golan Heights) south to the Dead Sea. The Bible links the Rephaim tribes to the Amorites both directly and through alliance. Og, who ruled Bashan, was a king of the Amorites,[99] but he was also the last "of the remnant of the Rephaim."[100] We'll explore specific and spiritual connections between the Amorites and the Rephaim a little later.

About four hundred years before the battle between Israel and the forces of Og, a coalition of kings from eastern Mesopotamia led a military expedition against a group of rebellious people in the Transjordan:

> In the days of Amraphel king of Shinar, Arioch king of Ellasar, Chedorlaomer king of Elam, and Tidal king of Goiim, these kings made war with Bera king of Sodom, Birsha king of Gomorrah, Shinab king of Admah, Shemeber king of Zeboiim, and the king of Bela (that is, Zoar). And all these joined forces in the Valley of Siddim (that is, the Salt Sea). Twelve years they had served Chedorlaomer, but in the thirteenth year they rebelled. **In the fourteenth year Chedorlaomer and the kings who were with him came and defeated the Rephaim in Ashteroth-karnaim, the Zuzim in Ham, the Emim in Shaveh-kiriathaim, and the Horites**

in their hill country of Seir as far as El-paran on the border of the wilderness. Then they turned back and came to En-mishpat (that is, Kadesh) and defeated all the country of the Amalekites, and also the Amorites who were dwelling in Hazazon-tamar. (Genesis 14:1–7, ESV; emphasis added)

Scholars have tried to identify the kings from the east ever since the modern archaeological age dawned about two hundred years ago. For a time, it was thought that Amraphel, king of Shinar (Sumer) was none other than Hammurabi, the first great Amorite king of Babylon, but that idea has fallen out of favor. The War of Nine Kings was probably fought about a hundred years before Hammurabi's reign.

We can make pretty good guesses about the homes of the other kings from the east. Elam was an ancient kingdom in what is today northwestern Iran, sitting on the east coast of the Persian Gulf. Chedorlaomer's name was probably something like Kudur-Lagamar, which means "servant of the goddess Lagamar." Unfortunately, archaeologists haven't found a complete list of ancient Elamite kings yet, so we can't say for sure whether a king named Kudur-Lagamar ever existed.

Arioch may have been a king of Larsa[101] in what is today southeastern Iraq. Larsa was one of the Amorite city-states that emerged to fill the power vacuum after the collapse of the last Sumerian kingdom around 2000 B.C. The king of Goiim, Tidal, bears a name that's similar to one that was common among later Hittite kings, Tudhaliya. But since the Hittites were based in what is now central Turkey, it's not likely that Tidal was a Hittite. Some scholars speculate that Goiim, which is Hebrew for "Gentiles," refers to Gutium, a nomadic people who lived in the Zagros mountains between Iraq and Iran.

That fits the time and place of the raid. It's likely that the Sumerian Third Dynasty of Ur collapsed around 2004 B.C., weakened by Amorite tribes that had been moving into southern Mesopotamia for centuries, and then finished off by an invasion of Elamites from the east and Gutians from the northeast. After the fall of Ur, a dark period of about a hundred years clouds the history of Mesopotamia. The fog had begun to lift by the nineteenth century B.C., when Abraham arrived in Canaan, but a king of Elam at that time could have had influence as far west as modern-day Israel.

As with nearly all invasions of the Levant, Chedorlaomer and his allies approached from the north. Crossing the Syrian desert from the east would have been foolish. Water, food, and fodder for animals is more plentiful along the Euphrates. Armies on the march would have followed the river northwest from Babylon to Mari, near the modern border between Iraq and Syria, and then turned west on the caravan trail through Tadmor (Palmyra) and Damascus, before turning south at the Anti-Lebanon mountains, the southernmost peak of which is Mount Hermon.

The first battle of the campaign was at Ashteroth-karnaim, a city in Bashan east of the Sea of Galilee. Clashes with the Rephaim continued as the coalition moved south, probably following the ancient King's Highway. The tribes along the road occupied lands that made up the later kingdoms of Ammon, Moab, and Edom, who called them Zamzummim, Emim, and Horim, respectively.[102]

Reestablishing control of the King's Highway may have been the main reason for Chedorlaomer's raid. The road was an important trade link between Egypt and Mesopotamia. If the Bible's account of the way travelers were treated by the people of Sodom is in any way accurate, commerce between Africa and Mesopotamia may have been disrupted by the rebel kings from the Valley of Siddim, or maybe the rebels were taking too big a piece of the action. There aren't many natural resources in that part of the world other than asphalt and rock, so trade caravans were a major source of wealth for kings and chieftains along the King's Highway.

By the time Moses arrived with two million Israelites, the kingdom of Og was all that was left of the territory that had been controlled by Rephaim in Abraham's day, although similar tribes still held the hill country of Judah. A careful reading of the book of Joshua reveals that his strategy for occupying the Holy Land was focused on taking out the Anakim, who, according to Deuteronomy 2:11, were "counted as Rephaim."

Indeed, the Rephaim disappear from history after the Israelite conquest of Canaan—as flesh-and-blood, mortal men and women. However, they're described elsewhere in the Bible as spirits of the dead. We just don't always recognize the Rephaim because they're not always called by name. For example:

The dead [*rapha*] tremble
under the waters and their inhabitants.
Sheol is naked before God,
and Abaddon has no covering. (Job 26:5, ESV)

Do you work wonders for the dead?
Do the departed [*rapha*] rise up to praise you? *Selah*
Is your steadfast love declared in the grave,
or your faithfulness in Abaddon? (Psalm 88:10, ESV)

This depiction of the *rapha* (Rephaim) as inhabitants of the netherworld is consistent with their description in the texts found at Ras Shamra. But to the citizens of Ugarit around the year 1200 B.C., and probably for hundreds of years before, the powerful spirits of these particular dead played an important role in their religion.

The Great Ones

Moses didn't invent the Rephaim to demonize (literally) Israel's enemies in the war for Canaan. The Rephaim were well known in the ancient Near East. It wasn't always by that name, but they were an integral part of the religion of the Amorites, who dominated the culture of the Near East from the time of Abraham until the time of the Exodus. The nomadic, tribal life of the Amorites is the milieu that produced the Hebrew patriarchs. In fact, the lives of Abraham, Isaac, and Jacob, which spanned the time from the founding of Babylon to the peak of the Hyksos kingdom in northern Egypt, were typical for Amorite herdsmen and traders.

Now, that's not to suggest they *were* Amorites. But their lives had far more in common with the Amorites of Syria than with the city-dwelling Sumerians of what is now southeastern Iraq. Cyrus H. Gordon, a renowned scholar of the ancient Near East, made a convincing case in a 1958 paper that Abram, son of Terah, came not from Ur in Sumer, but from Ura, a town known for traveling merchants located somewhere along the upper Euphrates in northern Mesopotamia.[103] In fact, it was generally believed that Abraham came from the north until the 1920s, when the great archaeologist Sir Leonard Woolley discovered the ruins of Sumerian Ur. As fabulous artifacts of gold, bronze, and lapis lazuli began to emerge from the Iraqi sand, it was decided that the royal city of Ur was a more fitting hometown for the father of nations than a nondescript village still hidden beneath the earth somewhere in southern Turkey.

But besides the similarities in the lifestyles of the patriarchs and the nomadic Amorites, if Abram's father had really meant to travel from Ur to Canaan, the route he chose was the worst possible. As I wrote in *The Great Inception*:

> Logistically, Harran was way too far north and east for Abraham's father Terah to have made it a stop on the way to Canaan if he'd been traveling from Ur in Sumer. There were much shorter routes between Sumer and Canaan—for example, a trade route used by Amorites that linked Mari on the Euphrates to Damascus via Tadmor (Palmyra).
>
> In other words, Mesopotamians in the 21st century B.C. would have mocked anyone from Sumerian Ur who tried to get to Canaan by way of Harran. Ending up at Harran would have required missing one turn completely and then taking another in the wrong direction, away from Canaan. Put it this way: Traveling to Canaan from Ur by way of Harran is like driving from Nashville to Kansas City by way of Minneapolis.[104]

("Harran," by the way, is usually spelled with a double *R* outside the Bible—just so you know that I did that on purpose.)

Searching for hints about the Rephaim in texts outside the Bible gets more difficult as you go farther back in history. As we noted, most scholars lean toward a definition of the Semitic root *rp'* as "healers," but another meaning has been proposed:

> In the light of the repeated occurrence of *rp'um* in military and heroic contexts and the inadequacy of alternative hypotheses, the significance of Ugaritic *r-p-'* might best be understood in the light of Akkadian *raba'um* "to be large, great", and its derivative *rabium* (< *rabûm*) "leader, chief". Thus, the *rp'um* would be "the Great Ones" or "the Mighty Ones."[105]

Not only is this a completely different sense than "healers," it also suggests that the Rephaim were revered at least as far back as the time of Abraham and probably earlier. We'll explore this in an upcoming section when we examine the etymology of the most famous Amorite king, Hammurabi.

Several important texts have been discovered at Ras Shamra in Syria, site of Ugarit, a small but wealthy kingdom during during the second millennium B.C. that reached the peak of its power around the time of the Exodus. The so-called Rephaim Texts, designated KTU 1.20–1.22 by scholars, yield important insights into what the Amorites believed about the Rephaim during the time of the Judges. Generally speaking, the three texts deal with the *rpum*, venerated dead Amorite kings, who are summoned to a ritual meal much like the *kispum*.[106]

> The saviours [*rpum*] will feast:
> seven times the divinities [*ilnym* (elohim)],
> eight times the dead. …
> The saviours hurried to his sanctuary,
> to his sanctuary hurried the divinities.[107]

Note that the word rendered "saviours" is the Ugaritic *rpum* (Rephaim), and "divinities" is translated from the Ugaritic word *ilnym*, which appears to be a cognate for the Hebrew *elohim*. (Note that these are small-*E* elohim, denizens of the spirit realm, not Yahweh.) So, at Ugarit in the time of the judges, the Rephaim were believed to be more than just the dead. They were honored, venerated spirits, a subset of the realm of the elohim.

The sanctuary mentioned in the text above belonged to the Canaanite creator-god, El. All three of the Rephaim texts refer to El's sanctuary, palace, house, plantations, and threshing floor, where a banquet awaits the Rephaim. Based on several lines toward the end of KTU 1.22, which describe El's abode as a "lofty banqueting-house on the peak in the heart of the Lebanon,"[108] it's probable that the location of El's sanctuary was located on Mount Hermon,[109] a significant detail. It's also important to note that some scholars translate KTU 1.22, column i, lines 8 and 9, to read, "There rose up Baal Rapiu, the warriors of Baal and the warriors of Anat [Canaanite war-goddess]."[110]

Although not all scholars agree on that interpretation, you'll see as we get deeper into this book that it's the best fit with what the Bible reveals about the Rephaim. Full disclosure: There are key pieces of information in the Rephaim Texts that we're holding back for a later chapter.

Anyway, invoking the power of the dead through rituals is necromancy, a practice specifically forbidden by God.[111] Obviously, the Amorite neighbors of ancient Israel didn't care much for Yahweh's standards of right and wrong. As we discussed earlier in this chapter, necromancy was not only allowed in Amorite society, it was expected.[112]

Also obviously, the depiction of the Amorites' honored dead, the Rephaim, is very different in the Bible than in the Amorite religious texts dug out of the ground at Ras Shamra.

Lucifer and the Rephaim

One of the most famous passages of the Old Testament is a very specific reference to the divine rebel from Eden:

How art thou fallen from heaven, O Lucifer, son of the morning! how art thou cut down to the ground, which didst weaken
the nations! **For thou hast said in thine heart, I will ascend into
heaven, I will exalt my throne above the stars of God: I will sit
also upon the mount of the congregation, in the sides of the
north: I will ascend above the heights of the clouds; I will be like
the most High.** Yet thou shalt be brought down to hell, to the
sides of the pit. (Isaiah 14:12–15, KJV; emphasis added)

Even though I normally prefer the English Standard Version, which
is a modern, word-for-word translation, the King James Bible better cap-
tures the sense of what happened. While Isaiah's taunt was directed at the
king of Babylon, the Chaldean king is compared to the supernatural rebel
who tempted Adam and Eve in Eden. By so doing, this remarkable chapter links the Rephaim to Baal, and to Gog, the chief prince of Magog in
Ezekiel's prophecy of a war to end all wars.

This means the Rephaim are connected to Zeus, a storm-god like
Baal, and thus to Kronos (aka Baal Hammon, El, and Dagan), and, of
course, the Watchers and Nephilim. And, through Gog of Magog, we can
connect the Rephaim to Armageddon. (We'll show you the evidence for
that in an upcoming chapter.)

Oh, yes—and Satan.

The passage above describes the divine rebel's demotion from anointed
cherub to lord of the dead. And the Rephaim were there to greet the rebel
upon his arrival in the underworld. Here is that section of Isaiah 14 from
the ESV:

Sheol beneath is stirred up
to meet you when you come;
**it rouses the shades [*rapha*] to greet you,
all who were leaders of the earth;
it raises from their thrones
all who were kings of the nations.**

All of them will answer
and say to you:
"You too have become as weak as we!
You have become like us!"
Your pomp is brought down to Sheol,
the sound of your harps;
maggots are laid as a bed beneath you,
and worms are your covers.
How you are fallen from heaven,
O Day Star, son of Dawn!
How you are cut down to the ground,
you who laid the nations low!
You said in your heart,
"I will ascend to heaven;
above the stars of God
I will set my throne on high;
I will sit on the mount of assembly
in the far reaches of the north;
I will ascend above the heights of the clouds;
I will make myself like the Most High."
All the kings of the nations lie in glory,
each in his own tomb;
but you are cast out, away from your grave,
like a loathed branch,
clothed with the slain, those pierced by the sword,
who go down to the stones of the pit,
like a dead body trampled underfoot. (Isaiah 14:9–19, ESV;
emphasis added)

Here, Isaiah describes how Satan was kicked out of Eden and greeted by the Rephaim on landing. This depiction of the *rapha*, the Rephaim, as "leaders of the earth" and "kings of the nations," is consistent with how they were perceived by the Amorites.

Now, because you pay attention to details, you may be waving a red flag right about now. How could the Rephaim already be in Sheol if Lucifer had just been kicked out of Eden? Weren't Adam and Eve the only humans? Weren't the Nephilim, who produced the spirits called Rephaim in Isaiah, created long after Adam and Eve were tossed out of Eden? Good questions.

Remember, Satan still had access to the throne room of God at least until the time of Job. Based on clues in the Bible, Job probably lived in the third millennium B.C., after Babel but before Abraham. So, Satan's ejection from the divine council may not have occurred until about the time God called Abram out of a town in northern Mesopotamia, or even later. Another possibility is that "the satan," which is how the Hebrew literally reads in the Old Testament, was a job title like "prosecuting attorney" that was held by different elohim over the centuries.

Back to point: Isaiah's reference to the "mount of assembly" is far more significant than most of us have been taught. Let's break this down.

In my first book, *The Great Inception*, I illustrated the importance of holy mountains in the Bible. Controlling the mount of assembly (in Hebrew, the *har mô 'ēd*) is the objective of the enemy's rebellion. Isaiah made that clear in the passage above. What most of us have not been taught, however, was that Eden was the original *har mô 'ēd*, the holy mountain of God:

> Because your heart is proud,
> and you have said, 'I am a god,
> I sit in the seat of the gods,
> in the heart of the seas,' [...]
> **You were in Eden, the garden of God;**
> every precious stone was your covering,
> sardius, topaz, and diamond,
> beryl, onyx, and jasper,
> sapphire, emerald, and carbuncle;
> and crafted in gold were your settings

and your engravings.
On the day that you were created
they were prepared.
You were an anointed guardian cherub.
I placed you; you were on the holy mountain of God;
in the midst of the stones of fire you walked.
You were blameless in your ways
from the day you were created,
till unrighteousness was found in you. (Ezekiel 28:2, 13–15, ESV;
emphasis added)

Most scholars agree that the lament over the king of Tyre in Ezekiel 28 is a parallel to Isaiah 14. Both prophets used the divine rebel from Eden to illustrate their polemics against the physical enemies of God's people, Israel. The guardian cherub, the serpent (Hebrew *nachash*), was in the garden, yes, but it was a garden on the holy mountain of God—the mount of assembly, the "seat of the gods."

God has always lived on mountains: first, Eden; then Sinai; now (and forevermore), Zion—the Temple Mount in Jerusalem:

For the LORD has chosen Zion;
he has desired it for his dwelling place:
"This is my resting place forever;
here I will dwell, for I have desired it. (Psalm 132:13–14, ESV)

On that day [the Day of the LORD; i.e., Judgment Day] the LORD
will punish
the host of heaven, in heaven,
and the kings of the earth, on the earth.
They will be gathered together
as prisoners in a pit;
they will be shut up in a prison,
and after many days they will be punished.

Then the moon will be confounded
and the sun ashamed,
for the LORD of hosts reigns
on Mount Zion and in Jerusalem,
and his glory will be before his elders. (Isaiah 24:21–23, ESV)

The "host of heaven," including the moon and sun, represented the gods of the ancient Near East[113] and those small-*G* gods are real. Isaiah was not using symbolic language. A day is coming when *those gods will die.* Read Psalm 82 for the courtroom scene where God delivered His sentence on the rebellious sons of the Most High.

The Mountain of God

The Bible is a chronicle of the long war by the fallen elohim, their demonic offspring, and human collaborators against the authority of our Creator. Mountains have played a key role in this rebellion.

The concept of the mount of assembly was known to the pagan neighbors of the ancient Israelites. As far back as the time of Sumerian dominance in Mesopotamia, the third millennium B.C. (3000–2000 B.C.), it was believed the divine council led by the chief god, Enlil, met at his temple in the city of Nippur, the *E-kur* (House of the Mountain). Remember, Enlil himself was called "Great Mountain."

To the Canaanites in the time of the Judges, roughly 1300–1200 B.C., their creator-god El met with his "assembled congregation" (in Ugaritic, *pḫr m 'd*) on Mount Hermon in the "tents of El." Although scholars would present this the other way around, the tents of El reflect the dwelling of Yahweh, the Tent of Meeting and the tabernacle, which housed the Ark of the Covenant for more than three hundred years before Solomon built the Temple on Mount Zion.

You see, this whole war is about the mountain. The divine rebel's goal is to establish *his* mount of assembly above that of Yahweh's. That is still his greatest wish. (It may be the goal of many of these rebel gods, actually.

The history of war between nations suggests that there may be as much competition between the fallen elohim as there is between the Fallen and Yahweh.) The prophets, psalmists, and apostles knew about this war for the mount. As you read the Bible with a careful eye, you'll see references to other mountains that the Fallen hoped to establish as the *har mô ʿēd*.

So, which mountain did Isaiah identify? According to scholar Edward Lipinski, El's mount of assembly was probably Mount Hermon,[114] but that isn't the one in view in Isaiah 14. The Hebrew phrase *yerekah tsaphon*, rendered "far reaches of the north," is the key to identification. The phrase is used only three places in the Hebrew Bible, so looking at the other occurrences gives us important context.

For example, in Psalm 48, the psalmist compares Zion to *yerekah tsaphon*:

> Great is the LORD and greatly to be praised
> in the city of our God!
> His holy mountain, beautiful in elevation,
> is the joy of all the earth,
> Mount Zion, **in the far north** [*yerekah tsaphon*],
> the city of the great King. (Psalm 48:1–2, ESV; emphasis added)

How do we know the psalmist's intent? Well, first of all, Mount Zion isn't in the "far north." Everyone in David's day knew there was plenty of real estate north of Zion, even inside Israel. Second, while Zion is beautiful, it's a bit short on elevation. It's not even the tallest peak in Jerusalem. At 2,428 feet, the Temple Mount is almost a hundred feet lower than the modern Mount Zion (the former Western Hill was thought to be more fitting for David's palace, so it was renamed Zion in the first century), and almost three hundred feet below the highest spot on the Mount of Olives. In short, the psalmist was making a point about theology, not geography.

The "far north" in Psalm 48:2 refers to another cosmic mountain, a mount of assembly (*har mô ʿēd*) that everyone in the ancient world knew was the home of the palace of the king of the Canaanite gods, Baal:

A seat was prepared and he was seated at the right hand of Valiant Baal, until the gods had eaten and drunk. Then Valiant Baal said, "Depart, Kothar-and-Hasis! Hasten! Build a house indeed; hasten! Construct a palace! Hasten! Let them build a house; Hasten! **Let them construct a palace, in the midst of the uttermost parts of Zaphon. A thousand square yards let the house take up, ten thousand acres the palace!**"[115] (Emphasis added)

Baal sits like the base of a mountain
Hadad [proper name of the storm-god, Baal] **settles as the ocean, in the midst of his divine mountain Zaphon,**
in the midst of the mountain of victory.
Seven lightning-flashes [...],
eight bundles of thunder,
a tree-of-lightning in his right hand.[116] (Emphasis added)

Highlight this, at least in your mind: The mount of assembly of the divine rebel in Eden is the holy mountain of the Canaanite storm-god Baal.

In other words, the rebel from Eden evidently manifested to later humans as the storm-god—Baal to the Canaanites and Israelites, Zeus to the Greeks, Jupiter to the Romans, Teshub to the Hurrians, and Tarhunz to the Hittites (and maybe even Indra to the Indians, Thor to the Norsemen, and so on). This is not only a key historical detail, it's important to understanding end-times prophecy.

Why? Because we know exactly where this mountain is. Mount Zaphon is known today as Jebel al-Aqra, a 5,600-foot peak in Turkey on the border with Syria, near the mouth of the Orontes River on the Mediterranean Sea. The Amorite kingdom of Ugarit was based only twenty-five miles south of Zaphon.

Besides being the home of Baal's palace, it was believed to be the holy mountain of Teshub and the place where Zeus battled the chaos-monster, Typhon. That conflict was very similar to Baal's battle with the chaos god of the sea, Yamm, both of which echo the original story, Yahweh's defeat of Leviathan.[117] Zaphon was so important in ancient Israel that its name became the Hebrew word for the compass point "north."[118]

Now, let's add a couple more bits of data to chew on. The fourteenth chapter of Isaiah is even more intriguing than it appears. First, let's look closer at verses 18 and 19:

> All the kings of the nations lie in glory,
> each in his own tomb;
> **but you are cast out, away from your grave,**
> **like a loathed branch,**
> clothed with the slain, those pierced by the sword,
> who go down to the stones of the pit,
> like a dead body trampled underfoot.
> (Isaiah 14:18–19, ESV; emphasis added)

What did the prophet mean by calling the rebel from Eden "a loathed branch"? Most English translations agree that the Hebrew word *netser* means "branch," although a couple opt for "shoot." The range of adjectives chosen by translators includes "loathed," "repulsive," "rejected," "worthless," and "abominable," but they convey the same sense—something utterly detestable. But even allowing for differences in culture and language over the last 2,700 years, the phrase "loathed/worthless/abominable branch" seems odd. It is not at all clear what connection there could have been between graves and branches, abominable or otherwise, in the eighth century B.C.

Scholar Christopher B. Hays has suggested an explanation: Perhaps Isaiah meant something different because the Hebrew word *netser* might not have been the word he used.

> [The] term is best explained as a loanword from the common Egyptian noun *ntr*. **Ntr is generally translated "god," but is commonly used of the divinized dead and their physical remains.** It

originally came into Hebrew as a noun referring to the putatively divinized corpse of a dead king, which is closely related to the Egyptian usage.[119] (Emphasis added)

Considering what we've just discussed in the previous sections about the Rephaim, the "kings of the nations," being the venerated dead kings of the Amorites (in other words, the "divinized dead"), Hays' proposal rings true.

Now, why a loanword from Egypt? The influence of Judah's southwestern neighbor is evident in the book of Isaiah. The prophet warned Hezekiah not to trust in an Egyptian alliance to protect his kingdom (Isaiah 30:1–2, 31:1–3), which Isaiah called "a covenant with death" (Isaiah 28:15). However, recently discovered seals from King Hezekiah feature the image of a scarab (dung beetle), a sacred symbol in Egypt.[120] So, borrowing an Egyptian word would not have been unusual for Isaiah, especially given the poor opinion he had of Judah's neighbor.

The adjective translated "abhorred" or "abominable," Hebrew *ta`ab*, is significant. It modifies the noun *netser*, which would normally have a positive connotation. In this context, *ta`ab* may suggest "ritually impure."[121] If so, then Isaiah made a profound declaration here about the rebel from Eden: The "loathed branch" was actually an "unclean god," and in the context of the Rephaim greeting the rebel upon his arrival in Sheol, it would describe an unclean god of the dead—exactly the role assigned to Lucifer after he was kicked out of Eden.

If that wasn't enough to make you wonder where that verse has been hiding all this time, let's look at another plausible loanword in Isaiah 14. Dr. Michael S. Heiser, author of the highly recommended books *The Unseen Realm* and *Reversing Hermon*, has made a good case for the derivation of the word "Nephilim" from an Aramaic noun, *naphil(a)*, which means "giant."[122] It's similar to the Hebrew word *naphal*, "to fall," which has led many to conclude that *nephilim* essentially means "fallen ones." While they certainly were that, Heiser points out that the rules of Hebrew would make the plural form *nephulim*, while "those who fall away" would be *nophelim*.[123] In other words, "Nephilim" is based on an Aramaic word, because in Hebrew, even though the words look and sound the same, you just can't get there from here.

The point is this: Heiser has speculated that something similar might be obscuring a more intriguing reading of the end of Isaiah 14:

> May the offspring of evildoers
> nevermore be named!
> Prepare slaughter for his sons
> because of the guilt of their fathers,
> lest they rise and possess the earth,
> and fill the face of the world with cities. (Isaiah 14:20b–21, ESV)

That's odd. I'm from Chicago. What's so bad about cities?

Here's the key: The Hebrew word for "city" is `iyr`. In Aramaic, the very same word means "Watcher." The plural forms are `iyrim` and `iyrin`, respectively. Thanks to Dr. Heiser, we have a good example above of an Aramaic word that was imported into the Bible and then corrected with the *-im* plural suffix, transforming *naphil(a)* into *nephilim*, according to Hebrew rules of word formation.[124] It's possible that Hebrew scholars in the centuries after Isaiah opted for "cities" to obscure the influence of the hated Watchers.

Now, because you're very perceptive, you see right off how that would change the passage above in an important way:

> Prepare slaughter for his sons
> because of the guilt of their fathers,
> lest they rise and possess the earth,
> and fill the face of the world **with Watchers**.
> (Isaiah 14:21, ESV, modified)

That puts a new spin on the verse—and on the whole chapter, for that matter. Isaiah may have intended to record God's judgment against the offspring of the rebel angels on Hermon, the Watchers, and their progeny, the Nephilim. But this isn't the only place in Isaiah where a Watchers-for-cities swap makes sense.

> **Behold, their heroes cry in the streets;**
> **the envoys of peace weep bitterly.**
>> The highways lie waste;
>> the traveler ceases.
>> Covenants are broken;
>> **cities are despised;**
>> there is no regard for man.
>> The land mourns and languishes;
>> **Lebanon is confounded and withers away;**
>> Sharon is like a desert,
>> **and Bashan and Carmel shake off their leaves.**
>> (Isaiah 33:7–9, ESV; emphasis added)

This is another fascinating section of Scripture. The word translated "heroes" in verse 7 is the Hebrew *'er'el.* Elsewhere in the Bible, it's transliterated into English as "Ariel," which means "lion of God." While we don't want to follow unbiblical notions too far, we note that later Jewish tradition was that the Arielites were angels.[125] And that isn't entirely out of context here. The "ariels" in verse 7 are paralleled by "envoys," which in Hebrew are *malakim*, a word that means "messengers," but that often refers to the lowest class of angel. So, reading "ariels" here as "angelic beings" may not be a reach.

Looking back three hundred years before Isaiah, "ariel" was a puzzling reference to one of the exploits of David's mighty men:

And Benaiah the son of Jehoiada was a valiant man of Kabzeel, a doer of great deeds. **He struck down two ariels of Moab.** He also went down and struck down a lion in a pit on a day when snow had fallen. (2 Samuel 23:20, ESV; emphasis added)

Compare that to the King James translation:

And Benaiah the son of Jehoiada, the son of a valiant man, of
Kabzeel, who had done many acts, **he slew two lionlike men of
Moab**: he went down also and slew a lion in the midst of a pit in
time of snow. (2 Samuel 23:20, KJV; emphasis added)

Were the lionlike men of Moab like the descendants of the giants
(*yâlîyd rapha*, "sons of the Rephaim") encountered by David during
his wars with the Philistines?[126] In other words, were the ariels, like the
Nephilim, human-angel hybrids? The Bible doesn't tell us, so we can't
know for sure. Rather than speculate, the ESV translators played it safe by
leaving the word "ariels" untranslated.

However, the context of Isaiah 33 suggests that the ariels, the "heroes"
of verse 7, were more than human. Besides the pairing with the *malakim*
of peace, the references to Lebanon, Bashan, and Carmel, a mountain
known as a holy site for centuries before Isaiah,[127] indicate either a lament
for a supernatural event that had just occurred or dread of something
that was about to happen. And that, of course, makes the substitution of
Watchers for cities not only plausible, but logical:

The highways lie waste;
the traveler ceases.
Covenants are broken;
Watchers are despised;
there is no regard for man. (Isaiah 33:8, ESV, modified)

Now, here's a hint without revealing a spoiler for what's ahead in this
book: Make a mental note to remember the word "traveler." It's important. You'll look back at this section and understand why we made this
detour.

So, yes, some of this is speculative, but it's based on the original languages and the cultural-religious world in which Isaiah lived. Yes, Isaiah

14:21 was a condemnation of the king of Babylon, but it appears it was also God's death sentence on the Nephilim, the sons of the Watchers. And if we consider that alongside the possibility that the "loathed branch" of verse 19 was in fact an unclean god, then Isaiah revealed a lot more about the war between God and the gods than we've been taught.

Isaiah 14 Summary

Summing up: The supernatural rebel known to Hebrews as Helel ben Shachar and to us as Lucifer, one of the cherubim and possibly a guardian of the throne of Yahweh, was kicked out of Eden for rebellion. His plan was to establish a new mount of assembly, Zaphon, as supreme in the cosmos, ruling above the throne of Yahweh Himself. Instead, the rebel was thrown down to the underworld, cast out as an "unclean god" to become lord of the dead, where he was greeted in Sheol by the Rephaim, former "leaders of the earth" and "kings of the nations."

This, by the way, fulfilled in part the judgment against him for his rebellion:

> Because you have done this,
> cursed are you above all livestock
> and above all beasts of the field;
> on your belly you shall go,
> and dust you shall eat
> all the days of your life. (Genesis 3:14, ESV)

Most of us read this verse and assume that this is when snakes lost their legs and humans learned to hate them. Not so. Adam and Eve weren't fooled by a talking snake. References to the divine rebel in Ezekiel 28 and Isaiah 14 make it clear the serpent was a supernatural entity, a guardian cherub—a divine throne guardian who got above his raising and was taken down for his hubris.

The interesting bit here, which my wife, Sharon, called to my attention, is the dust eating. You know enough biology to realize snakes don't eat dust. So, God may have been speaking metaphorically to the *nachash*. Or, as Sharon pointed out, God may have been alluding to the common belief in ancient Mesopotamia that the dead spend the afterlife wandering about the netherworld eating dust and clay. That's exactly how serpents were depicted in ancient Near Eastern texts such as *Descent of Inanna*.[128]

In other words, Genesis 3:14 telegraphs Isaiah 14:9–11. The pinnacle of God's creation, "full of wisdom and perfect in beauty," was cast down from the holy mountain of God to become the abominable, loathed, unclean lord of the dead, the *rapha*—the Rephaim.

Over time, the rebel *nachash* established himself among mankind as the storm-god and king of the pantheon under names such as Hadad (Baal), Tarhunz, Zeus, and Jupiter. We'll address the connections between the divine rebel, the storm-god, and Satan in a later chapter.

But even though the storm-god ruled the pagan cosmos for about two thousand years up to the time of Jesus, Hadad/Zeus is only one cog in a vast supernatural conspiracy against Yahweh. You see, the old gods are down—but they're not quite out.

FROM MESOPOTAMIA TO GREECE

Y ou have probably deduced from the title of this book that my goal is to show the connections between Greek mythology and the Bible, and especially Bible prophecy.

You are, of course, correct. We're getting to that, but we have to lay a lot of groundwork to get from points A (Amorites), B (Babylon), and C (Canaan), all the way to point G (Greece).

We've briefly discussed the foundations of the case:

The Nephilim were the giant offspring of rebellious angels and human women.

The rebellious angels were the Watchers. They were punished by being sent to Tartarus, where they are still in chains waiting for the final judgment.

Other elohim were placed over the nations after the Tower of Babel. They also rebelled and set themselves up as the gods of the pagans.

The Amorite neighbors of ancient Israel venerated their ancestors, and especially their dead kings, whom they believed to be the Rephaim. Ancestors and Rephaim alike were honored and provided for by summoning them to meals with necromancy rituals.

With me so far? Good. At this point, we need to introduce a gentleman who's written several paradigm-shifting academic papers for those of us trying to understand the long war of the Fallen.

Amar Annus is an Estonian scholar whose specialty is the cosmology of the ancient Near East. In 2010, his paper, "On the Origin of Watchers: A Comparative Study of the Antediluvian Wisdom in Mesopotamian and Jewish Traditions," connected some very important dots. Annus demonstrated that the Watchers were not a creation of the ancient Hebrews, but were well known to their Mesopotamian predecessors as *apkallu*.[129] The brief summary that follows is drawn from his study.

Briefly, the *apkallu* were primordial sages sent by the Sumerian god Enki (called Ea by the later Akkadians), the lord of the *abzu*—the abyss. They were believed to have brought the gifts of civilization to humanity, although there were times when they malicious, demonic beings capable of witchcraft.

There were three types of *apkallu*: A bearded man with wings; a winged, bird-headed humanoid; and a fish-cloaked man who has been mistakenly identified for more than 150 years as the god Dagon or one of his priests.[130]

Interestingly, in Babylon they connected the disappearance of the *apkallu* to the great flood. The chief god of their pantheon, Marduk, claimed to have punished them for something:

> Once long ago, indeed I grew angry, indeed I left my dwelling, and caused the deluge! When I left my dwelling, the regulation of heaven and earth disintegrated. [...] I sent those craftsmen down to the depths [Apsû], I ordered them not to come up.[131]

In other words, just like the Watchers, who were *tartaróō* (thrust down to Tartarus) by God for corrupting humanity, the Amorites of Babylon believed the *apkallu* had been banished to the Abyss by Marduk for some unspecified transgression, and at exactly the same time—the great flood.

Same story, different worldview.

Old Gods of the Greeks

Now, let's bring in the Greeks. As we discussed in the previous chapter, religions of the ancient Near East followed a pattern: Over time, old gods were replaced or overthrown by successive generations of younger gods. To the Greeks, these generational roles were filled by sky-god Ouranos, the grain-god Kronos, and the storm-god, Zeus.

Briefly, Ouranos caused his wife, Gaia (Earth), great pain by locking away in her belly their eldest children, the giant Kyklopes and Hekatonkheires (also called the Centimanes, or Hundred-Handers). Gaia persuaded their other children, the Titans, to rebel. With the help of four of his brothers, the youngest, Kronos, castrated Ouranos with an adamantine sickle. But instead of freeing his siblings, Kronos and his bunch drove the Kyklopes and the Hundred-Handers into Tartarus, where they were bound with heavy chains. Kronos then assumed kingship over the Titans and married his sister, Rhea.

The era of Kronos' rule was called the Golden Age by later Greeks, a time when everyone had enough and there was no need of laws, because everyone did the right thing. We'll come back to that in a bit.

Ouranos, probably looking to stir up trouble to get a little payback, prophesied that Kronos "was destined to be overcome by his own son, strong though he was."[132] Trying to prevent the prophecy from being fulfilled, Kronos proceeded to eat his children as soon as Rhea gave birth, dispatching Demeter, Hestia, Hera, Hades, and Poseidon in that fashion. However, with advice from Gaia, Rhea secretly gave birth to Zeus on the island of Crete and then presented Kronos with a stone wrapped in swaddling, which he promptly swallowed. Good thing for Zeus that Kronos wasn't a picky eater.

Well, Zeus grew to adulthood and managed to force Kronos to disgorge his siblings. Then he freed the Kyklopes and Hundred-Handers, and together with the rest of the Olympians, Zeus overthrew Kronos and the Titans in an epic war called the Titanomachy, which concluded with most of the Titans locked up in Tartarus.

There are different accounts of what eventually happened to Kronos. In some accounts, he was banished to Tartarus permanently, while in others, he was released to rule over Elysium, a section of the afterlife reserved for heroes (the demigods), the righteous, and those related to the gods. In one account, Virgil's *Aeneid*, Kronos (Saturn) escaped from the Abyss to emerge as king and lawgiver at Latium, the part of Italy where Rome was founded.

You undoubtedly noticed that Kronos and his bunch were sent to Tartarus, the very place reserved for the angels who sinned in Genesis 6. You might dismiss that as a coincidence or conclude that Peter simply named Tartarus as their place of punishment because it was familiar to readers in a world that had been dominated by Greek thought for nearly four hundred years.

I think not. Remember, 2 Peter 2:4 is the only verse in the Bible where Tartarus is mentioned. The usual term for the dwelling of the disobedient dead was Hades. Did Peter know the difference? Yes. He referred to Hades in his sermon on Pentecost (Acts 2:27, 30). Besides, where did Peter get his theological training? And did he write under the guidance of the Holy Spirit or not? (That's not an answer that will satisfy secular scholars, but we don't have time to dig all the way down to Christian Apologetics 101 in this book.)

At the risk of putting too fine a point on it: The Mesopotamian *apkallu*, the angels who sinned, called Watchers in 1 Enoch, and the Greek Titans were one and the same. So, it's possible that Kronos, king of the Titans, was known to the ancient Hebrews as Shemihazah, leader of the Watchers who descended on the summit of Hermon.

Dead Kings and Rephaim

Now, here's where it gets weird.

The ancestor veneration at Ugarit includes a group we mentioned in the last chapter, an ancient Amorite tribe called the Tidnum, or Tidanu, by the last Sumerian kings of Mesopotamia. At Ugarit, they were called the Ditanu or Didanu. This was the tribe that was so frightening, the Sumerians of Ur built that 170-mile long wall to "keep Tidnum away."

Archaeologists have found texts that show the Amorite founders of Babylon and the ruling house of the Kingdom of Upper Mesopotamia (eighteenth century B.C., the time of Isaac and Jacob) traced their ancestry back to this tribe.[133] However, by the time of Ugarit, the Ditanu/Didanu appear to be a legendary group rather than historical, definitely among the pantheon of gods.

In a Ugaritic ritual text only translated about forty years ago, the Didanu are among a number of spirits summoned during a ritual that was apparently performed at the coronation of the last king of Ugarit, Ammurapi III:

"Sacrifice of the Shades" liturgy:

You are summoned, O Rephaim of the earth,
You are invoked, O council of the Didanu!
    Ulkn, the Raphi', is summoned,
    Trmn, the Raphi', is summoned,
    Sdn-w-rdn is summoned,
    Tr 'llmn is summoned,
    the Rephaim of old are summoned!
You are summoned, O Rephaim of the earth,
You are invoked, O council of the Didanu![134]

Like the Rephaim, the council of the Didanu holds an honored place among the spirits. Other texts from Ugarit suggest that kings aspired to be counted among that number upon their deaths. For example, in the *Legend of Keret*, El blesses the king thus:

Be greatly exalted, Keret,
among the *rpum* of the underworld,
in the convocation of the assembly of Ditan.[135]

This further links the Rephaim (*rpum*) to the council/assembly of the Didanu. And a fragmentary ritual text, RS 24.248 (KTU 1.104), mentions "the temple of Ditanu," making it clear that this council or assembly was more than just the honored dead, they were counted among the gods.[136] In fact, in my view, the name of the greatest king of the Amorites confirms this.

The etymology of the name of Hammurabi, the famous lawgiver of the Amorite dynasty that founded Babylon, is usually explained thus: *Ammu* ("father" or "paternal kinsman") + *rapi* ("healer"). But, as we explained earlier, scholars can't point to any texts outside the Bible where the Akkadian and Ugaritic cognates to *rp'*, the root behind Rephaim, means "healer." Instead, as we noted earlier, it's more likely related to the Akkadian word meaning "to be large, great," and by extension, "leader" or "chief."

Since *rapi* is obviously the theophoric element (the god-name) in *Ammu-rapi*, it's more plausible to render Hammurabi as "my fathers are the Rephaim" or "my fathers are the Great Ones."

By the way, there were at least five other Amorite kings named Hammurabi over a period of more than five hundred years, from the great lawgiver to the last king of Ugarit, Ammurapi III. Through their names, the kings of the Amorites claimed a direct link to the Rephaim, who were the demigod sons of the Watchers, the Nephilim.

Greek Rephaim

The link to the Greek pantheon, not surprisingly, also comes from groundbreaking work by Amar Annus. His 1999 paper, "Are There Greek Rephaim? On the Etymology of Greek *Meropes* and *Titanes*," is the source for most of what follows.[137] The subject matter of his paper is dense. It's way outside our scope to reproduce his chain of logic entirely, so I'll summarize as best I can.

The Greek word *merops*, not surprisingly, roughly means "healer." *Merops* has a West Semitic origin, the same root (*rp*), from which we get Ugaritic *rpum* and Hebrew Rephaim. The Greek poets Hesiod and Homer used the phrase *meropes anthropoi* (μερόπων ἀνθρώπων)[138] to describe the "golden race of mortal men who lived in the time of Kronos when he was reigning in heaven."

Hesiod provides another clue to the identity of the *meropes anthropoi*:

> When they died, it was as though they were overcome with sleep, and they had all good things; for the fruitful earth unforced bare them fruit abundantly and without stint. They dwelt in ease and peace upon their lands with many good things, rich in flocks and loved by the blessed gods. **But after earth had covered this generation—they are called Pure Spirits (*daimones hagnoi*) dwelling on the earth**, and are kindly, delivering from harm, and guardians of mortal men; for they roam everywhere over the earth, clothed in mist and keep watch on judgements and cruel deeds, givers of wealth; for this royal right also they received.[139] (Emphasis added)

Note Hesiod's description of the fate of the *meropes anthropoi*: At death, they became *daimones*—demons.

Giants and Demons

The Greek story of the origin of demons is consistent with Jewish beliefs, although they had very different views on the nature of those spirits. In 1 Enoch, demons were the spirits of the giants born to human woman from their union with the angelic Watchers:

> **But now the giants who were begotten by the spirits and flesh— they will call them evil spirits on the earth**, for their dwelling will be on the earth. **The spirits that have gone forth from the body of their flesh are evil spirits,** for from humans they came into being, and from the holy watchers was the origin of their creation. Evil spirits they will be on the earth, and evil spirits they will be

called. The spirits of heaven, in heaven is their dwelling; but the spirits begotten on the earth, on the earth is their dwelling. And the spirits of the giants <lead astray>, do violence, make desolate, and attack and wrestle and hurl upon the earth and <cause ill-nesses>. They eat nothing, but abstain from food and are thirsty and smite. These spirits (will) rise up against the sons of men and against the women, for they have come forth from them.

From the day of the slaughter and destruction and death of the giants, from the soul of whose flesh the spirits are proceeding, they are making desolate without (incurring) judgment. Thus they will make desolate until the day of the consummation of the great judgment, when the great age will be consummated.[140] (Emphasis added)

Now, there are good reasons that the Book of Enoch is not included in the canon of Scripture. A good bit of what's in Enoch can't be confirmed by the Bible, and so the book as a whole should mainly be taken as evidence of what Jews of the Second Temple period (530 B.C.–A.D. 70) thought about the spirit realm.

But remember, that period of history includes the writings of the later prophets and the entire apostolic age, so Enoch is a helpful guide to understanding and adding context to what they wrote. If Enoch was completely unreliable, Jesus would have told the apostles, and the Holy Spirit would have prevented all references to it. But that happens not to be the case. Jude quotes 1 Enoch 1:9 in verses 14 and 15 of his short epistle, and Enoch's account of the origin of demons was the common belief among the early church fathers:

"And when the angels of God saw the daughters of men that they were beautiful, they took unto themselves wives of all of them whom they Chose." Those beings, whom other philosophers call demons, Moses usually calls angels; and they are souls hovering in the air. (Philo, *On the Giants 6*)

In my opinion, however, it is certain wicked demons, and, so to speak, of the race of Titans or Giants, who have been guilty of impiety towards the true God, and towards the angels in heaven, and who have fallen from it, and who haunt the denser parts of bodies, and frequent unclean places upon earth, and who, possessing some power of distinguishing future events, because they are without bodies of earthly material, engage in an employment of this kind, and desiring to lead the human race away from the true God. (Origen, *gainst Celsus 4.92;* emphasis added)

God...committed the care of men and of all things under heaven to angels whom He appointed over them. **But the angels transgressed this appointment, and were captivated by love of women, and begot children who are those that are called demons;** and besides, they afterwards subdued the human race to themselves, partly by magical writings, and partly by fears and the punishments they occasioned, and partly by teaching them to offer sacrifices, and incense, and libations, of which things they stood in need after they were enslaved by lustful passions; and among men they sowed murders, wars, adulteries, intemperate deeds, and all wickedness. (Justin Martyr, *2 Apology 5;* emphasis added)

Note that Justin Martyr understood that the angelic Watchers not only fathered the giants, who in turn became demons, they lured humans into worshiping them as gods and sowed the seeds of evil that matured into "all wickedness."

Heroes

Now, here's another link in the chain of evidence showing how classical Greece and Rome inherited much of its religion from the East, in this case, it appears, specifically from the Amorites.

The word "hero" has a much different meaning today than it did two thousand years ago. For us, a hero is a soldier, a firefighter, a police officer, or a star athlete. To the ancient Greeks, a *heros* was a dead person who remained powerful in death and was therefore venerated by the living. Heroes were believed to be historical persons, often ancestors. Like the Amorite kings of Ugarit, then, the living could aspire to becoming a *heros* after death.[141]

Heroes were expected (or feared) to show supernatural power after death. Epic heroes were elevated to the status of protector of their cities,[142] such as Theseus at Athens and Herakles, under the Phoenician name Melqart, at Tyre. While there was no standard form for the cult of heroes, there was one common element:

> The one central feature of heroic cult, though, is the common meal at the *hērōion* as an expression of the importance which the hero has for the community gathered around his cult-place; from it, heroic iconography develops the meal scene as a standard theme in its iconographic repertoire.[143]

So, it appears that the Greeks inherited the Amorite practices of venerating the demigods, whom they considered their ancestors, and something like the *kispum* ritual as well. What's startling, however, is that this practice was brought into the Christian church by the well-intentioned but misguided Augustine:

> Christian writers first accepted the term [*daimones*] and the concomitant belief in dangerous and demonic dead (Tertullian, *De an.* 49, 2). Augustine, however, argued for a positive connotation of the term and a differentiation from the negative *daemones*: in the Christian sense, heroes were the martyrs (*CD* 10, 21). This not only followed a use of the word already known in Christian poetry, but laid the theoretical foundation for the cult of the saints as the Christian hero cult.[144]

Did you catch that? Augustine, by trying to rehabilitate Greek hero worship, established a theological basis for canonizing and venerating saints, a practice that continues in Roman Catholic and Orthodox churches to this day. And it can be linked directly to the Amorite cult of the Rephaim.

The bottom line: The Greek *meropes anthropoi* of the Golden Age, who were the heroes of the Golden Age ruled by Kronos, were one and the same with the giants—the Nephilim. And just like the Rephaim venerated by the Amorites, the demigods of the Greeks received worship and sacrifices.

Funny how that part of the story never makes it into the movies or novels marketed to our kids.

Titans and Amorites

Now, here's a mind-blower: Further confirmation that we're absolutely correct to identify the Titans as the biblical Watchers and the Greek heroes as the Nephilim/Rephaim is the etymological link between the venerated ancestral tribe of the Amorite kings, the Didanu/Tidanu, and the old gods of the Greeks:

> Then it may not be overbold to assume that **Greek *Titanes* originates from the name of the semi-mythological warrior-tribe (in Ugarit) *tdn*** — mythically related with *Rpum* in the Ugarit, and once actually tied together with Biblical Rephaim in II Sam 5:18-22, where we have in some manuscripts Hebrew *rp'm* rendered into LXX [Greek] as Titanes.[145] (Emphasis added)

Did you catch that? The ancient Amorite tribe the Ditanu/Tidanu—remember, the one that freaked out the last Sumerian kings of Mesopotamia—was not only venerated by the Amorites of Ugarit, *it's where the Greeks got the name of the Titans.* The Watchers, the angels who "kept not their first estate," were called Titans by the Greeks—the name of an ancient Amorite tribe.

The Amorites dominated the world of Abraham, Isaac, and Jacob. They founded Babylon and its occult system, which was condemned in the Bible by everyone from Moses to John the Revelator. *And their kings claimed to be descended from the Titans.*

At least one of the Greek heroes of the Golden Age clearly has origins in the Near East. The name of Bellerophon, who tamed the flying horse Pegasus and is called by some "the greatest hero and slayer of monsters, alongside Cadmus and Perseus, before the days of Herakles,"[146] may be "a transparent transcription of West Semitic *Ba`al Rapi'u*"[147]—that is, "lord of the Rephaim."[148]

As the story goes, Bellerophon, son of the sea-god Poseidon and a mortal woman named Eurynome, decided after a series of heroic adventures that he'd earned the right to live in Olympus with the gods. As he flew Pegasus toward the mountain, a gadfly sent by Zeus startled the horse, throwing Bellerophon back to earth. Blinded upon landing, Bellerophon wandered the earth the rest of his life miserable and alone, hated by gods and men.

Because you're a sharp reader, you no doubt noticed a similarity to the story of the other Baal-Rapi'u, the one who was thrown down from Heaven in Isaiah 14 to become lord of the Rephaim. Like Bellerophon, Helel ben Shachar—Lucifer, if you prefer—wanted to storm the mount of assembly. And, like Bellerophon, he was cast down from Heaven in disgrace. The parallels are startlingly obvious, but they escape most students of Greek mythology. That's why Bellerophon's name is usually interpreted as "Wielder of Missiles," from the Greek words *belos* and *phoreô*.[149]

Apkallu, Watchers, Titans

So, let's put together what we've got so far: At some point in ancient history, the *apkallu*/Watchers/Titans descended to the earth and corrupted humanity by exchanging forbidden knowledge for pleasures of the flesh.

For their sin, the Watchers were thrust down to Tartarus, which we equate with the Abyss.

Their children, the Nephilim/Rephaim/*meropes anthropoi*, were remembered as men of renown, heroes of the pre-Flood Golden Age ruled by Kronos. After death, which for most of the Nephilim occurred during the Flood of Noah, the spirits of the Watchers' offspring became *daimones*/demons, evil spirits, condemned to wander the earth until the judgment.

About the time of the Judges, around 1200 B.C., the Amorites of Ugarit were summoning the "council of the Didanu"—i.e., the Titans of Greek mythology (or ancestral spirits conflated with the Titans)—to bless their new king. Evidence from Babylon suggests that this ritual wasn't new or unique to the Amorites of Ugarit.

What is new and unique, at least to you and me, is this: The Titans of myth were real, they were worshiped by the pagan neighbors of the ancient Israelites, and they're mentioned in the Bible—and not in a metaphoric sense, either.

V

THE TITANS

We've looked at what the Amorites believed about their gods, including their venerated dead, the Rephaim, and the Council of the Didanu, whom we believe were the same entities known to the later Greeks and Romans as the Titans.

What do we know about these elder gods that we haven't told you already? As a group, the Greeks and Romans generally considered them a wild and dangerous group, "notorious for their bad and lawless behavior."[150] About the individual Titans, we don't know much. As we told you in the previous chapter, the Titans were born to Ouranos (Heaven) and Gaia (Earth). There were fourteen—seven male and seven female—according to the earliest lists. The oldest was Okeanos; his brothers were Koios, Hyperion, Kreios, Iapetus, Phorkys, and the youngest, Kronos.

Scholars believe the names of the female Titans were late inventions by Greek poets,[151] but we can learn some interesting things about the back story of the Titans from the brothers.

It's understandable that Okeanos was considered the oldest. Anyone who's looked out on the ocean has been awed by the power and timelessness of the water. And since the Greeks, who were excellent sailors, couldn't very well have the Titan representing the ocean locked up in Tartarus, they believed that Okeanos decided to sit out Kronos' rebellion against Ouranos, for which Zeus apparently spared the oldest Titan the punishment he inflicted on the rest.

Very little is known about Kreios and Phorkys. Koios (or Coeus) is mainly remembered as the father of Leto, the mother by Zeus of the twins Apollo and Artemis.

The name of Iapetus is very similar to that of Noah's middle son, Japheth, father of the people who lived north of the Near East. Iapetus was considered one of the oldest deities in Greece,[152] best known as father of the twins Prometheus, who stole fire from the gods and gave it to mankind (a spin on the stories of the *apkallu* and Watchers, who were likewise remembered for sharing information from the spirit realm with humanity), and Epimetheus, who was given Pandora by the gods as a gift.

Kronos, however, is a different matter. He is the only one of the Titans who played a significant role in the cosmological history of the universe, and he alone among his brothers and sisters was honored by cults and festivals. Further, his cult, the etymology of his name, and even his use of a sickle to castrate his father, Ouranos,[153] support our theory that Kronos and the Titans weren't invented by the Greeks. Rather, the stories of the Titans were Greek interpretations of ancient history inherited from the Near East. And it's with Kronos that the practice of child sacrifice was spread from the Topheth of Jerusalem across the Mediterranean.

An annual festival called the Kronia was celebrated in Lycia, a region of southwest Turkey,[154] from which it apparently spread to the nearby island of Rhodes. The philosopher Porphyry of Tyre, writing in the third century A.D., recorded that the annual festival on Rhodes, held on the 16th of Metageitnion (roughly August/September), involved the sacrifice of a prisoner who'd been convicted of a crime and sentenced to death.[155] An older festival had existed on Crete, according to Porphyry,[156] and in the fifth century B.C. the Greek playwright Sophocles noted that "from ancient times the barbarians have had a custom of sacrificing human beings to Kronos."[157]

We've already mentioned the Phoenician practice of sacrificing to Baal Hammon and identified the Phoenicians as the descendants of the Amorites. And remember that Baal Hammon is one and the same as Kronos, also known as El, Dagan, and Enlil to the Amorites. The arrow of history points from right to left, from east to west. The lands of the Bible are the place of origin for the story of the Titans and their fall.

The Kronia, a Greek precursor to the Roman Saturnalia (since Kronos = Saturn), involved abandoning typical social roles as part of the festivities, with masters waiting on slaves as part of a ritual of reversal. The roots of this festival point to an earlier origin in the Near East. In 1983, a text in both the Hittite and Hurrian languages was found at the site of the ancient Hittite capital, Hattuša. The document was dated to about 1400 B.C., just about the time of Joshua's war against the Amorite and Anakim tribes in Canaan. The text included an *Epic of Release*, something like the Hebrew Jubilee, during which slaves were freed and debts were forgiven.[158] The ritual wasn't found with the text, but it did preserve the accompanying myth.

In that myth, the king of the gods, the storm-god Teshub (the Hurrian equivalent of Baal and Zeus), has a ritual meal with the sun-goddess of the earth, Allani, and the "primeval gods" who'd been banished to the underworld. These primeval gods are not only at the table; they sit at Teshub's right hand. Apparently, this suspension of order in the heavens reflected the temporary suspension of the social order on earth, which was commemorated at annual festivals like the Kronia.[159]

While that myth suggests that the Greek memories of Kronos and the Titans were inherited from the Hittites of Anatolia and Hurrians of upper Mesopotamia, the strongest evidence of east-to-west transmission is a group of Hurro-Hittite texts first published in 1952 called *The Kumarbi Cycle*. They describe a story that sounds very familiar to anyone who's read basic Greek mythology: The supreme deity, Anu the sky-god (equivalent to Ouranos), was overthrown by the grain-god, Kumarbi. Like Kronos, the Hurro-Hittite grain-god castrated his father, although in this case it was with his teeth. (Ugh.) Without getting too graphic, as a result, Kumarbi became pregnant and gave birth to the storm-god Teshub (Baal/Zeus) in what must have been the world's first delivery by caesarean section.

The similarities between Kronos and Kumarbi are so obvious that previous theories of Indo-European origins for Greek and Roman mythology, independent of Semitic influence, went out the window. It's clear that the Titans and Olympians originated not with the proto-Greeks but with the Hurrians and Hittites, and in turn *their* gods came from the lands of the Bible.

Yet it goes even deeper into history. As with Greek myth and *The Kumarbi Cycle*, older texts from Mesopotamia record the transfer of power from generation to generation of gods—from sky-god Anu to "lord of the air" Enlil to Marduk, the patron god of Babylon. Along the way, the Anunnaki, once the most powerful gods of the Sumerian pantheon,[160] were reassigned to the underworld to serve as judges of the dead.

> West drew attention to **the conceptual similarity of the (Hittite) "former gods"** (*karuilies siunes*) **with the Titans,** called Πρότεροι Θεοί in *Theogony* 424, 486. Both groups were confined to the underworld (with the apparent exceptions of Atlas and Prometheus), and as Zeus banished the Titans thither, so Tešup [Teshub] banished the *karuilies siunes*, commonly twelve in number, like the Titans. **They were in turn identified with the Mesopotamian Anunnaki.** These were confined by Marduk to the underworld, or at least some of them were (half the six hundred, *Enuma Elish* vi 39–47, see 41–44), where they were ruled over variously by Dagan or Shamash.[161] (Emphasis added)

Working backward in time, we can link the Greek Titans to the Hittite "former gods" and then to the Mesopotamian Anunnaki. All of those groups are just different names for the "angels who sinned," the Watchers of the Bible.

In short: Titans = Hittite "former gods" = Anunnaki = *Apkallu* = Watchers.

By the Old Babylonian period, the time of Abraham, Isaac, and Jacob, the Anunnaki were no longer the gods who decreed the fates of the living, they were the gods of the underworld. That's why the reference to the Anunnaki in the Old Babylonian text of the Gilgamesh epic is so intriguing—it places their "secret dwelling" on and around Mount Hermon.[162] Since we discussed the connections between the dead and Hermon in an earlier chapter, you see the significance of the connection to the Anunnaki; it's more evidence that we're dealing with the same group of supernatural entities.

We can identify several common elements shared by the Watchers, *apkallu*, Anunnaki, Hittite "former gods," and the Titans: They ruled (or at least influenced, as messengers delivering the gifts of civilization to humanity) the natural realm in the distant past; they either transgressed against the high god or were overthrown by a new generation of gods; and they were subsequently banished or confined to the underworld by younger gods, a place identified by the Greeks and Hebrews as the abyss or Tartarus. In the case of the Watchers and *apkallu*, they were remembered also for having intimate relations with humans; and the leaders of the Titans and the "former gods," Kronos and Kumarbi, attained their kingship by castrating their fathers.

By connecting the myths of the ancient Greeks, Hittites, Hurrians, Amorites, and Sumerians, we've made a strong case that the characters we've known from high school mythology class, comic books, so-so Hollywood films, and novels aimed at young adult readers have a real basis in history. Not only that—they and their demigod offspring are in the Bible.

Let's dig a little deeper.

A Lot of Bull

We've already shown how the Greek word *titanes* was derived from the name of the ancient Amorite tribe, the Ditanu/Tidanu, which is also the root of the personal names Dedan and Dathan in the Bible. Dedan and

Sheba are mentioned in the prophecy of Ezekiel 38; earlier in the Bible, they're named as sons of Raamah, son of Cush (which makes Dedan a nephew of Nimrod). Dathan, you probably remember, was one of the ringleaders of Korah's rebellion against Moses. (You know, the character played by Edward G. Robinson in *The Ten Commandments*.)

The point here is that the word behind the name Dathan/Dedan/Ditanu is the Akkadian word *ditânu* ("aurochs," "bison," or "bull"). This is more evidence that the story of the Titans originated with the Semitic people of the Near East and not Indo-Europeans. In other words, the people who first encountered the Titans/Watchers lived in Mesopotamia, not Greece.

That's not all. Because of the connection between the king of the Titans and El, creator-god of the Canaanites, we can make a good case that the name Kronos probably has a Semitic origin, too:

> The bovid sense of the form Ditanu/Didanu is particularly intriguing in view of other tauromorph elements in the tradition. Thus, **the prominent Titan Kronos was later identified with El, who is given the epithet _tr_, "Bull", in Ugaritic and biblical literature.** Apart from this explicit allusion, we may well ask whether the name El, (Akkadian and Ugaritic *ilu*) does not already itself have a bovine sense. ... Does it perhaps mean "Bull", (perhaps more generically "male animal"), so that the epithetal title _tr_ is in effect a redundant gloss on it? ...
>
> Furthermore, the name Kronos may well carry the same nuance, since it may be construed as referring to bovine horns (Akkadian, Ugaritic *qarnu*, Hebrew *qeren*), which feature prominently in divine iconography in the Near East.[163] (Emphasis added)

It's interesting enough to see the additional link between Kronos and El through the bull imagery of their names, but did you notice there are references to "Bull El" in biblical literature?

In *biblical* literature?

Yes. In the book of Hosea, the prophet recalled the idolatry of Jeroboam, the man who led the rebellion against Solomon's son, Rehoboam:

I have spurned your calf, O Samaria.
My anger burns against them.
How long will they be incapable of innocence?
For it is from Israel;
a craftsman made it;
it is not God.
The calf of Samaria
shall be broken to pieces. (Hosea 8:5–6, ESV; emphasis added)

The phrase, "For it is from Israel," comes from the Masoretic Hebrew text, *kî miyyiśrā'ēl*, which literally means, "for from Israel."[164] That doesn't make sense. But separating the characters differently yields *kî mî šōr 'ēl*, which changes verse 6 to this:

For who is Bull El?
a craftsman made it;
it is not God.
The calf of Samaria
shall be broken to pieces.[165]
(Hosea 8:6, ESV, modified; emphasis added)

That's a huge difference! Jeroboam set up worship sites to rival the Temple for political reasons. If the northern tribes continued to travel to Jerusalem for the feasts, they might eventually switch their loyalty back to the House of David. Apparently, Jeroboam felt that the worship of El was close enough to do the trick. After all, didn't Yahweh reveal Himself to Abraham, Isaac, and Jacob as El Shaddai? Hence, the golden calves at Bethel and Dan.

Since El was Kronos, king of the Titans, he was also Shemihazah, leader of the rebellious Watchers on Mount Hermon thousands of years earlier. By erecting the golden calves, Jeroboam had drawn the northern tribes back into the worship of a god who introduced the pre-Flood world to the occult knowledge that Babylon was so proud of preserving. This crossed a big red line, and God made it immediately clear that it was completely unacceptable:

> You have done evil above all who were before you and have gone and made for yourself other gods and metal images, provoking me to anger, and have cast me behind your back, therefore behold, I will bring harm upon the house of Jeroboam and will cut off from Jeroboam every male, both bond and free in Israel, and will burn up the house of Jeroboam, as a man burns up dung until it is all gone. (1 Kings 14:9–10, ESV)

By reading "Bull El" in Hosea 8:6, instead of "Israel," the verse becomes a polemic directed not just at the idols of Jeroboam, but against the creator-god of the Canaanites as well. Frankly, it fits the context of the passage better than the common English rendering. And this isn't the only place in the Bible where that substitution may come closer to the Hebrew original.

The epithet has also been identified recently in a perceptive study of Deuteronomy 32:8 by Joosten, in which he proposed a similar consonantal regrouping in the expression *bny yśr'l* (*běnê yiśrā'ēl*) to read (*běnê šōr 'ēl*). Since LXX (ἀγγέλων θεοῦ, some mss υἱῶν θεοῦ), and one Qumran text, 4QDeut^j (*lmspr bny 'lhym*), already read a divine reference here, rather than the "Israel" of MT, this proposal has much to commend it:

> *yaṣṣēb gĕbulōt 'ammîm* **he set up the boundaries of the nations** *lĕmisparbĕnê šōr 'ēl* **in accordance with the number of the sons of Bull El.**[166] (Emphasis added)

As noted earlier, most English translations render Deuteronomy 32:8 "number of the sons of Israel." A few, such as the ESV, follow the Septuagint ("angels of God" or "divine sons") and the text of Deuteronomy found among the Dead Sea scrolls ("sons of Elohim"). What scholars Simon and Nicolas Wyatt propose is reading the Hebrew as "sons of Bull El" instead at the end of the verse. And to be honest, it fits.

That may sound borderline heretical, like we're playing fast and loose with the text. But note: As pointed out earlier, in the Genesis 10 Table of Nations, there are seventy names, and in Canaanite religious texts, El had seventy sons.[167]

Coincidence?

Bulls of Bashan

While it doesn't change the net effect of what happened (Yahweh allocating the small-G gods to the nations after the Tower of Babel incident), reconstructing Deuteronomy 32:8 to read "sons of Bull El" gives it a new, perhaps deeper, meaning. Since we've identified El as Kronos, leader of the Titans, which presumably also makes him Shemihazah, ringleader of the rebellious Watchers, it may explain why God divided the world into seventy nations.

This is admittedly confusing. Whether they were sons of Bull El or El Shaddai (Yahweh), why seventy sons? Why would God put powerful supernatural entities with a rebellious streak in charge of His creation anyway?

As for the number, we can't know for sure. It's symbolic, no question. The number of the elders of Israel[168] and the number of disciples sent ahead of Jesus into Galilee[169] matched the number of these divine sons. That was no accident. But why that specific number? Maybe there were exactly seventy tribes or nations at the time God stopped the workmen at Babel, or maybe, as we'll see shortly, it's related to the belief in the ancient Near East that seventy symbolized a complete set, the full amount.

Now, why did God delegate authority to elohim that He knew would rebel? Remember, this was punishment for the rebellious humans of Nimrod's day. They'd tried to build the Tower of Babel as an artificial "cosmic mountain," an abode for the gods, and they did it just three generations after God sent a devastating Flood as a consequence for getting too cozy with an earlier group of Watcher-class angels. God's response was to give humanity what it wanted, and so "the sun and the moon and the stars, all the host of heaven" were "allotted to all the peoples under the whole heaven."[170]

We can assume that these seventy sons of El were not among the two hundred who descended on Mount Hermon in the days of Jared. The Watchers that Enoch knew were punished for their sin, chained in gloomy darkness until the final judgment, according to Peter and Jude. So, in what sense were these seventy post-Babel angels the sons of El?

This is speculation, you understand, since we're working without a biblical net here. The term "sons" is not to be taken literally, in the human sense. While we know from Jesus that the angels in Heaven don't marry,[171] Genesis 6:1–4 is clear that they can procreate, at least with human partners. But the Bible never shows us female angels, even though some of the most popular pagan deities are female. Without scriptural support, we can't say that angels reproduce. So, our best guess is that the sons of Bull El were his children in the same way the Pharisees of Jesus' day were "of [their] father, the devil"—[172] spiritual descendants rather than genetic and physical offspring.

It's interesting, isn't it, that while El was chained in Tartarus with the rest of the Watchers, his seventy "sons" were believed to congregate on Mount Hermon? Remember that, because Jesus certainly did.

The pagans didn't recognize El as a god trapped in the underworld, but these spirits lie. Do the fallen angels chained in Tartarus still influence what happens here on the surface? You'd think not, but maybe the angels who rebelled later, after the Tower of Babel incident, found it useful for their cause to preserve the name and memory of El/Kronos/Baal Hammon, and their colleagues, even if their spiritual "father" and his gang of two hundred were indisposed. But those Watchers are coming back for one last shot at the throne of God. More on that later.

Bearing in mind the importance of Mount Hermon to the spirit realm, consider the deeper meaning within the messianic prophecy of Psalm 22:

My God, my God, why have you forsaken me?
Why are you so far from saving me, from the words of my
groaning? [...]
Many bulls encompass me;
strong bulls of Bashan surround me;
they open wide their mouths at me,
like a ravening and roaring lion.
(Psalm 22:1, 12–13, ESV; emphasis added)

You recognize the first verse of Psalm 22 because Jesus spoke it from the cross. This was obviously a prophecy of what was to happen on Calvary. But the psalmist wasn't shown a vision of angry bulls from the Golan Heights surrounding Christ on the cross. He was given a glimpse into the future at *spirits* from Bashan, demonic entities represented by bulls, who surrounded the cross to celebrate what they thought was their victory over the Messiah.

Confirming this interpretation of Psalm 22:12, Old Testament scholar Dr. Robert D. Miller II recently used archaeological and climatological evidence to prove that "the phrase Bulls of Bashan refers not to the bovine but to the divine, [and] moreover that Iron Age Bashan would have been a terrible land for grazing and the last place to be famous for beef or dairy cattle."[173]

How about that? Soil samples confirm the truth of the Bible!

Feast of Booths

Now, let's add another bit of historical detail that may be relevant. The Feast of Tabernacles, or Sukkot (literally "Feast of Booths"), was one of the annual festivals that God directed the Israelites to keep when He gave the Law to Moses. It's a seven-day festival that begins on the

15th of Tishrei, the seventh month of the Hebrew calendar. That puts it exactly six months after the Feast of Unleavened Bread, which begins on the 15th of Nisan, the first month of the calendar. Those two along with Shavuot, the Feast of Weeks (Pentecost), were the three Pilgrimage Festivals in the Hebrew calendar that required Jewish men to appear before God at the Tabernacle, and later, at the Temple from the time of Solomon until the first century A.D.[174]

Interestingly, the pagan religious calendar in the ancient Near East featured a festival called the *akitu* that dates back at least to the middle of the third millennium B.C.[175] It was thought to be a new year festival held in the spring to honor the chief god of Babylon, Marduk, but more recent discoveries have shown that there were two *akitu* festivals, one in the spring, the harvesting season, and the other in the fall, the planting season, and some of them were performed to honor other gods. For example, the oldest known *akitu* is documented at ancient Ur in Sumer, which was the home city of the moon-god, Sîn.[176]

The *akitu* festivals began on the 1st of Nisan and 1st of Tishrei, close to the spring and fall equinoxes. Although the length of the festivals changed over the years, it appears they generally lasted eleven[177] or twelve days.[178] So, the Jewish festivals began a few days after their pagan neighbors finished their harvesting and planting rituals.

Sukkot is a seven-day festival. It's especially interesting because of the sheer number of sacrificial animals that were required, and especially because they were bulls. Numbers 29:12–34 spells out the requirements for the Feast of Booths.

Day 1	Day 2	Day 3	Day 4	Day 5	Day 6	Day 7
13 bulls	12 bulls	11 bulls	10 bulls	9 bulls	8 bulls	7 bulls
2 rams	2 rams	2 rams	2 rams	2 rams	2 rams	2 rams
14 lambs	14 lambs	14 lambs	14 lambs	14 lambs	14 lambs	14 lambs
1 goat	1 goat	1 goat	1 goat	1 goat	1 goat	1 goat

The Feast of Unleavened Bread, which was likewise a seven-day festival, required only one ram and seven lambs each day. But the biggest difference between the two feasts is that only two bulls were sacrificed each day during the Feast of Unleavened Bread.[179] In fact, none of the other festivals ordained by God for Israel required the sacrifice of more than two bulls per day.

This suggests that Sukkot was unique in the annual calendar. In fact, in several places in the Old Testament it's simply called "the festival" or "the feast."[180] But why? Why so many *bulls* at this particular feast? And why the decreasing number of bulls slaughtered each day?

We may never know specifically, but it's fascinating to note that a similar festival called the *zukru* was performed regularly during the time of the Judges (fourteenth through 12th centuries B.C.) in Emar, a city in what is today northern Syria.

> It was celebrated in Emar on the first month of the year, called SAG.MU—namely, the "head of the year". On the first day of the festival, when the moon is full, the god Dagan—the supreme god of Syria— and all the other gods in the pantheon were taken outside the temple and city in the presence of the citizens to a shrine of stones called *sikkānu*. [...]
> The first offerings of the *zukru*-festival were sacrificed on the fourteenth of the month of the "head of the year":
> On the month of SAG.MU (meaning: the head of the year), on the fourteenth day, they offer seventy pure lambs provided by the king...for all the seventy gods [of the city of] Emar.[181]

Seventy lambs for the seventy gods of Emar, headed up by Dagan, sacrificed over seven days during a festival that began in the first month "when the moon is full," just like at Sukkot.

Quickly: How many bulls were sacrificed at Sukkot?

13 + 12 + 11 + 10 + 9 + 8 + 7 = **70**

Remember from an earlier chapter the link between the underworld and Dagan, the *bēl pagrê*, "lord of the corpse," or "lord of the dead." Recall also that the similarities in their roles and descriptions helped us identify Dagan as the Hurrian grain-god Kumarbi and the king of the Titans, Kronos—which brings us back to the Canaanite creator-god El and his seventy sons on Mount Hermon. And then connect Dagan/El, "lord of the dead," to Mount Hermon, which towers over Bashan, the entrance to the Canaanite underworld.

Is it possible that the festival of the Israelites was intended as a message to the small-*G* gods who had deceived the nations in and around the land God had chosen for His people—that the seventy bulls sacrificed to Yahweh represented the seventy gods who'd sworn allegiance to Dagan/ El? Or was it simply to commemorate Israel's rescue from the gods of the nations—to remind the people that they were Yahweh's allotted heritage?

Given the bull imagery of the pagan gods and demons of the ancient Near East, the answer to both questions may be, "Yes."

The Seventy Sons of El

Now, how do we make sense of the relationships between the king of the rebel gods—Dagan, El, Kronos, Shemihazah, or whatever name he used—and his seventy "sons" or the seventy "gods of the city"? That's a good question. We can only speculate. In fact, we don't know for sure that the number of "sons" was exactly seventy. You see, in the ancient Near East, the number seventy represented completion, totality, the full amount.

> The Aramaean inscription from Zinjirly of Bir-Rakib concerning of his father Panamuwa notes that Bir-Ṣur from Šam'al's seventy brothers were killed by an usurper. The Tel-Dan Inscription (line 6) notes that King Hazael slew seventy kings. In the biblical texts, Abimelech slaughtered Gideon's seventy sons (Judg[es] 9:5–6) and Yehu Ahab's seventy sons (2 K[in]gs 10:6–7). In all these instances, the number seventy is symbolic of complete destruc-tion, not one person escaping.[182]

In this context, it seems reasonable to interpret the Sukkot sacrifices the same way. It appears God directed the Israelites to send an annual reminder to the "bulls of Bashan," the Titans and their sons, that they would meet their doom one day and not one of them would escape, regardless of the actual number. Psalm 82 records God's sentence of death on the rebel gods.

God has taken his place in the divine council;
in the midst of the gods he holds judgment:
  "How long will you judge unjustly
  and show partiality to the wicked? *Selah*
  Give justice to the weak and the fatherless;
  maintain the right of the afflicted and the destitute.
  Rescue the weak and the needy;
  deliver them from the hand of the wicked."
  They have neither knowledge nor understanding,
  they walk about in darkness;
  all the foundations of the earth are shaken.
  I said, "You are gods,
  sons of the Most High, all of you;
  nevertheless, like men you shall die,
  and fall like any prince."
  Arise, O God, judge the earth;
  for you shall inherit all the nations!
  (Psalm 82:1–8, ESV; emphasis added)

"Death of the gods" has a ring to it, doesn't it? That day is coming. Maybe that's another reason the rebels are so unhappy with humanity.

Other Supernatural Bulls

There are other verses in the Old Testament that could be interpreted as references to the Canaanite deity El instead of God, but the passage above from Hosea is the most obvious. There are two takeaways from this section: First, the bull-like imagery—"tauromorphic," for you scholars—associated with the Titans in general and Kronos in particular did not originate with the Greeks. It's much older, which points to the Near East, and specifically to Syria.[183] And second, it's another reminder that the Bible wasn't written in a vacuum. References to other gods in Scripture do not imply polytheism or a pantheon of gods who are roughly co-equal. The spirit realm is a lot more complicated than we've been led to believe. Trying to understand what the prophets and apostles knew about the religions of their neighbors will help us sort it out.

Now, because you know your Bible, the episode with the golden calf at the foot of Mount Sinai probably just came into your mind. You may well be right, although the idol at Sinai probably represented a deity other than El.

Quick historical review: Although the Bible tells us the Israelites were descended from Shem while the Amorites came from Canaan, son of Ham, Israel emerged from a cultural milieu that was established and dominated by Amorites. The Amorites first showed up in Near Eastern history around 2500 B.C. By the time of Abraham, c. 1900 B.C., Amorite kingdoms ruled what we know today as Iraq, Syria, Jordan, Kuwait, Lebanon, Israel, and northern Arabia, and they were making inroads into northern Egypt, which they controlled by the time of the Jacob.

Abraham was a product of this culture. As I mentioned in earlier chapters, the Ur from which the patriarch was called was not the Sumerian Ur in southeastern Iraq. Abraham's home was near Harran (modern Haran) in southern Turkey. Harran, like Sumerian Ur, was a major center of the cult of the moon-god, Sîn, whose importance to the Amorites (and to the world today) will be the focus of a future book, God willing. The most famous Amorite king, Hammurabi the Great (probably a contemporary of Isaac and Jacob), in the prologue and epilogue of his famous law code, "states explicitly that he is the seed of a dynasty which Sîn created, and that Sîn created him personally."[184]

In Sumer, Sîn, called Nanna by the Sumerians, was referred to as the "frisky calf of heaven."[185] So, the golden calf at Mount Sinai, in the Wilderness of Sin, was more likely a representation of Sîn than of Bull El. No doubt you noticed that the desert and the mountain were named for the moon-god.[186] Note also that manna began to fall on the very day the Israelites entered the Wilderness of Sin (see Exodus 16). It's not hard to imagine that the Israelites assumed the source of their blessing was Sîn, not Yahweh, especially when Moses didn't come back down the mountain right away.

But bovid imagery doesn't end with just El and Sîn. The Akkadians believed that the primordial chaos-dragon Tiamat was served by a host of demonic creatures, one of which was the *kusarikku*, or "bison-man."[187] This chimera was human above and bovid below, a sort of bullish centaur but with horns on a human head. The *kusarikku* was defeated by the god Ninurta but it was also associated with—surprise!—the Titans, by way of the ancient Amorite Ditanu tribe.

> Let us consider first the equation *alim* = *ditânu* [Note: here he cites several lexical lists showing equivalent words in Sumerian and Akkadian], which means "bison, bull." Free variant of Sumerian *alim* is *gud-alim*, from which derives *kusarikku*, the name of a demonic "bison-man." This bison-man is for unclear reasons associated with the sun-god. The head of the bison (*sag-alim*) is "emblem of Utu" [the Sumerian sun-god] and he himself is called *gud.dumu.^{d}utu* "bison-son of the Sun" or *gud.dumu.an.na* "the bison-son of heaven."[188]

Scholar Amar Annus, mentioned earlier, goes on to highlight connections in Greek myth between a Titan named Titan (oddly enough) and the sun. These connections may be memories of the stories first put into writing by Akkadians and Sumerians more than a thousand years before the oldest Greek myths, and it's more evidence of the bull imagery associated with the old gods.

So, where does the connection between the bull and the pagan gods come from in the first place? Would you believe the cherubim?

Cherubim

We actually know more than we think about the entities that occupy the spirit realm. We're going to take an extended look at a class of angel that's best described as a throne guardian, because the imagery connected to these creatures is consistent with other depictions of supernatural entities in the ancient world.

In Ezekiel 28, God tells the divine rebel from Eden:

> You were an anointed guardian cherub.
>   I placed you; **you were on the holy mountain of God;**
>   in the midst of the stones of fire you walked.
>   (Ezekiel 28:14, ESV; emphasis added)

As we've pointed out in this book, you'll notice many references to God's holy mountain in the Old Testament. The prophets knew that the war between the rebellious fallen gods and the Creator is all about who would establish their holy mountain—the "mount of assembly" or "mount of the congregation"—as supreme.

Let's go back to the beginning of the story. We've already established that the rebel in Eden wasn't a talking snake. Who or what was the serpent in the garden? Most of us assume it was Satan, but maybe not. The serpent isn't named in the book of Genesis. In fact, Satan wasn't even a personal name in the Old Testament.

Satan means "accuser," written *ha-shaitan* in the OT. It's a title, like "*the* Satan." It really means "the accuser." Think of it as a job title, like prosecuting attorney.

As we mentioned earlier, *nachash* is the Hebrew word translated into English as "serpent." It's based on an adjective that means bright or brazen, like shiny brass. The noun *nachash* can mean snake, but it also means "one who practices divination."

In Hebrew, adjectives are frequently converted into nouns—the term is "substantivized."[189] If that's the case here, *nachash* could mean "shining one." That's consistent with other descriptions of the satan figure in the Old Testament. For example, in Isaiah 14, the character called Lucifer in the King James translation, based on the Latin words chosen by Jerome (*lux* + *ferous*, meaning "light bringer"), is named in Hebrew Helel ben Shachar—"shining one, son of the dawn."

Interestingly, Shachar was a Canaanite deity, the god of dawn, so a better translation of the verse is "Day Star, son of Dawn." Shachar was believed to be one of the sons of El, a twin to Shalim the god of dusk. And that leads to some interesting speculation about the nature of Helel. If Helel was the son of Shachar, what did the Canaanites think they knew about the divine rebellion? Were Helel and Shachar two of the fallen Watchers who rebelled against Yahweh? Titans by different names? But I digress.

Consider this in Daniel 10:

> I lifted up my eyes and looked, and behold, a man clothed in linen, with a belt of fine gold from Uphaz around his waist. His body was like beryl, **his face like the appearance of lightning, his eyes like flaming torches, his arms and legs like the gleam of burnished bronze**, and the sound of his words like the sound of a multitude. (Daniel 10:5–6, ESV; emphasis added)

Obviously, the angel who battled the prince of Persia, another supernatural being, to bring his message to Daniel was a "shining one." This seems to be a common trait of supernatural beings when they appear in the natural realm, and it's possible that Helel ben Shachar was the same type of entity as the angel who visited Daniel.

About nine hundred years before Daniel, God sent fiery serpents (Hebrew *saraph nachash*) to torment the Israelites when they began to complain on their way out of Egypt (see Numbers 21:4–9). *Saraph* is the root word of "seraphim," which roughly means "burning ones." But the key point of the verses in Numbers 21 is that the Hebrew words *saraph* and *nachash* are used interchangeably. So rather than "fiery serpents," the translation should read "*saraph* serpents."

Recalling the incident later, Moses praised Yahweh for bringing Israel through "the great and terrifying wilderness, with its fiery serpents"[190] (again, *saraph nachash*), reinforcing the interchangeability of *saraph* and *nachash*.

Now, if the mental image of flaming snakes isn't weird enough, the prophet Isaiah twice referred to "flying" serpents in Isaiah 14:20 and 30:6 (*saraph `uwph*). And in his famous throne room vision, Isaiah saw:

> …the Lord sitting upon a throne, high and lifted up; and the train of his robe filled the temple. Above him stood the seraphim. Each had six wings: with two he covered his face, and with two he covered his feet, and with two he flew. (Isaiah 6:1–2, ESV)

Again, the root word of seraphim is *saraph*, the same word translated "serpent" in Numbers and Deuteronomy.

The flying serpent was a well-known symbol in the ancient Near East, especially in Egypt, so it would have been very familiar to the Israelites. The uraeus, a cobra standing on its coil with its hood extended, was a royal symbol of protection used by pharaohs and Nubian kings. Tutankhamun's death mask is an excellent example; the uraeus' hood on his mask is depicted with six distinct sections that look a lot like wings. Of course, some scholars take this as evidence that the Hebrews' understanding of seraphim was either influenced by or borrowed from the Egyptians.

The bottom line is this: What Adam and Eve saw in the Garden wasn't a talking snake, but a *nachash*—a radiant, supernatural entity, and one that may have had a serpentine appearance.[191]

Remember that the divine rebel in Eden, the *nachash* of Genesis 3, was called a guardian cherub in Ezekiel 28. As we just showed you, *nachash* and *saraph*, the singular form of seraphim, are interchangeable terms. But if the rebel in Eden was one of the seraphim, how could he also be one of the cherubim?

Good question. Cherubim are mentioned more frequently than seraphim in the Old Testament, usually in descriptions of the Ark of the Covenant or carved decorations in Solomon's Temple. The exceptions are the cherubim who guard the entrance to Eden and the four cherubim Ezekiel saw in his famous "wheel within a wheel" vision by the Chebar canal.

The modern image of cherubim has been shaped by artists in the Middle Ages. Think "cherub" and you probably imagine a cute, chubby little boy with dinky wings. Nothing could be farther from the biblical and archaeological truth.

To be blunt, cherubim are seriously bad dudes you do *not* want to mess with.

The cherubim of the mercy seat on the Ark of the Covenant are usually shown as a matched pair of easily recognizable angels perched on top of the ark with their outstretched wings touching in the middle. The thing is, the Bible doesn't really describe these cherubim. We read only that they have wings and faces. Why is that?

Well, probably because everybody in the ancient Near East knew what a cherub looked like, and they knew it was right and proper for them to serve as Yahweh's throne-bearers. You see, contrary to the nonsense in *Raiders of the Lost Ark*, it wasn't a radio to talk to God. The Ark of the Covenant was literally God's throne on earth, and He appeared to men above the mercy seat "enthroned on the cherubim."[192]

But the cherubim that Ezekiel saw weren't the standard-issue winged angels we're used to. These things were straight out of a nightmare:

> This was their appearance: they had a human likeness, but each had four faces, and each of them had four wings. Their legs were straight, and the soles of their feet were like the sole of a calf's foot. And they sparkled like burnished bronze.
>
> Under their wings on their four sides they had human hands. And the four had their faces and their wings thus: their wings touched one another. Each one of them went straight forward, without turning as they went.

> **As for the likeness of their faces, each had a human face. The four had the face of a lion on the right side, the four had the face of an ox on the left side, and the four had the face of an eagle.**
>
> Such were their faces. And their wings were spread out above. Each creature had two wings, each of which touched the wing of another, while two covered their bodies. And each went straight forward. Wherever the spirit would go, they went, without turning as they went.
>
> As for the likeness of the living creatures, **their appearance was like burning coals of fire, like the appearance of torches moving to and fro among the living creatures. And the fire was bright, and out of the fire went forth lightning.**
>
> And the living creatures darted to and fro, like the appearance of a flash of lightning. (Ezekiel 1:5–14, ESV; emphasis added)

While these living creatures aren't identified as cherubim in these verses, they are specifically called cherubim in Ezekiel 10. How do we read this? These creatures sound nothing like shining serpentine seraphim. It could be that this just illustrates how difficult it is to describe beings that may operate in dimensions we can't see.

What's even more confusing is the description Ezekiel gives of another type of angelic being, the *ophanim*. Those are the wheels that UFO/ancient alien hunters love to call spacecraft. They seem to be related somehow to the cherubim:

> And I looked, and behold, there were four wheels beside the cherubim, one beside each cherub, and the appearance of the wheels was like sparkling beryl. And as for their appearance, the four had the same likeness, as if a wheel were within a wheel. When they went, they went in any of their four directions without turning as they went, but in whatever direction the front wheel faced, the others followed without turning as they went. And their whole body, their rims, and their spokes, their wings, and the wheels

were full of eyes all around—the wheels that the four of them had. As for the wheels, they were called in my hearing "the whirling wheels."

And every one had four faces: the first face was the face of the cherub, and the second face was a human face, and the third the face of a lion, and the fourth the face of an eagle. (Ezekiel 10:9–14, ESV; emphasis added)

Wait a minute—if these are the same entities Ezekiel saw in chapter 1, why is there a cherub instead of an ox for the fourth face? Is there some connection between the cherub and the ox?

Well, yes—actually, there is. The word "cherub" probably comes from the Akkadian *karibu*.[193] (The "ch" should be a hard *k* sound, although we English speakers don't usually say it that way.) It means "intercessor" or "one who prays."[194]

Here's the significance of this for the chapter we're in: The *karibu* were usually portrayed as winged bulls with human faces. Huge statues of the *karibu* were set up as divine guardians at the entrances of palaces and temples. This is like the role of the cherubim placed "at the east of the garden of Eden...to guard the way to the tree of life."[195]

Think about that. The divine rebel in Eden, the anointed guardian cherub called Helel ben Shachar by Isaiah, might have protected the tree of life once upon a time. Or could he have been the guardian of the tree of the knowledge of good and evil? Did Adam and Eve believe the rebel's lie because he was a regular in the garden?

Cherubim were apparently the gold standard for guarding royalty in the ancient Near East. Giant stone statues of winged bulls with human faces guarded the entrance to the palaces of Assyrian kings at Nimrud and Nineveh, where they were called *lamassu* and *shedu*.[196] Although they didn't share the form of the cherubim entirely, having just the one face, the *lamassu* and *shedu* were very similar in function.

Statues of the winged bull-men are best known from the Neo-Assyrian period, which roughly coincided with the divided monarchy in Israel. The

Assyrians destroyed the northern kingdom based in Samaria in 721 B.C., and twenty years later, during the reign of Hezekiah, Sennacherib led the Assyrian army against the fortified cities of Judah. However, images of the human-headed, winged bull a thousand years older were found at the ancient city of Ebla in Syria.[197]

As mentioned previously, a similar creature called the *kusarikku,* or bison-man, was also a common figure in Mesopotamian religious art as far back as the Sumerian Early Dynastic period (2900–2350 B.C.). The bison-man was a type of demon, possibly originally associated with the sun-god Shamash; but later, in the Babylonian creation myth, the *kusarikku* appears in the army of the chaos serpent Tiamat in her battle against Marduk.[198]

And now here's where things get really interesting.

In the epic poem *Erra and Ishum,* dated to the Neo-Assyrian period, the war-god Erra sends his vizier Ishum to punish a wicked tribe of Amorites, the Suteans. They lived on a mountain called Sharshar, which may have been Jebel Bishri.[199] Remember that Jebel Bishri in Syria is the first recorded homeland of the Amorites (c. 2500 B.C.). The Suteans were infamous in the ancient Near East for their bad behavior.[200] (You'll find out just how bad in an upcoming chapter.)

The point is that the Suteans and the demonic *kusarikku* are linked to the Titans.

> The mountain or the mountain range Sharshar also had another name, Tid(a)nu, "the mountain of the Amorites". Among the Amorite tribal names *sutu* and *tidnu,* the latter with variants *tidanu* or *ditnu,* were often interchangeable and denoted the same group of nomads. **Tid(a)nu was the name of its deified eponymous ancestor, who had an iconographic representation of human-faced bull or bison.** This monstrous being was subordinated to sun-god Shamash, who, in his capacity as a warrior god held it under his control. Under its Akkadian name *kusarikku,* the human-faced bull firmly belonged to the inventory of Mesopo-

tamian demons. According to the Anzu epic, Ninurta [Mesopotamian warrior-god] had defeated *kusarikku* in "the midst of the sea" as a specimen of his exploits. On some pictorial representations Shamash subdues the human-faced bison, who is leaning against a mountain, being the personification of Mount Sharshar. Apparently some myth or oral tradition told how Shamash defeated human-headed bull Ditanu, of which event no written testimony is available. However, this explains why the beast was associated with sun-god in art and literature.[201] (Emphasis added)

"Deified eponymous ancestor" is a fancy way of describing the ancestor for whom the Ditanu/Tidanu tribe was named, who was worshiped by the tribe as a god. But if, as we believe, there's something more to this bovid imagery than coincidence, we may have another explanation.

Horns were associated with the gods in the very earliest Sumerian artwork. The easy way to spot a deity in a carving or on a cylinder seal is to look for the horned cap. They're easy to find because they usually have three or more sets of horns.

Let's consider the evidence. A group of gods was known to the later Greeks and Romans as the Titans, which is a name we can trace back to an Amorite tribe infamous in the Near East centuries before Abraham was born. That name derives from an Akkadian word that means "aurochs," "bison," or "bull." Imagery based on the bull is associated with demons, divine throne guardians, and even the Canaanite creator-god, "Bull El," who is one and the same as the king of the Titans, Kronos, whose name was apparently based on a Semitic word meaning "horns"—and, remember, he's the only Titan for whom there was any religious role or cult.

Coincidence?

Where are we going with this? I suggest we consider another possibility: Rather than believing that the Titans were simply invented by Greek poets, let's extrapolate from Ezekiel's visions to connect some dots. While the cherubim in Ezekiel 1 were described as having four faces (man, ox, eagle, lion), "the soles of their feet were like the sole of a calf's foot."[202] In chapter 10, the cherubim are likewise described with four faces, but "the first face was the face of the cherub, and the second face was a human face, and the third the face of a lion, and the fourth the face of an eagle."[203]

Identifying the face of a cherub as that of an ox, plus hooves in place of feet, suggests that the cherubim were primarily winged bull-men, similar to the demonic, bison-like *kusarikku* or the colossal *lamassu* and *shedu* of the Assyrians. If that's what cherubim looked like, is it too far-fetched to speculate that the rebellious Watcher-class angels who descended on Mount Hermon looked more or less the same?

If that theory holds water, descriptions of the rebellious *bene elohim* could have been handed down from the eight survivors on Noah's ark. Since the rebels were confined to Tartarus for their disloyalty, the only source of information about their appearance may have been tales told by the descendants of Noah, unless other Watchers made themselves known to humans in the post-Flood world. (Which is possible: The Hebrew in Genesis 6:4 translated, "The Nephilim were on the earth in those days, and also afterward, when the sons of God came in to the daughters of man," can also mean, "*whenever* the sons of God came in to the daughters of man.")[204]

In short, the biblical cherubim may give us a picture of what the Titans/Watchers actually looked like. It may explain the bovid associations with the names Titan and Kronos, and with the bull images associated with gods and demons in ancient Mesopotamia.

All this evidence makes for interesting reading if you like history and Greek mythology. But does it really matter?

That's a good question. Apparently, the Jewish translators of the Septuagint thought so, because the Titans are in their translation of the Old Testament.

Titans in the Bible

Yes, the Titans are in the Bible. But they probably aren't in the version you read, unless you prefer the Septuagint. That translation was the work of seventy-two Jewish scholars in the third century B.C. who produced a version of the Hebrew Scriptures in Koine Greek at the direction of Ptolemy II, the Greek king who'd inherited the Egyptian chunk of Alexander the Great's divided empire. Ptolemy apparently wanted to add the Torah to the famous library of Alexandria in a language his constituents could understand.

We've already showed the connection between the Titans and the Watchers, the sons of God of Genesis 6, the angels who sinned mentioned by Peter and Jude. The references in the Septuagint, however, are more obvious.

And the Philistines heard that David was anointed king over Israel; and all the Philistines went up to seek David; and David heard of it, and went down to the strong hold. And the Philistines came, and assembled in the **valley of the giants** (*Titânes*)...

And the Philistines came up yet again, and assembled in the **valley of Giants** (*Titânes*), (2 Samuel 5:17–18, 22; Septuagint translation by Lancelot C. L. Brenton, 1851; emphasis added)

References to the Valley of Rephaim/Titans also occur in 2 Samuel 23:13 and 1 Chronicles 11:15. Another mention of the Titans occurs in the apocryphal book (for Protestants) of Judith:

The Assyrian came down from the mountains of the north;
    he came with myriads of his warriors;
    their numbers blocked up the wadis,
    and their cavalry covered the hills.
    He boasted that he would burn up my territory,
    and kill my young men with the sword,
    and dash my infants to the ground,
    and seize my children as booty,
    and take my virgins as spoil.
    But the Lord Almighty has foiled them

by the hand of a woman.

For their mighty one did not fall by the hands of the young men,

nor did the sons of the Titans strike him down,

nor did tall giants set upon him;

but Judith daughter of Merari

with the beauty of her countenance undid him.

(Judith 16:3–6, NRSV; emphasis added)

Since the oldest text of Judith available to us today is from the Septuagint, we don't really know the book's original language.[205] It may have been composed in Greek, since the earliest Hebrew copy is from the Middle Ages.

The point: By the time the Greeks controlled the lands of the Bible, after the conquests of Alexander the Great in the fourth century B.C., the religious scholars and scribes of the Jews had no problem directly linking the Titans to the Rephaim, and identifying them specifically as giants. In the religion of the Greeks, Jewish scholars recognized their own stories of the Watchers, the Nephilim, and the rebel gods who'd rejected the authority of the Creator, Yahweh.

GOD'S WAR AGAINST THE TITANS

Discovering that the Greek myths we studied in high school are a twisted retelling of key biblical theology is at the same time exciting and disappointing. On the one hand, finding that the stories of the Olympians, Titans, giants, and monsters are based on history is a thrill. On the other, I wish somebody had taught me this stuff when I was in junior high! Church would have been *so much cooler.*

Let's be honest: The Bible has been drained of the really exciting stuff because we've been taught that most of the important characters in it are make-believe. The gods of the pagan world are dismissed as though the greatest civilizations of the ancient world—Sumer, Babylon, Egypt, Assyria, Persia, Greece, and Rome—were built by grown-ups who talked to imaginary friends.

Really? Our ancestors were that primitive? They built towers out of mud brick before they developed writing, but they were too simple to realize that their gods were lifeless blocks of wood and stone?

I don't think so. God called them "gods," so I'm pretty sure these things are real.

Now, here's a question for you: Why Og? Have you ever wondered about that? Why did God direct Moses to lead the Israelites against Og of Bashan first, before crossing the Jordan River? After all, the Promised Land, Canaan, was *west* of the river. Og's kingdom was on the east side. What was so special about Og and Bashan that Yahweh was compelled to make Og's small kingdom the first military objective of the campaign?

Okay, yes; Og was the last of "the remnant of the Rephaim." Hopefully, that phrase has more meaning now than it did before you read the last couple of chapters of this book. The Rephaim weren't just a warlike tribe who made traveling the King's Highway dangerous; they were heirs of a tradition that took pride in its alleged origin as the union of gods and men.

So, was Og literally a hybrid, part angel and part human? The Bible doesn't tell us, but it doesn't matter. Why? Because it's not what's in one's blood that condemns a man. It's what's in the thing that pumps the blood—the heart.

Whether or not Og was a giant is irrelevant. Moses, under God's direction, made it clear that Og represented the wickedness God had mentioned to Abraham more than four hundred years earlier—the iniquity of the Amorites. Let's review the clues.

First of all, it's a pretty safe bet that Og was the intended first target of the Israelites all along. His fellow Amorite king, Sihon of Heshbon, was given an opportunity to let Israel pass through his territory but opted for the sword instead. Sihon's capital city, Heshbon, was due east of Jericho, so if the Jordan River crossing had been Israel's immediate objective, Moses wouldn't have offered to pass through Sihon's territory on the King's Highway, which carried the people north. Moses would have simply ordered the people to make a hard left through Sihon's front yard on their way to knocking over Jericho's walls. But God had other plans.

Og, as we've mentioned, was king of a land with a bad reputation. Deuteronomy 1:4 notes that "Og the king of Bashan…lived in Ashtaroth and in Edrei." Remember that the Rephaim defeated by the Chedorlaomer coalition four hundred years earlier also lived at Ashtaroth. But Bashan was also the home of something else.

May Rapiu, King of Eternity, drink [wi]ne,
    yea, may he drink, the powerful and noble [god],
    the god enthroned in Athtarat [Ashtaroth],
    the god who rules in Edrei. [206]

We mentioned this entity earlier. At the time of the conquest, the Canaanites believed a god named Rapi'u, the singular form of Rephaim, ruled the underworld from exactly the same two cities in Bashan that were the center of Og's kingdom. The text cited above appears to be a ritual inviting a number of deities, including the war-goddess Anat and plague-god Resheph, to a feast at which Rapi'u asks Baal to "transmit the powers of the *Rapa'ūma* [Rephaim] to the living king."[207]

There's more. The home city of Rapi'u, Ashtaroth, identifies the King of Eternity with a mysterious god whose career we traced in a previous chapter:

Mother *Šapšu*, take a message
    To *Milku* in *'Aṯtartu* [Ashtaroth]:
    "My incantation for serpent bite,
    For the scaly serpent's poison."[208]

Mother *Šapšu* was the sun-goddess in Ugarit. In this ritual, she was asked to carry a message to a god of the underworld ruling in Ashtaroth—*Milku*, which was another form of the name Molech.

In short, Bashan was the entrance to the Amorite underworld. Og was its king, the last of the remnant of the living Rephaim. But Og had the power of the dead Rephaim on his side, or so he thought, and that's why he had to go. To be sure his readers knew just how evil Og was, Moses gave us the dimensions of Og's bed: Nine cubits by four cubits, or about thirteen and one-half feet by six. So, Og was a giant, right?

Not necessarily. Yes, the Rephaim had a reputation, and there are definite connections between the Rephaim and the pre-Flood Nephilim giants. But that connection may be mostly spiritual—as in occultic and demonic. That's the point Moses was making in Deuteronomy.

As I wrote in *The Great Inception*:

Every year at the first new moon after the spring equinox, Babylon held a new year festival called the *akitu*. It was a twelve-day
celebration of the cycle of regeneration, the beginning of a new
planting season, and it included a commemoration of Marduk's
victory over Tiamat. The entire celebration, from Yahweh's perspective, was a long ritual for "new gods that had come recently"[209]
involving all manner of licentious behavior.

The highlight of the festival was the Divine Union or Sacred
Marriage, where Marduk and his consort, Sarpanit, retired to the
cult bed inside the Etemenanki, the House of the Foundation
of Heaven and Earth, the great ziggurat of Babylon. Although
scholars still debate whether the Sacred Marriage was actually performed by the king and a priestess, it didn't matter to Yahweh.
The idea that a bountiful harvest in the coming year depended on
celebrating Marduk's sacred roll in the sack was abhorrent.

Now, here's the key point: Guess how big Marduk's bed was?

"…*nine cubits [its long] side, four cubits [its] front, the bed; the
throne in front of the bed*".[210]

Nine cubits by four cubits. Precisely the same dimensions as
the bed of Og. That is why Moses included that curious detail! It
wasn't a reference to Og's height; Moses was making sure his readers understood that the Amorite king Og, like the Amorite kings
of Babylon, was carrying on pre-flood occult traditions brought to
earth by the Watchers.[211]

If all that mumbo-jumbo about an underworld god ruling Bashan
had been invented by the priests of the Amorites, then God might have
ignored Og. From a military or economic perspective, Bashan, which
roughly covered the modern Golan Heights, wasn't exactly Babylon,
Egypt, or Assyria. There was no strategic benefit to picking that fight.
The goal was Canaan, west of the Jordan. Fighting Og meant marching a

couple million people with flocks and herds to the north end of the Jordan valley, fighting a battle, and then turning around and marching back south to cross the river near Jericho. Why do it, if Og was nothing more than a local warlord? Why give the Amorites west of the Jordan more time to prepare their defenses?

The Bible doesn't say so specifically, but in the context of what the Amorite neighbors of Israel believed about Bashan, the gods who lived there, and the spiritual power of the Rephaim, it seems clear that this was more than just a fight for control of some real estate. This was war in the spirit realm. Just as Yahweh humiliated Baal at the Red Sea forty years earlier, the Battle of Edrei against Og of Bashan was a clear message to the "warriors of Baal," the Rephaim.

And their allies in Canaan were next.

The Titans in Prophecy

The victories over Og of Bashan and his ally, Sihon of Heshbon, were the last two battles fought by the Israelites under Moses. Since you've read your Old Testament, you know that Moses didn't live much longer after the clash at Edrei. The Israelites retraced their steps along the King's Highway, and then turned west at Heshbon to camp in the Plains of Moab, across the Jordan River from Jericho. That takes place toward the end of the Book of Numbers, just before the fascinating encounter with the prophet-for-profit Balaam.

An inscription discovered in 1967 at Deir Alla, a town about twenty-five miles north of the Plains of Moab, three miles east of the Jordan River in modern-day Jordan, mentions Balaam, son of Beor by name. While the text is probably from the eighth century B.C., about 650 years after the incident with Balaam (around 1406 B.C.), it confirms that there were people who believed a prophet named Balaam son of Beor, a "divine seer," was a historical character. And this evidence was found about a two-day journey from where the king of Moab, Balak, offered Balaam the going rate for a high-quality curse. Instead, Balaam delivered several blessings on

Israel. To his credit, at least the prophet refused to say anything Yahweh didn't put in his mouth.

Before parting ways with the furious king of Moab, Balaam offered one of the best-known prophecies in the Old Testament, one that is clearly messianic:

> I see him, but not now;
>> I behold him, but not near:
>> a star shall come out of Jacob,
>> and a scepter shall rise out of Israel;
>> it shall crush the forehead of Moab
>> and break down all the sons of Sheth.
> (Numbers 24:17, ESV)

Scholars have argued for literally thousands of years about the exact meaning of this passage. Some have believed there is no messianic application to Balaam's prophecy. For example, Martin Luther just couldn't accept that God would use a devious pagan like Balaam that way. Of course, that ignores Numbers 24:2, which tells us that "the Spirit of God came upon him". Others believe the passage was fulfilled by David; still others think the process began with David but won't be completed until the Messiah returns.

I'm setting aside all of that to focus on the very last line of Balaam's oracle.

Have you ever read this verse and wondered who, exactly, are the sons of Sheth? Some translations render the name "Seth," and a few read "sons of tumult" instead of Seth or Sheth. Which Seth are we talking about here? Allow me to put forward two possibilities I doubt you've heard before.

First, consider the possibility that the sons of Sheth are followers of a pagan god. Seth and Sheth are alternate transliterations of the name of Egyptian chaos-god, Set (also spelled Sutekh, Setekh, and Setesh). During Egypt's Second Intermediate Period, Lower Egypt (that is, northern Egypt) was ruled by a Semitic-speaking people called the Hyksos, who were almost certainly Amorites.[212] The most important god in their pantheon was Baal, who was merged by the Hyksos with Set.[213]

The timing of the end of the Hyksos era in Egypt is fuzzy, but most scholars place it about a hundred years or so before the Exodus. They were driven out after a series of wars led by native Egyptian rulers based at Thebes. While it would be convenient to think that the Hyksos were destroyed by the Egyptians or simply disappeared from history, that's unlikely. It's more probable that they were driven out of Egypt and into the Transjordan or Arabia, absorbed into the native population, or a bit of both. Since Baal-Set was worshiped in Egypt for at least two hundred years after the Exodus, that may be closest to what happened.[214]

Is it possible that the prophecy refers to David's defeat of Set-worshiping desert nomads southeast of the Dead Sea? Maybe. To be honest, I was more excited about that idea a year and a half ago when I wrote *The Great Inception*. Now, not so much. Let's try another one on for size.

Amar Annus has linked the name Sheth/Seth to that infamous Amorite tribe we met in a previous chapter, the Suteans. He notes that the Egyptian term for the Suteans, *Šwtw*, a form of the Akkadian *Shutu*, appears in one of the Execration Texts from the nineteenth or eighteenth centuries B.C., about the time of Abraham, Isaac, and Jacob.

> The Ruler of Shutu, Ayyabum, and all the retainers who are with him; the Ruler of Shutu, Kushar, and all the retainers who are with him; the Ruler of Shutu, Zabulanu, and all the retainers who are with him.[215]

As we mentioned in the first chapter, the Execration Texts were like ancient Egyptian voodoo dolls. The names of enemies were inscribed on pottery, which were ritually cursed and then smashed. In a nutshell, "Sheth," "Shutu," and "Sutean" are the same name processed through different languages and types of writing.[216] Other Egyptian texts place the Shutu/Sheth in the central and northern Transjordan, which, significantly, includes Bashan—Rephaim territory.[217]

Other fascinating tidbits from the Execration Texts: The Shutu leaders were listed just after the "Rulers of Iy-'anaq"—the Anakim tribes that Joshua and the Israelites would fight for control of Canaan about four hundred years later. Also, the Shutu leader named Ayyabum bears the same name as the biblical Job. Now, this was probably not the Job of the Old Testament, but the Egyptian curse does locate him in the Transjordan, the same general area that was home to the long-suffering Job[218] and exactly where the Bible places the Rephaim tribes. And because you've read your Old Testament, you've noticed that the other Shutu leader, Zabulanu, has a name that Jacob would later give to one of his sons, Zebulon.

Here's the key link: Annus points to an Akkadian lexical list (that's like an ancient clay tablet version of Google Translate) that specifically equates *ti-id-nu* and *su-tu-u*—Tidanu and Sutean.[219] Citing Michael Heltzer's 1981 book *The Suteans*, Annus continues:

> In Ugaritic literature Suteans are mentioned in the epic of Aqhatu, where the antagonist of the *mt rpi* ["man of the Rephaim"] Dnil is a nomadic Ytpn, *mhr št*—"warrior of the Sutû, Sutean warrior."
> …In the epic of Keret Suteans are mentioned as *dtn*, spelled also as *ddn*, and it "must be understood as the *Di/Tidânu* tribe, a part of common Amorite stock. It is even likely that this term was used in Mesopotamia at the end of the 3rd millennium to designate tribes later known as Suteans.[220]

Highlight that! The Ugaritic *Epic of Keret* links the Amorite Sutean tribe, the Egyptian Shutu and the biblical sons of Sheth, with the Ditanu—the Titans.

Here's one more bit of historical evidence for your consideration: The Shutu are also identifed in later Egyptian texts as the Shasu,[221] probably as language and pronunciation changed over the centuries. About two hundred years after the Exodus, Ramesses II ("the Great") fought an epic battle against the Hittites at Qadesh, a city on the Orontes River near the modern border between Syria and Lebanon. According to the Egyptian account of the battle, Ramesses encountered a pair of Shasu nomads who told him the Hittites were about 125 miles away, near Aleppo, because the Hittite king, Muwatalli II, was "(too much) afraid of Pharaoh...to come south."[222]

Turned out that was a lie. The Shasu had been sent by the Hittites to fool the Egyptians into relaxing their guard, a ruse that was discovered when a member of Ramesses' bodyguard arrived with two Shasu prisoners who admitted that the full Hittite army was...well, right over there.[223]

Only some quick thinking and what was apparently incredible personal bravery by the pharaoh prevented the Battle of Qadesh from becoming Ramesses' Last Stand. The point is this: A surviving inscription commemorating the battle shows two Shasu prisoners, possibly the two who confessed to Ramesses, taking a beating from Egyptian soldiers. Here's the thing: The Shasu spies are as tall *on their knees* as their captors.

I can't emphasize this enough: This is not typical. Normally, defeated enemies were depicted as much smaller than the "good guys" in ancient artwork. Even 3,500 years ago, governments understood the power of propaganda. Yet, the Shasu captives were depicted as more than a head taller than the Egyptians soldiers around them.

This tracks with another Egyptian text that mentions the extraordinary height of the Shasu. A letter from an Egyptian scribe named Hori to another named Amenemope describes a mountain pass near Megiddo as "infested with Shasu." According to Hori the scribe, "some of them are of four cubits or of five cubits, from head to foot."[224] Since the Egyptian royal cubit was a little over twenty and one-half inches, that makes those Shasu between 6'8" and 8'6". Bear in mind that was when average Egyptian men stood between 5'2" [225] and 5'6".[226]

In other words, Egyptian evidence documents a nomadic people called the Shasu or Shutu, the Bible's sons of Sheth, who scholars identify as an Amorite tribe called the Suteans. They lived in the Transjordan from the time of Abraham through the time of the Judges (roughly 1900–1200 B.C.). That was Rephaim territory. These people, like the Rephaim, were exceptionally big—two and a half to three feet taller than most Egyptians.

As the Israelites prepared to invade Canaan, the prophet Balaam foresaw a messianic figure, "a star," who would come out of Jacob to "break down all the sons of Sheth." These were the Suteans, Amorite nomads living in Rephaim country east of the Jordan. The Suteans were known in former days throughout Mesopotamia as the Ditanu/Didanu or Tidanu, dead kings of old who were linked to the Rephaim in ritual texts at Ugarit. And the Dit/Did/Tidanu was the tribe from which the Greeks got the name of their old gods, the Titans.

Here's the short equation: Sheth = Shutu/Shasu = Suteans = Ditanu/Tidanu = Titans. In other words, the sons of Sheth were the Rephaim.

Let's complete the picture. Because "the Spirit of God came upon him," we'll take Balaam seriously: It appears the pagan prophet foresaw not just the conquest of the nomads living in the Syrian desert, but *the Messiah's ultimate destruction of the sons of the Titans.*

Whoa! Greek myth overlapping Bible prophecy? You bet. Who were the sons of the Titans? The offspring of the Watchers, the Nephilim, whose spirits are the demons who torment humanity to this day.

Psalm 82 records God's sentence of death on the rebel gods. Numbers 24 appears to be an inspired prophecy of the destruction of their demon spawn. And Ezekiel tells us when and where that will happen.

But before we get there, a bit more history.

Joshua vs. the Giants

Think I'm reaching? I don't blame you. Let's continue with our examination of the evidence.

Even though Og, last of the (living) Rephaim, was dead, his allies, the Anakim, were important enough that their utter destruction was Joshua's main objective in the conquest of Canaan. Remember, the Anakim were specifically linked to the Rephaim by Moses:

Do not harass Moab or contend with them in battle, for I will not give you any of their land for a possession, because I have given Ar to the people of Lot for a possession. (**The Emim formerly lived there, a people great and many, and tall as the Anakim. Like the Anakim they are also counted as Rephaim, but the Moabites call them Emim.**… And when you approach the territory of the people of Ammon, do not harass them or contend with them, for I will not give you any of the land of the people of Ammon as a possession, because I have given it to the sons of Lot for a possession. (**It is also counted as a land of Rephaim. Rephaim formerly lived there—but the Ammonites call them Zamzummim—a people great and many, and tall as the Anakim;** but the LORD destroyed them before the Ammonites, and they dispossessed them and settled in their place. (Deuteronomy 2:9b–11, 19–21, ESV; emphasis added)

While the Book of Joshua goes into some detail about his campaigns against all the "—ites" (Canaanites, Amorites, Hittites, Perizzites, Jebusites, etc.), when it summarizes the result of the war, the Anakim are singled out for special mention:

And Joshua came at that time and cut off the Anakim from the hill country, from Hebron, from Debir, from Anab, and from all the hill country of Judah, and from all the hill country of Israel. Joshua devoted them to destruction with their cities. There was none of the Anakim left in the land of the people of Israel. Only in Gaza, in Gath, and in Ashdod did some remain. So Joshua took the whole land, according to all that the LORD had spoken to Moses. And Joshua gave it for an inheritance to Israel according to their tribal allotments. And the land had rest from war. (Joshua 11:21–23, ESV)

In short, Joshua's conquest of Canaan was a war against the giants. Taking out Og, last of the Rephaim, was the first objective, and the war in Canaan was focused on "cutting off" the Anakim. Remember, according to the spies Moses sent into the land, the Anakim were unusually large:

The land, through which we have gone to spy it out, is a land that devours its inhabitants, and all the people that we saw in it are of great height. **And there we saw the Nephilim (the sons of Anak, who come from the Nephilim), and we seemed to ourselves like grasshoppers, and so we seemed to them.** (Numbers 13:32b–33, ESV; emphasis added)

And there's the reason for their size—the Anakim came from the Nephilim.

There are some who debate this passage, trying to erase the giants from history by arguing that the spies lied and that's what is meant by their "bad report." In fact, some English translations lean toward that reading of the text, preferring "false report," "rumors," or "lies" to describe their assessment of the enemy. But then it would seem the Egyptians were also lying about giants in the land.

Please understand, we're not claiming that monsters thirty feet tall roamed Canaan in the days of Moses. But when you're 5'2", a guy big enough to play professional basketball looks like a giant, especially when he's pointing the business end of a spear at you. The important point is not their height, it's that the Anakim, Rephaim, and their Amorite allies had *spiritual* connections to the Nephilim and their fathers, the Watchers.

Backing up a step: Did you notice the phrase, "devoted to destruction," in Joshua 11:21? That's translated from the Hebrew word *kherem*. It's used a lot in Joshua, especially chapters 10 and 11, but you find it twenty-nine times in the Old Testament. It essentially means someone or something that must be destroyed because it's taboo, under the ban, or spiritually contaminated.[227]

So, the people and goods that were "devoted to destruction" by Joshua and the Israelites were condemned, offered as a sort of sacrifice to Yahweh. Why? Maybe the better question is, "Who?" Who did God declare *kherem*, devoted to absolute destruction? Well, not the Israelites' cousins in Edom, Moab, and Ammon. Even though the later prophets had some harsh words from Yahweh about the descendants of Esau and Lot, God declared that they were not to be touched during the conquest of Canaan.

Likewise, Joshua was free to make treaties and spare the lives of citizens from cities far away. But God was explicit in His instructions to Moses about what was to happen to those in Canaan, and why:

> But in the cities of these peoples that the LORD your God is giving you for an inheritance, you shall save alive nothing that breathes, but you shall devote them to complete destruction, the Hittites and the Amorites, the Canaanites and the Perizzites, the Hivites and the Jebusites, as the LORD your God has commanded, **that they may not teach you to do according to all their abominable practices that they have done for their gods, and so you sin against the LORD your God.** (Deuteronomy 20:16–20, ESV; emphasis added)

That's the reason. The people occupying Canaan were sold out to rebel gods and had been drawn into "abominable practices." Such as? Sacrificing children to gods of the underworld was just one of their crimes. Read through Leviticus and Deuteronomy sometime, but don't read them out loud with children in the room.

It's hard for us twenty-first-century types, especially in the postmodern West, to really understand why God commanded Israel to wage a war of extermination against the Amorites and Anakim. We've lost the sense of gravity that this spiritual conflict deserves. Somewhere along the way, we've forgotten that we're in the middle of a war for control of *eternity*.

Joshua understood it. Did the Israelites fighting for him? Some, probably. Others, no, like Achan, son of Carmi. In Joshua 7, we read that after the destruction of Jericho, Achan couldn't resist helping himself to a fine cloak from Sumer, two hundred shekels of silver (about five pounds), and a gold bar weighing fifty shekels (about twenty ounces, worth more than $26,000 at the time of this writing!). Because of his sin, the army of Israel was routed by a much smaller force at the city of Ai.

When God revealed the presence of "devoted things" in the Israelite camp, the punishment was severe. Achan, his wife, their sons and daughters, and his livestock were stoned and then burned with the stolen goods. Why so harsh? Because, according to God, the mere presence of devoted things in the camp meant that the Israelites themselves had "become devoted to destruction."[228]

That's how serious this is. Be glad we're not asked to fight that way today. We don't have to, because Jesus did it on the cross.

But before He was led to Calvary, Jesus, like Joshua, had to contend with giants.

Jesus vs. the Nephilim

Jesus battled the Nephilim.

Wait—before you chuck this book into the circular file, consider this: If our working theory on the origin of demons is correct, then the demons Jesus cast out were spirits of the giants destroyed by Noah's Flood. So, Jesus and the apostles literally waged spiritual war against the Nephilim—the sons of the Titans.

Think about that for a minute. If there is any truth at all to the mythology of the ancient Greeks and Romans, then their demigod heroes like Theseus (son of Poseidon), Bellerophon (ditto), Perseus (son of Zeus), and Herakles (ditto) were Nephilim.

Imagine that. Can't you just see the Apostle Paul tangling with the spirit of Herakles during one of his missionary trips through Greece? We'll never know, but it's a cool idea for a graphic novel.

Seriously, though, Jesus' mission to drive the demons out of the Holy Land was more than a ministry to help the demon-oppressed and possessed. Israel, land and people, belonged to Yahweh. Demons were not welcome. They were trespassers.

Why were there so many in Israel in Jesus' day? Have you ever noticed that the Old Testament prophets never cast out demons? In fact, the word translated "demon" in the OT only appears twice. The fact is there was more demonic activity during Jesus' ministry than any other period in the Bible. Coincidence? Not on your life.

There are a couple of reasons for this. While demons are mentioned, like the "demons that were no gods"[229] to which the Israelites sacrificed in the desert, the emphasis in the Old Testament is on God and His sovereignty. Yes, demons existed, but it's only in passing when they're mentioned at all. And many of those references are hidden because their names are translated into English words like plague, pestilence, destruction, and terror. They're treated as forces of nature rather than literal entities. Texts from the cultures around ancient Israel confirm that Resheph ("plague"), Deber ("pestilence"), Pachad ("terror"), Gad ("fortune"), Meni ("destiny"), and others found in the Old Testament were considered pagan gods or demons, even by the prophets.

Jesus' ministry was the spiritual equivalent of hand-to-hand combat, and demons are the enemy's foot soldiers. His mission was to repel the enemy that had encroached on holy ground, something that had been going on for a long time.

The concept of holy ground in the Bible dates back to the Tower of Babel. It's another aspect of the incident that Moses repeated for the Israelites in Deuteronomy 32:8–9:

> When the Most High gave to the nations their inheritance, when he divided mankind, he fixed the borders of the peoples according to the number of the sons of God. **But the LORD's portion is his people, Jacob his allotted heritage.** (ESV; emphasis added)

God reserved Israel for Himself. The small-*G* gods had been allotted to the rest of the nations (Deuteronomy 4:19–20), but Jacob was *His* inheritance. Israel, the people and the land, belonged to Yahweh, just as Moab belonged to Chemosh and Ammon belonged to Molech. However, since Israel had been out of the land since the days of Jacob, Joshua had to wage a holy war to reclaim it from the rebel gods and their human minions for Yahweh and His people.

Those rebel gods want to take Yahweh's mount of assembly for themselves, and they've never stopped trying to take back the Holy Land. Human history revolves around the Fallen trying to destroy God's chosen people, or at least drive them away from His holy mountain, Zion. This is the sense behind David's distress at Saul's attempt to chase him out of Israel:

> And he said, "Why does my lord pursue after his servant? For what have I done? What evil is on my hands? Now therefore let my lord the king hear the words of his servant. If it is the LORD who has stirred you up against me, may he accept an offering, but if it is men, may they be cursed before the LORD, for they have driven me out this day that I should have no share in the heritage of the LORD, saying, 'Go, serve other gods.'" (1 Samuel 26:18–19, ESV)

David was afraid that he would not be able to worship Yahweh outside of Israel because the lands beyond its borders belonged to other gods.[230]

Another illustration of the concept is in the story of the commander of the Syrian army, Naaman. He came to Israel, desperate for a cure for his leprosy. After he was miraculously healed, Naaman had an odd request for the prophet Elisha:

> Please let there be given to your servant two mule loads of earth, for from now on your servant will not offer burnt offering or sacrifice to any god but the LORD. (2 Kings 5:17, ESV)

The Syrian soldier knew that Yahweh was the one true god, and to be sure he worshiped only Yahweh, Naaman returned to Damascus with two mule loads of holy dirt.

So, back to the New Testament: When Jesus cast out demons, he wasn't just delivering the oppressed and possessed. He was telling those foul spirits, the sons of the Titans, "Get off my land."

Assault on Mount Hermon

You've got to admit that's pretty cool. But it gets even better. Toward the end of His third year in ministry, Jesus went on the offensive and invaded *their* turf.

> And Jesus went on with his disciples to the villages of Caesarea Philippi.…
>
> And after six days Jesus took with him Peter and James and John, and led them up a high mountain by themselves. And he was transfigured before them, and his clothes became radiant, intensely white, as no one on earth could bleach them. And there appeared to them Elijah with Moses, and they were talking with Jesus. And Peter said to Jesus, "Rabbi, it is good that we are here. Let us make three tents, one for you and one for Moses and one for Elijah." For he did not know what to say, for they were terrified. And a cloud overshadowed them, and a voice came out of the cloud, "This is my beloved Son; listen to him." And suddenly, looking around, they no longer saw anyone with them but Jesus only.
>
> And as they were coming down the mountain, he charged them to tell no one what they had seen, until the Son of Man had risen from the dead. So they kept the matter to themselves, questioning what this rising from the dead might mean. (Mark 8:27a, 9:2–10, ESV)

Caesarea Philippi was at the foot of Mount Hermon, which is the only high mountain in the neighborhood. Remember, this was not only where the two hundred Watchers swore an oath to corrupt humankind, it was the mount of assembly for the creator-god of the Canaanites, El, where he held court with his consort, Asherah, and their seventy sons.

Here's the point: Jesus climbed the rebels' mount of assembly and transformed Himself into a being of light:

Behold, a bright cloud overshadowed them, and a voice from the cloud said, "This is my beloved Son, with whom I am well pleased; listen to him." When the disciples heard this, they fell on their faces and were terrified. (Matthew 17:5–6, ESV)

Could He have been any more obvious? As our friend Dr. Michael Heiser describes it, this was a cosmic poke in the eye. It's like Jesus shot a flare gun into the heavens! Then He came down the mountain and, after casting a demon out of a boy at the foot of Mount Hermon, Jesus made sure the message was received, loud and clear:

After these things **the Lord appointed other seventy also, and sent them two and two before his face into every city and place,** whither he himself would come. (Luke 10:1, KJV; emphasis added)

Some manuscripts read "seventy-two," but the theological point is the same. As noted in an earlier chapter, the number was a reference to the complete set—in other words, all of them. El, Asherah and their seventy sons—i.e., the gods of all the nations—claimed Mount Hermon as their holy mountain. Jesus climbed their mountain, had a meeting with the Father, Elijah, and Moses on the summit, and then came down to demonstrate that *His* seventy was better than El's. Like so many other events in the Bible, this was not a coincidence.

And that's not all. This remarkable event may have been an echo of a military campaign led by Yahweh.

> **O mountain of God, mountain of Bashan;**
> **O many-peaked mountain, mountain of Bashan!**
> Why do you look with hatred, O many-peaked mountain,
> at the mount that God desired for his abode,
> yes, where the LORD will dwell forever?
> **The chariots of God are twice ten thousand,**
> **thousands upon thousands;**

the Lord is among them; Sinai is now in the sanctuary.
You ascended on high,
leading a host of captives in your train
and receiving gifts among men,
even among the rebellious, that the LORD God may dwell
there. (Psalm 68:15–18, ESV; emphasis added)

The psalmist's "many-peaked mountain" is Hermon, the southern-most peak in the Anti-Lebanon mountains. Now, because you're sharp, you know that Mount Hermon is not the mountain of God. That's Zion, in Jerusalem—the "mount that God desired for His abode." However, the Hebrew phrase *har elohim* can be singular or plural, depending on the context. In this passage, considering the history of Mount Hermon, reading the verse "O mountain of *the gods*, mountain of Bashan" is a better fit.[231] At some point in history, Yahweh led His heavenly army against Hermon and returned to His abode with a host of captives.

What was *that* about? It's hard to say. Scholars aren't in agreement on the meaning of this psalm, but since Paul quoted it to describe Christ's victory over the dark domain (Ephesians 4:8), we can assume that the psalmist likewise had some sort of battle in the spiritual war in mind.

It was not chance that Jesus began His last journey to Jerusalem right after descending from Mount Hermon. He'd picked a fight with the Fallen and it was time to complete the last phase of His mission. Notice that in the chapters of Matthew, Mark, and Luke describing the events that took place after the Transfiguration, it appears that Jesus took His time getting to Jerusalem, and He made the journey as public as possible.

Quick rabbit trail: Have you ever wondered why Jesus rode a donkey into Jerusalem? Yes, it was a fulfillment of prophecy:

Rejoice greatly, O daughter of Zion! Shout aloud, O daughter of Jerusalem! Behold, your king is coming to you; righteous and having salvation is he, humble and mounted on a donkey, on a colt, the foal of a donkey. (Zechariah 9:9, ESV)

However, that doesn't answer the question. Why did Zechariah prophesy a donkey colt for the Messiah? Was it to demonstrate the Savior's humility? Maybe. It certainly fits the image of the suffering servant, a Messiah who washed the feet of His disciples to demonstrate that "the Son of Man came not to be served but to serve, and to give his life as a ransom for many."[232]

From our modern perspective, we assume kings always rode horses, noble steeds worthy of their riders' royal image. But this is another example of us reading our modern worldview backwards into the Bible. Imagining John Wayne, the Marlboro man, or a medieval knight in shining armor on a powerful stallion clouds our understanding of what was really going on. Jesus' entry into Jerusalem on the back of a donkey was a clear message to the principalities and powers behind the people who had dominated the culture of the Near East since the time of the patriarchs, the Amorites.

You see, Amorite kings didn't ride horses. In their world, the royal ride was a donkey. (The donkey was a powerful sacrificial animal, too. Donkey sacrifices were common among the Amorites.) In fact, around the time of Isaac and Jacob, an Amorite official in the kingdom of Mari, which was based on the Euphrates River near the modern border between Syria and Iraq, offered advice to his king, Zimri-Lim:

> "May my lord honor his kingship. Since you are the king of Hanean (tribesmen), and also are the king of the Amorites, may my lord not ride horses; instead, he ought to ride a chariot or mules, so that he could honor his kingship." Therefore, when Christ entered Jerusalem on a donkey, the population, as well as the authorities, knew how to read the symbolism at stake (Matthew 21).[233]

Of course, Jesus will come back on a horse, but we'll discuss that in an upcoming chapter. But just before His triumphant entry into Jerusalem, Jesus sent yet another message to the spirit realm.

We've already mentioned the story of Lazarus (John 11:1–44). He was the brother of Martha and Mary, the woman who anointed Jesus with ointment and wiped His feet with her hair. Oddly, when word reached Jesus of Lazarus' illness, He didn't seem bothered by the news. He stayed two days longer where He was before announcing to His disciples that it was time to return to Judea.

Jesus and His entourage arrived at Bethany to find Mary and Martha in mourning. Lazarus had already died; in fact, he'd been in the tomb for four days. This was deliberate. Jesus had waited until He knew Lazarus was dead before departing for Judea (John 11:14). It appears He had waited long enough so that there was no question in the minds of the mourners that Lazarus was truly dead before Jesus called him out of the tomb to the shock and awe of the crowd. As you can imagine, this attracted the attention of the authorities:

> When the large crowd of the Jews learned that Jesus was at Bethany, they came, not only on account of him but also to see Lazarus, whom he had raised from the dead. So the chief priests made plans to put Lazarus to death as well, because on account of him many of the Jews were going away and believing in Jesus. (John 12:9–11, ESV)

Do you get that? The chief priests were so desperate to keep their jobs that they not only wanted to kill Jesus, they planned to assassinate a man God raised from the dead!

There was a spiritual source behind their hubris. Jesus purposefully timed His arrival in Bethany to make it clear to all parties, human and spirit, that He'd literally revivified His friend. I think it was a message to a specific group of spirits.

Who were they, and why would they care? You've probably already guessed that I believe this was directed at the spirits of the Rephaim—the Nephilim, the sons of the Titans.

Correct. Here's where I reveal some of the information from the Canaanite Rephaim texts that I held back earlier.

All three of the texts describe the spirits of these venerated dead as traveling to a ritual meal, something that appears similar to the *kispum* for the dead we described earlier. The meal is held in the house, sanctuary, plantations, or threshing-floor of the creator-god of the Canaanites, El, which was on Mount Hermon.[234] Pay special attention to the travel time of the Rephaim:

> The [Rephaim] hurried to his sanctuary,[235]
>> to his sanctuary hurried the [elohim].
>> The chariots they harnessed;
>> the horses they hitched, …
>> They mounted their chariots,
>> they came on their mounts.
>> **They journeyed a day**
>> **and a second.**
>> **After sunrise on the third**
>> **the [Rephaim] arrived at the threshing-floors,**
>> **the [elohim] at the plantations.**[236] (Emphasis added)

> To his sanctuary, [Rephaim], hurry indeed.
>> to his sanctuary hurry indeed, [elohim].
>> *[Note: El begins speaking here]*
>> my banquet
>> Therefore…
>> as my shepherd.
>> **Now I shall journey a day and a second;**
>> **after sunrise on the third I shall arrive at my house,**
>> **I shall come into the midst of my palace.**[237] (Emphasis added)

> To his sanctuary the [Rephaim] hurried indeed,
>> to his sanctuary hurried indeed the [elohim].
>> They harnessed the chariots;
>> the horses they hitched.
>> They mounted their chariots,

they came on their mounts.
They journeyed a day
and a second.
After sunrise on the third
the [Rephaim] arrived at the threshing-floors,
the [elohim] at the plantations.[238] (Emphasis added)

The Amorite neighbors of the ancient Israelites summoned the spirits of the Rephaim to ritual meals in their honor on El's mount of assembly, Mount Hermon. The travel required two full days, and they arrived after *dawn on the third day.*

No doubt you grasp the significance, but let me add one more bit of information. Some scholars interpret the Rephaim text KTU 1.22 as a ritual to bring the Rephaim back to life.

There, shoulder to shoulder were the brothers,
whom El made to stand up in haste.
    There the name of El revivified the dead,
    the blessings of the name of El revivified the heroes.
There rose up Baal Rapiu,
the warriors of Baal and the warriors of Anat.[239]
(Emphasis added)

Baal Rapiu ("Lord Rapi'u") may refer to Rapi'u, the underworld god who ruled from Ashtaroth and Edrei in Bashan, or it may be an epithet ("Lord of the Rephaim") of the storm-god Baal, king of the Canaanite pantheon. Other scholars translate that sentence, "There rose up the Rephaim of Baal,"[240] which fits with the following sentence describing them as warriors of Baal and the war-goddess Anat.

To be clear, the scholars who believe the Rephaim texts were rituals to raise the god-kings of old back to life are in the minority. The fact is those tablets are pretty beat up. They were buried under the rubble when Ugarit was destroyed by the Sea Peoples about 3,200 years ago, so it's amazing we can make out anything at all. Although the theory does have some evidence, most Ugaritic scholars just don't believe there's enough evidence to read these texts as resurrection rituals.

Still, it's clear that the Amorites believed the dead weren't gone, they still had power to affect the living, and the Rephaim were an exalted group in the afterlife who served the great gods Baal and El.

And remember the travel time from the abode of the dead to the sanctuary of El: They arrived after dawn of the third day. Scholars agree on that detail, and it's important. To put a finer point on it:

> The Lord Jesus on the night when he was betrayed took bread, and when he had given thanks, he broke it, and said, "This is my body, which is for you. Do this in remembrance of me." In the same way also he took the cup, after supper, saying, "This cup is the new covenant in my blood. Do this, as often as you drink it, in remembrance of me." For as often as you eat this bread and drink the cup, you proclaim the Lord's death until he comes. (1 Corinthians 11:23–26, ESV)

A meal. Not a ritual, exactly, but at the Last Supper Jesus gave His disciples a pattern for remembering His death until His glorious return. Then, after dawn of the third day:

> They went to the tomb, taking the spices they had prepared. And they found the stone rolled away from the tomb, but when they went in they did not find the body of the Lord Jesus. While they were perplexed about this, behold, two men stood by them in dazzling apparel. And as they were frightened and bowed their faces to the ground, the men said to them, "Why do you seek the living among the dead? He is not here, but has risen. Remember how he told you, while he was still in Galilee, that the Son of Man must be delivered into the hands of sinful men and be crucified **and on the third day rise**." (Luke 24:1–7, ESV; emphasis added)

Coincidence? The timing matches *exactly*. Jesus died on Friday. He traveled that day, and then another, and at dawn of the third day, like the Rephaim traveling from the land of the dead to El's mount of assembly, Hermon, Jesus arrived back in Jerusalem—the site of *His* mount of assembly, Zion.

What did He do during those three days?

> For Christ also suffered once for sins, the righteous for the unrighteous, that he might bring us to God, **being put to death in the flesh but made alive in the spirit, in which he went and proclaimed to the spirits in prison, because they formerly did not obey, when God's patience waited in the days of Noah,** while the ark was being prepared, in which a few, that is, eight persons, were brought safely through water. (1 Peter 3:19–20, ESV; emphasis added)

The meaning of this phrase has been studied and debated for about two thousand years. While it might appear that Jesus, as a spirit, "preached" (Greek *kērÿssō*) to human spirits in Hell, that's not what this means. "Proclaimed" or "declared" is a closer translation for *kērÿssō*. Jesus wasn't preaching; He was telling the spirits, "Listen—this is how it's going to be." And the context and grammar of the sentence make it clear that those spirits weren't human:

> The NT never uses the word for "spirit" in an unqualified fashion to refer to the human soul. Therefore, the reference in 1 Peter 3:19 may point to nonhuman supernatural beings. This interpretation is strengthened when the passage is read in the context of Genesis 6–9 because of the reference to Noah and the flood in 1 Pet[er] 3:20. The flood reference also draws in the traditions of 1 Enoch, so the **"spirits in prison" may have been understood to be the fallen angels or "sons of God" of Genesis 6:1–4.**[241] (Emphasis added)

Bingo! Jesus traveled to a supernatural prison to deliver a proclamation to spirits who'd been locked up for their disobedience since the days of Noah. Given that Peter wrote that the angels who sinned were chained in Tartarus "until the judgment," it's a safe bet that this was the same group.

Do you see the significance? The ancient Amorites of Ugarit performed rituals to summon the spirits of the Rephaim/Nephilim, the sons of the Watchers/Titans, to a ritual meal on El's mount of assembly, Mount Hermon. The journey of those dead kings of old took two days, and they arrived "after sunrise on the third." More than a thousand years later, shortly after His Transfiguration on their mount of assembly, Jesus was crucified. He died on Good Friday. In the spirit, He spent two days declaring His victory to the Watchers in Tartarus, and then rose to *His* mount of assembly, Jerusalem, at sunrise of the third day!

Hallelujah!

Jesus is coming back, and this time on a white horse. And here we get to the heart of this book: The prophets knew that the Messiah's enemy on that day would be the rebel gods of the pagan world and the demon offspring of the old gods who walked the Earth before the Flood.

EZEKIEL

One of the most intriguing mysteries in the Bible is the identity of Gog of Magog. Let me state for the record, with all due respect, that most scholars and students of end-times prophecy are looking in the wrong place for an answer.

I don't mean just geographically, I mean in the wrong plane of existence. Gog will not be human.

A human actor will be involved, no question. But the one who drives the action—or, more accurately, is led into action, since he's dragged by hooks in his jaw, is supernatural. And it's easier to identify him with some confidence than to guess whether Gog is Vladimir Putin, Recep Tayyip Erdogan, or some other political leader in the Middle East.

First, historical context. The prophet Ezekiel wrote his book while living as an exile in greater Babylonia beginning around 593 B.C. He was in the first group of captives taken from Judah by Nebuchadnezzar, the Chaldean king of Babylon. From the first chapter of his book, we learn that he lived along the Chebar canal, which diverted water from the Euphrates River near Babylon through the city of Nippur. This was in what is now Iraq, about a hundred miles southeast of modern Baghdad.

The older I get, the more believe that God put nothing in the Bible that isn't relevant. What seem like minor details prove to be very important when we understand the context. If something looks unimportant, it's probably because we just don't understand it correctly. (Or, in the words of Dr. Michael Heiser, "If it's weird, it's important.")

So it is with Ezekiel's location. The Chebar canal is only mentioned by Ezekiel, but he saw fit to mention it eight times. It was where he saw several visions from God, including the famous one that has UFO believers so needlessly excited, Ezekiel's wheel.[242]

His home was Tel Abib, a community that gave its name to the second-largest city in modern Israel, Tel Aviv (spelled differently; pronounced the same). Nearby Nippur was one of the most important religious sites in the ancient Near East, the holy city of the god Enlil and the home of his temple, the *E-kur* ("House of the Mountain"). As related in an earlier chapter, Enlil was the chief god in the Mesopotamian pantheon for centuries. He replaced the sky-god, Anu, and was in turn replaced as king of the gods by the city god of Babylon, Marduk.

Nippur, or Nibru in Sumerian, was where ancient Sumerians and Akkadians believed the gods met—the location of their divine council. Beginning in the late 1960s, authors like Erich von Däniken and Zecharia Sitchin, inspired by writers like horror fiction author H. P. Lovecraft,[243] tortured the texts of the ancients to support their belief that the chief gods of Sumer, the Anunnaki (apparently, before they were demoted to the netherworld), arrived on Earth hundreds of thousands of years ago from a planet called Nibiru, whereupon they created humanity through genetic engineering to serve as slaves.

The irony is that the nonsense peddled by ancient astronaut theorists pales in comparison to the truth. The reality is *way* more interesting! Apparently, Nippur/Nibru *was* important in the cosmic scheme in the distant past. For His reasons, which aren't entirely clear, God called a prophet who lived near Nippur to prophesy a war that results in the death of the gods—the last clash of the Titans.

Gog

Ezekiel's visions of the war of Gog and Magog is where Bible prophecy meets Greek myth. So, let's dig in:

> The word of the LORD came to me: "Son of man, set your face toward Gog, of the land of Magog, the chief prince of Meshech and Tubal, and prophesy against him and say, Thus says the Lord GOD: Behold, I am against you, O Gog, chief prince of Meshech and Tubal. And I will turn you about and put hooks into your jaws, and I will bring you out, and all your army, horses and horsemen, all of them clothed in full armor, a great host, all of them with buckler and shield, wielding swords. Persia, Cush, and Put are with them, all of them with shield and helmet; Gomer and all his hordes; Beth-togarmah from the uttermost parts of the north with all his hordes—many peoples are with you." (Ezekiel 38:1–6, ESV)

Let's stop and unpack that. In recent years, Magog has often been interpreted as southern Russia, hence the idea that a Russian-led coalition will attack Israel. This is taken as a given in some prophecy circles these days, where the identity of Magog isn't even questioned. This is an error we need to correct.

Russia, Russia, Russia

This particular interpretation of Ezekiel 38 began in the nineteenth century when prominent scholars Wilhelm Gesenius and C. F. Keil translated the Hebrew word *rosh* in Ezekiel 38:3 as a proper noun,[244] which changes the verse from "Gog, chief prince of Meshech and Tubal" to "Gog, prince of Rosh, Meshech, and Tubal." Bear in mind, however, that the study of ancient Hebrew has advanced a great deal over the last century, and even in their day other respected scholars, including Keil's instructor in

Hebrew, disagreed with their interpretation.[245] But it was the publication of the *Scofield Reference Bible* in 1909, which was revised in 1917, that mainstreamed the belief that Russia would lead a world coalition in a war against Israel in the last days:

> **That the primary reference is to the northern (European) powers, headed up by Russia, all agree.** The whole passage should be read in connection with Zechariah 12:1–4; 14:1–9; Matthew 24:14–30; Revelation 14:14–20; 19:17–21. "Gog" is the prince, "Magog," his land. **The reference to Meshech and Tubal (Moscow and Tobolsk) is a clear mark of identification.** Russia and the northern powers have been the latest persecutors of dispersed Israel, and it is congruous both with divine justice and with the covenants… that destruction should fall at the climax of the last mad attempt to exterminate the remnant of Israel in Jerusalem. The whole prophecy belongs to the yet future "day of Jehovah" (Isaiah 2:10–22; Revelation 19:11–21) and to the battle of Armageddon (Revelation 16:14) but includes also the final revolt of the nations at the close of the kingdom-age (Revelation 20:7–9).[246] (Emphasis added)

The American political climate since the Cold War, and especially since the election of Donald Trump, has created a body of believers primed to accept Russia as the great end-times enemy of God and Israel.

It seemed to fit world conditions a hundred years ago, too. World War I destroyed the sunny optimism of amillennialism, a belief that the Millennium is spiritual rather than physical and identical with the current Church Age. At the end of this age, whenever that is, Jesus returns to take over from the Church.

It was understandably much harder to believe that things were getting better and better in the middle of a war that killed more than sixteen million people. Then the Spanish flu came along in the fall of 1918 and took another twenty to fifty million lives. Scofield's premillennial interpretation of Bible prophecy made sense of a world gone mad. But that doesn't make him right about Russia as Magog.

Here's the key question: How would readers in Ezekiel's day have understood the prophecy? He wasn't writing just for readers in the United States of America 2,600 years in the future. His primary audience was Jews of the sixth century B.C. What would they take away from this text?

Well, it's a safe bet they wouldn't have read *rosh* as a name. It means "chief" or "head," as in Rosh Hashanah ("head of the year"), the Jewish New Year. In the Bible, when *rosh* doesn't refer to somebody's head, it's used the way we English speakers use the word "head"—head of the company, head of the nation, heads of their fathers' houses, etc. Thus, *Gog ro'sh nasiy' Meshek Tuwbal* is "Gog, chief prince of Meshech and Tubal," or possibly, "Gog, the prince, chief of Meshech and Tubal."[247] The meaning is clear.

But, some argue, the hordes of Magog come from the "uttermost parts of the north." Take a world map and draw a straight line north from Jerusalem. There is nothing farther north than Russia. Case closed, right?

Well, no. We've already shown that the Hebrew *yerekah tsaphon* points to Mount Zaphon, Baal's mount of assembly. By examining the rest of the Hebrew underlying our English translations, it is clear that Russia is nowhere in view here:

> Verse 2b appears to place Gog at the head of Meshech and Tubal, though the syntax of *něśî' rō'š mešek wĕtubāl* is problematic. The issue revolves around whether *rō'š* is the name of an ethnic group or a common noun. Both LXX ἄρθοντα Ρως and the construct pointing of the Masoretes argue for the former. But who then is this Rosh? The popular identification of Rosh with Russia is impossibly anachronistic and based on a faulty etymology, the assonant similarities between Russia and Rosh being purely accidental.[248]

In plainer English, it's pure coincidence that *rosh* and Russia sound anything alike. Further, the people called the Rus', who were actually

Vikings from Sweden, didn't arrive in what became Russia before the ninth century A.D., nearly 1,500 years after Ezekiel's prophecy. There is no evidence from the ancient Near East, the time and place in which Ezekiel lived and wrote, that a people or country called Rosh existed anywhere.

So, identifying Russia with the word "Rosh," Moscow with "Meshech," or Tobolsk with "Tubal" because they sound alike is just bad hermeneutics. The *Expositor's Bible Commentary* puts it this way: "There is no etymological, grammatical, historical, or literary data in support of such a position."[249]

Magog and Friends

So, then, who *were* these people? Let's get the easy ones out of the way first: Persia is Iran, Cush is Ethiopia and/or Sudan, and Put is Libya. That's simple and well-documented from ancient sources. While it's easy to see Iran as an enemy of Israel, it's harder to see Ethiopia and Libya as part of a terrifying end-times army, especially since Libya isn't even a functioning state in 2018. We'll address that in a bit.

The other players are harder to pin down because their names have faded from history. There are no ambassadors at the United Nations from Magog, Meshech, Tubal, Gomer, and Beth-Togarmah. But we can and do know where on the globe Ezekiel was pointing. All of them are place names in what used to be called Anatolia, which is modern-day Turkey.

Our first clue is chapter 10 of Genesis. We find all these names in the Table of Nations:

> The sons of Japheth: **Gomer, Magog,** Madai, Javan, **Tubal, Meshech,** and Tiras. **The sons of Gomer:** Ashkenaz, Riphath, and **Togarmah.** The sons of Javan: Elishah, Tarshish, Kittim, and Dodanim. From these the coastland peoples spread in their lands, each with his own language, by their clans, in their nations. (Genesis 10:2–5, ESV; emphasis added)

The Hebrew name *Gomer* probably refers to the Cimmerians (Akkadian *Gimirru*, which means "complete"), who migrated south from the Eurasian steppes and attacked Assyria in the late seventh century B.C. The Assyrians called them *Gimmerai*; the Cimmerian king Teushpa was defeated by Assarhadon of Assyria sometime between 681 and 668 B.C.[250] Because of the military power of the Assyrians, the Cimmerians usually raided west, into Anatolia. They conquered the kingdom of Phrygia in what is today west-central Turkey, thus putting an end to the reign of the legendary king Mita, better known to us by his Greek name, Midas.[251] The Cimmerians eventually settled in Cappadocia in what's now eastern Turkey and gradually faded from history after the seventh century B.C.

Beth-Togarmah, or "House of Togarmah," was apparently referred to in Assyrian texts as *Til-garimmu*.[252] The Assyrian king Sennacherib campaigned against the city in 695 B.C. Hittite texts refer to a city and district of Tegarama on the upper Euphrates in Turkey, which was captured by their king Suppiluliuma along with other parts of the kingdom of Mitanni, in the mid-fourteenth century B.C.[253] Again, the location is definitely within modern Turkey.

Like Beth-Togarmah, Meshech and Tubal are mentioned earlier in the Book of Ezekiel, in chapter 27, alongside Javan (Greece) in a list of trading partners of the Phoenician city-state of Tyre. Akkadian texts mention *tabal* and *mushki*, nations in eastern Asia Minor—Turkey. Tabal was a landlocked kingdom between the Halys River and the Taurus River in Asia Minor, bounded on the west by Meshech and by Beth-Togarmah on the east.[254]

Two different groups were called *Mushki* in Assyrian sources, one from the twelfth to the ninth centuries near the confluence of the Murat and the Euphrates ("Eastern Mushki") and the other from the eighth to the seventh centuries in Cappadocia and Cilicia ("Western Mushki").[255] By now, you've guessed that both of those regions were in modern-day Turkey.

The men of Meshech first appear in secular history around 1100 B.C. in the Prism Inscriptions of Tiglath-pileser I, king of Assyria. The Assyrian king tells of fighting five kings of the Mushki, who'd led a coalition south from what is today Armenia to threaten the security of the core of Assyria.[256] The Mushki appear in the records of later Assyrian kings, but most often in the Annals and Pavement Inscriptions of Sargon II (722–705). Their king, Mita/Midas, was apparently a formidable adversary. The Assyrians formed military alliances and built border fortresses specifically to punish these warlike people.

Interestingly, the war between Assyria and the Mushki was over control of Tabal, a strategically important buffer state between the two. After long years and many battles, the Mushki were finally forced to submit and pay tribute. Then the Cimmerians invaded, and it was game over for Midas.[257]

As for Magog: Not to get ahead of ourselves, but Ezekiel 39:6 gives us a clue to the location of Magog's homeland. The war will bring "fire on Magog and on those who dwell securely in the coastlands." This points to western Asia Minor and the islands of the Aegean—in other words, Javan (Greece). Remember, Genesis 10 tells us the sons of Japheth include Javan and Tiras, who is often identified as the father of the *Teresh*, one of the Sea Peoples who swarmed from the Aegean[258] and overran much of the eastern Mediterranean around 1150 B.C. Ultimately, the Tirasians appear to have migrated west to Italy and established the Etruscan civilization.[259] In other words, based on the promise of its fiery doom, we should look for Magog along the coastlands of the Aegean, western and/or southwestern Turkey.

Some scholars cite Josephus, the Jewish historian of the first century A.D., as a source for the Russian connection to Magog. Josephus believed Magog referred to the Scythians,[260] a nomadic people who occupied the lands north of the Black Sea for most of their history. However, in Ezekiel's day, the Scythians had pushed southward across the Caucasus mountains into what is now Armenia, Turkey's eastern neighbor. So, even if Josephus, who wrote six hundred years after Ezekiel, was correct to link Magog to the Scythians, Ezekiel was still pointing to Anatolia, not the Eurasian steppe.

In short, the people Ezekiel saw coming from the north against Israel in the last days will be from Turkey, not Russia.

Where Is the Uttermost North?

If Russia is not the rally point for the hordes of Magog, then where is it? The problem of identification is compounded by an overly literal interpretation of English translations of Ezekiel 38:6, which describe a place in "the far north," "the uttermost parts of the north," "the remote (or remotest) parts of the north," or "the north quarters."

The key is not to look at a map, but at the Hebrew—and *then* at a map. You see, based on the original language, it appears we should be looking at *cosmic* north—supernatural north—rather than the northernmost country on a map from Israel. The phrase in Ezekiel 38:6, which is repeated in 38:15 and 39:2, is one we mentioned earlier in this book: *yerekah tsaphon.* It is used only two other places in the entire Old Testament. Examining those uses might shed some light on just where Ezekiel located "the uttermost parts of the north."

First, Psalm 48:

> Great is the LORD and greatly to be praised
> in the city of our God!
> > His holy mountain, beautiful in elevation,
> > is the joy of all the earth,
> > Mount Zion, **in the far north,**
> > the city of the great King. (Psalm 48:1–2, ESV; emphasis added)

You have to read between the lines, but this passage is a polemic against Baal. As mentioned earlier, everyone in the ancient world knew that Mount Zaphon, the modern Jebel al-Aqra, was the home of Baal's palace. In the 48th Psalm, Yahweh's mount of assembly (Zion) is compared to Baal's (Zaphon) through of clever wordplay: *har Tsiyyon yerekah Tsaphon*:

> Psalm 48 makes a bold theological statement. It evicts Baal from his dwelling and boots his council off the property. The psalmist has Yahweh ruling the cosmos and affairs of humanity, not Baal. Psalm 48 is a backhanded smack in the face to Baal.
> So is Isaiah 14.[261]

Yes, we're back to that famous section of Isaiah. I cannot emphasize enough the importance of the 14th chapter of Isaiah to understanding the nature of the supernatural war and the prophecies of what will come in the last days. At the risk of boring you, here it is again—because this is the only other place in the Bible that mentions *yerekah tsaphon*:

> "How you are fallen from heaven,
> O Day Star, son of Dawn [Lucifer, son of the morning]!
>> How you are cut down to the ground,
>> you who laid the nations low!
>> You said in your heart,
>> "I will ascend to heaven;
>> above the stars of God
>> I will set my throne on high;
>> **I will sit on the mount of assembly**
>> **in the far reaches of the north;**
>> I will ascend above the heights of the clouds;
>> I will make myself like the Most High."
>> But you are brought down to Sheol,
>> to the far reaches of the pit.
>> (Isaiah 14:12–15, ESV; emphasis added)

Isaiah 14:13 is key. The rebel from Eden wants to establish *his* mount of assembly, Zaphon, as supreme above that of Yahweh, Zion. A few English translations reflect this desire:

I will sit enthroned on the mount of assembly, on **the utmost heights of Mount Zaphon.** (NIV)

You thought you would sit like a king on **that mountain in the north where the gods assemble.** (Good News Translation)

I will rule on the mountain of assembly on **the remote slopes of Zaphon.** (NET Bible)

Even the ESV offers this alternate translation for the last part of verse 13: "in the remote parts of Zaphon."

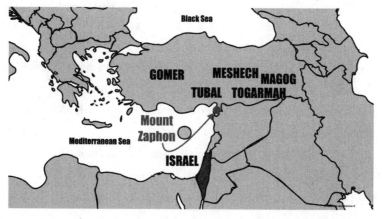

Ezekiel 38 points to Turkey, home of the divine rebel's mount of assembly.

The supernatural war is for control of the mount of assembly, the *har mô'ēd*. Isaiah 14 and Psalm 48 point to Baal's mount of assembly, Mount Zaphon. That's Jebel al-Aqra, on the Mediterranean shore in Turkey, just across the border from Syria. That is where we find the uttermost *spiritual* north, not Russia.

Gog

All this begs the question: Who or what is Gog?

Modern prophecy students look to political leaders such as Vladimir Putin, whose long tenure has made him an attractive candidate here in the West. But since we've placed the "uttermost parts of the north" inside the borders of present-day Turkey, should we consider its president as of this writing, Recep Tayyip Erdogan?

He's another attractive candidate for Gog of Magog because of his obvious neo-Ottoman ambitions. Erdogan has made it clear that the days of secular rule in Turkey are over. As I wrote in *I Predict! What 12 Global Experts Believe You Will See by 2025*:

> The rise of Erdogan's Justice and Development Party (AKP) has given Erdogan the clout to roll back some of the secular reforms of Mustafa Kemal Ataturk, who modernized Turkey and aligned it with the West after the collapse of the empire in 1923. Ottoman Turkish and Arabic script will again be taught in government schools, and the number of students enrolled in state-run Islamic seminaries has grown from 62,000 in 2002, when Erdogan first came to power, to over 1 million. Considering Erdogan's public call for Muslims to work toward wresting control of Jerusalem away from Israel, it is no surprise that some Middle East observers are asking in so many words: Is Turkey attempting to resurrect the Ottoman Empire on the back of the Islamic State?[262]

In December of 2017, Erdogan called on the fifty-seven member nations of the Organization of Islamic Cooperation to form a united military front against Israel.[263] If the political and religious rivalries within Islam could be overcome—which, to be clear, is not a sure bet to say the least—the OIC could theoretically field a five-million-man army backed by Pakistan's nuclear arsenal.

Not a pleasant thought. It makes you wonder how Israeli political and military leaders sleep at night. But the hatred that divides the factions within Islam is at least as strong as that between Islam and the *kafir*, which is anyone and everyone who rejects the teachings of Muhammad. It's not likely we'll see Sunnis and Shias on the same side of any battlefield, so the odds of an alliance between Turkey and Iran, or the Saudis and Iran, are pretty slim.

Similarly, the Sunnis of Turkey and their Sunnis of Saudi Arabia don't particularly like one another, either. With Erdogan flexing the muscle of Turkey's army, which is the second largest in NATO after the US,[264] the Saudis have grown increasingly suspicious of his intentions. Saudi Arabia has controlled Islam's holiest sites for nearly a century, after the collapse of the Ottoman Empire in the early 1920s, but the Turks haven't forgotten their glory years. The Ottomans controlled Mecca and Medina, the Levant, most of the Mediterranean, and southeastern Europe for more than six hundred years. It's hard for us Americans to grasp the impact of Islam in general, and the Ottomans in particular, on world history, but think about this: Sixty years after the Pilgrims landed at Plymouth Rock, the Ottoman Turks laid siege to Vienna. Check a map—Austria is a long way from Turkey.

The point is that Turkey, or at least the ruling AKP party of President Erdogan, wants to restore Turkey to great power status, at least in the Middle East. The Saudis aren't keen to give up that status. Their priority is containing the growing power of Iran, even if that means cooperating with Israel, which they've been doing through back channels. Just days before this book went to the editor, Saudi Crown Prince Mohammad bin Salman told Jewish leaders at a gathering in New York that the Palestinian Authority should accept the peace proposals put forward by the Trump administration "or shut up and stop complaining."[265]

Obviously, this isn't what Fatah or Hamas wanted to hear, and it's certainly a different tone from President Erdogan's call for a united Muslim army to march on Jerusalem. But it makes the point clear: Even the world's leading Sunni powers don't get along. So, the notion that they'll work together against Israel, especially with Israel useful to the Saudis as an ally against Iran, seems far-fetched. Without supernatural intervention, of course. And that's where I'm going with this:

> The battle of Gog and Magog would be something expected after the initiation of Yahweh's plan to reclaim the nations and, there-fore, draw his children, Jew or Gentile, from those nations. *The Gog invasion would be the response of supernatural evil against the messiah and his kingdom.* This is in fact precisely how it is por-trayed in Revelation 20:7–10.
>
> Gog would have been perceived as either a figure empowered by supernatural evil or an evil quasi-divine figure from the super-natural world bent on the destruction of God's people. For this reason, Gog is regarded by many biblical scholars as a template for the New Testament antichrist figure.[266]

While human actors will be involved, the true identity of Gog, leader of the Magog coalition, is found in the spirit realm. Ezekiel spelled it out for us by pointing to Isaiah 14. He may even have added a subtle clue in this verse:

> You will advance, **coming on like a storm**. You will be like a cloud covering the land, you and all your hordes, and many peoples with you. (Ezekiel 38:9, ESV; emphasis added)

By naming *yerekah tsaphon* as the point of origin for the armies of Gog, Ezekiel pointed to the mountain of the storm-god, Baal, the mount of assembly of the divine rebel from Eden, Helel ben Shachar, AKA Lucifer.

Does this mean Gog is Lucifer/Baal? No. Gog is the Old Testament Antichrist figure. John the Revelator clearly distinguishes between the Antichrist (the Beast) and Satan (the dragon).

Identifying Gog as the Antichrist is not a new idea. Our Jewish broth-ers and sisters have been aware of Gog's starring role in the end times for a long, long time:

An important part in the eschatological drama is assigned to Israel's final combat with the combined forces of the heathen nations under the leadership of Gog and Magog, barbarian tribes of the North. Assembled for a fierce attack upon Israel in the mountains near Jerusalem, they will suffer a terrible and crushing defeat, and Israel's land will thenceforth forever remain the seat of God's kingdom.[267]

In Jewish eschatology, Gog is the great end-times enemy who confronts YHWH and His people, Israel, in a climactic battle that coincides with the arrival of Messiah.[268] (Actually, Jews who believe in a coming Day of Yahweh expect *two* messiahs, one from the tribe of Joseph or Ephraim, who falls in the Gog-Magog war, and the second from the tribe of Judah, who defeats Gog and is universally accepted as king.) While there are as many differences of opinion about end-times prophecy among Jewish scholars as there are among Christians, it's clear that Gog was a prototype of the Christian Antichrist described by Paul and John. More on the Gog-Antichrist connection in a bit.

This view of Gog by Jews during the Second Temple period is hinted at by some of the choices made by translators of the Septuagint. For example, they made an interesting choice in rending the first two verses of Amos chapter 7. First, the ESV:

> This is what the Lord GOD showed me: behold, he was forming locusts when the latter growth was just beginning to sprout, **and behold, it was the latter growth after the king's mowings.** When they had finished eating the grass of the land, I said,
> "O Lord GOD, please forgive!
> How can Jacob stand?
> He is so small!" (Amos 7:1–2, ESV; emphasis added)

Contrast that with the way the Septuagint translators interpreted the verse:

Thus the LORD showed me, and behold, a swarm of locusts coming early, **and behold, one locust, Gog, the king**. And it came to
pass when he had finished devouring the grass of the land, that I
said, "Lord God, be merciful; who shall raise up Jacob? for he is
small in number." (Amos 7:1–2, Septuagint translation by Lancelot C. L. Brenton, 1851; emphasis added)

Explaining how the Jewish translators of the Septuagint rendered that
passage the way they did is way above my pay grade, but the bottom line
is this: The scholars saw an army of invading locusts, similar (or maybe
identical) to the supernatural army of Joel 2, and in trying to make sense
of a difficult phrase they chose to connect it to a natural villain—Gog, the
supernatural enemy of Israel in the last days.

Regardless which human face is worn by the commander of this great
end-times army, the real leader, Gog, is unquestionably a creature from
the abyss who leads an army from the cosmic (supernatural) north in a
final assault on the holy mountain of God.

Through a Glass, Darkly

The picture begins to come into focus. The hordes of Magog will be led
by a supernatural entity called Gog by the prophets Ezekiel and John the
Revelator. Let's be clear: This does *not* mean humans will play no part in
the great war led by Gog of Magog. Far from it. While I haven't settled
on a particular timeline for when in the last days this devastating war will
be fought, it seems clear to me that this will happen after the Rapture of
the church.

I hold to a premillennial, pretribulational view of prophecy that
informs my view of the Gog-Magog conflict. But I don't have the full
picture. None of us do. With all due respect to the great scholars of Bible
prophecy, some of whom I am honored and blessed to call friends, God
in His wisdom has not disclosed the fine details of His plan to the world.

As evidence, I point to the reactions of the apostles to the arrival of the Messiah. They learned directly from Jesus for more than three years and they *still* didn't get it:

> Jesus presented himself alive to them after his suffering by many proofs, appearing to them during forty days and speaking about the kingdom of God. And while staying with them he ordered them not to depart from Jerusalem, but to wait for the promise of the Father, which, he said, "you heard from me; for John baptized with water, but you will be baptized with the Holy Spirit not many days from now."
>
> So when they had come together, they asked him, "Lord, will you at this time restore the kingdom to Israel?" (Acts 1:3–6, ESV)

You can almost hear Jesus sigh before He replied. They were still looking for a geopolitical savior. The concept of the suffering servant was as alien to Jews then as it is now, which is why most of them rejected Jesus as the Messiah. In other words, the apostles, who had the best teacher of theology in all of history, didn't understand the prophecies of Messiah's coming. But here's the key point: The Fallen didn't get it, either:

> None of the rulers [archons] of this age understood this, for if they had, they would not have crucified the Lord of glory. (1 Corinthians 2:8, ESV)

The rulers Paul referred to weren't politicians and bureaucrats. The Greek word, *archōn*, is the same word used by Jesus in John 12:31 and 14:30 to describe Satan. It's likely that Paul was telling the church at Corinth that the principalities, powers, rulers, thrones, dominions, and their demonic henchmen thought they'd won a major victory when they manipulated their human dupes into putting Jesus on the cross. But that's exactly what He wanted them to do.

The takeaway is this: The apostles, who learned directly from Christ, and the evil intelligences who'd been plotting against Him for millennia didn't understand the prophecies of Messiah's First Coming. We don't understand the prophecies of His Second Coming any better. It's a military thing. Information is released on a need-to-know basis. Yahweh is called LORD of Hosts, which means "Yahweh of Armies." He's the greatest military mind in history, and we will know His plans in due time.

So, please take my analysis in that light. I reserve the right to change my mind as new information becomes available or as I grow in wisdom.

Valley of the Travelers

That said, I believe the texts from the ancient Amorite kingdom of Ugarit confirm my hypothesis that the giants of the ancient world, the Nephilim/Rephaim, have a role to play in the last great battle of human history. The clue is the location of Magog's defeat.

The picture is almost of a reluctant adversary:

And you, son of man, prophesy against Gog and say, Thus says the Lord GOD: Behold, I am against you, O Gog, chief prince of Meshech and Tubal. **And I will turn you about and drive you forward** [or, "drag you along"], **and bring you up from the uttermost parts of the north** [*yerekah tsaphon*, Baal's mount of assembly], and lead you against the mountains of Israel. Then I will strike your bow from your left hand, and will make your arrows drop out of your right hand. **You shall fall on the mountains of Israel, you and all your hordes and the peoples who are with you.** I will give you to birds of prey of every sort and to the beasts of the field to be devoured. You shall fall in the open field, for I have spoken, declares the Lord GOD. I will send fire on Magog and on those who dwell securely in the coastlands, and they shall know that I am the LORD....

On that day I will give to Gog a place for burial in Israel, the

Valley of the Travelers, east of the sea. It will block the travelers, for there Gog and all his multitude will be buried. It will be called the Valley of Hamon-gog. (Ezekiel 39:1–6, 11, ESV; emphasis added)

"The Valley of the Travelers, east of the sea." Many of us have read that verse and paid little attention to the name of Gog's burial place, assuming it was symbolic or just giving it a mental shrug. Okay, someplace "east of the sea."

If you assume the sea is the Mediterranean, that could be anyplace from Dan to Beersheba—in other words, just about anywhere in Israel. This has allowed prophecy scholars to keep the war of Gog and Magog separate from Armageddon, which many still incorrectly place at Megiddo. But "east of the sea" actually means ancient Moab, which was east of the Dead Sea. This opens a fascinating new look at the war of Gog and Magog.

The Hebrew word rendered "traveler" is *ōbĕrîm*, a plural form of the verb *'br*, which means "to pass from one side to the other."[269] In this context, then, a Traveler is a spirit that passes from one plane of existence to another, in the same sense that the ancient Greeks believed the dead had to travel across the River Styx to reach or return from the underworld.

It is interesting that this was the very place, just northeast of the Dead Sea, where Israel camped before crossing the Jordan to begin the conquest of Canaan. How do we know this? Because places where Israel stopped after the Exodus refer to the dead, and specifically to the Travelers.

And the people of Israel set out and camped in Oboth. And they set out from Oboth and camped at Iye-abarim, in the wilderness that is opposite Moab, toward the sunrise. (Numbers 21:10–11, ESV)

Oboth has the same sense as *ōbĕrîm*, although it's more specific. *Oboth* derives from *'ôb*, which refers to necromancy, the practice of summoning and consulting with spirits of the dead.[270] *'Ôb*, in turn, is related to the Hebrew word *'ab*, which means "father." In the Old Testament, the word "fathers" most often refers to one's dead ancestors. For example:

And when the time drew near that Israel must die, he called his son Joseph and said to him, "If now I have found favor in your sight, put your hand under my thigh and promise to deal kindly and truly with me. Do not bury me in Egypt, but **let me lie with my fathers** [*ăḇōṯ*]. (Genesis 47:29–30, ESV; emphasis added)

Oboth, then, means "Spirits of the Dead."[271] And, you've probably already noticed that the second half of the compound name Iye-abarim is very similar to *ōḇĕrîm*. Excellent work! Iye-abarim means "heaps (or ruins) of the Travelers."[272]

Not coincidentally, this area east of the Jordan Rift Valley, from ancient Moab to Bashan, southeast of Mount Hermon, is home to thousands of dolmens, megalithic tombs made from slabs of basalt and limestone that weigh as much as fifty tons.[273]

While dolmens are found all over the world, there are more of these tombs in Jordan and the Golan Heights than anywhere else. They are simple structures, mostly in a trilithon formation—two standing stones and a capstone, like a "table" across the top, with no cement holding the slabs

Dolmen at Tell Johfiyeh in northern Jordan, roughly twenty miles southeast of the Sea of Galilee.

together. Sometimes additional stones are placed at the front and back, occasionally with a porthole cut to include a frame around the opening cut to hold a removable flat stone. Skeletal remains have been found at enough of them to conclude that the primary function of these intriguing structures was burial of the dead.[274]

These ancient monuments are fascinating for a couple of reasons. First, although Iye-Abarim was located just northeast of the Dead Sea, the highest concentration of dolmens in the region is on and around the Golan Heights, where the Rapha king Og and the deity called Rapi'u, King of Eternity, once ruled. A recent survey of the Golan found more than five thousand megalithic burial sites, most of which are dolmens.[275] In Jordan, another twenty thousand dolmens have been found,[276] although many are threatened by the expansion of modern cities and quarrying for rock and gravel. (Which makes sense—dolmens were built where great big rocks were close to the surface and easy to find.) Secondly, and this is an interesting admission: Scholars really don't know anything about the people who built them.

The dolmens are generally dated to the third millennium (3000–2000) B.C. On the Golan Heights, they are more narrowly dated to between 2250 B.C. and about 1800 B.C.[277] Based on pottery shards found near some of the dolmens in Jordan, the megaliths closer to the Dead Sea may be as old as the beginning of the Early Bronze Age, circa 3300 B.C.[278]

If the Bible is accurate, and we believe it is, then the time and location suggest that the builders of the dolmens were the Rephaim tribes, who constructed them in the centuries before Abraham's arrival in the area. By the time the Israelites returned from Egypt around 1406 B.C., only Og's small kingdom remained of the Rephaim—possibly the last of the dolmen-builders in the Levant.

It's tempting to go overboard with speculation, but we don't serve our God well by wandering too far afield without evidence. Still, credentialed scholars link the megaliths to the Rephaim, although instead of identifying the dolmen-builders as Rephaim they tend to view things the other way around, believing the dolmens "were the basis for belief in giants, the Rephaim, Anakim, Emim, Zamzummim, and the like."[279] In other words, scholars think the people who moved into the lands alongside the Jordan River invented stories of giants because they imagined really big men must have moved those really big rocks.

Over the centuries, tomb robbers have removed most of the useful evidence from the dolmens. The few bones left behind in burial chambers don't show any evidence of giantism, or at least I haven't found any papers reporting it. Most of the dolmens are oriented north-south, although about 10 percent appear to be oriented east-west, perhaps to face the rising sun.

Is this significant? While it's interesting to note that the Pole Star was Thuban (*Alpha Draconis*) in the constellation Draco, the Dragon, when the dolmens were built, we don't know if that was relevant. In spite of their ability to lift stupendously heavy blocks of stone, the dolmen-builders weren't considerate enough to leave behind any written evidence.

That makes a recent discovery in the Golan all the more intriguing and frustrating at the same time. In 2012, archaeologists examined a massive, multi-chambered dolmen in the Shamir Dolmen Field on the western foothills of the Golan Heights, a site with over four hundred dolmens. What was truly remarkable about this particular dolmen was the discovery of rock art on the underside of the capstone, a basalt monster weighing about fifty tons.[280] (For comparison, that's about twice as heavy as a fully-loaded eighteen-wheel tractor-trailer in the United States.) That's the first time art has been found inside any of the thousands of dolmens in the region, possibly the first written or artistic record that might be connected directly to the biblical Rephaim.

The dolmen itself is surrounded by a tumulus, a burial mound of about four hundred tons of stone. Think about that! Four thousand years ago, maybe a century or so before Abraham arrived in Canaan, a government on the Golan Heights was powerful enough to organize the manpower and logistics (food, water, etc.) to move and assemble some eight hundred thousand pounds of stone into a multi-chambered tomb for— who? The king and his family? Archaeologists recovered enough bones and teeth to identify "an 8–10 year-old child, a young adult and a 35–45 year-old adult".[281]

Were they—dare I speculate—of the dynasty that produced Og, the enemy of Israel, about six hundred years later? Well, probably not. Most dynasties don't last that long. But it's interesting to wonder.

The engravings were fourteen figures comprised of a vertical line and a downturned arc. What did the symbol mean? No idea. Nothing like it has been found anywhere in the Levant or anywhere else.[282] It might be a representation of the human soul taking flight, but because the artist didn't leave a note, we're guessing. Or—and again, we're speculating—this could be an ancient symbol with occult meaning even today. Three-dimensional scanning of the images show that at least some of them look very much like the Greek character *psi*, which is a trident (and the logo for Indiana University), the three-pronged spear traditionally carried by the Greco-Roman god of the sea, Poseidon/Neptune. Today it's used, among other things, as a symbol for parapsychology, especially research into extrasensory perception, and in a mathematical formula that claims to guide occultists in how to perform rituals in chaos magick.

What did that symbol mean in the twentieth century B.C.? We have no way to know. It might have been doodling by a bored Bronze Age stonemason.

The takeaway for this section is this: For at least a thousand years, people living in lands the Bible identifies as the home of Rephaim tribes built burial tombs with massive slabs of limestone and basalt. And those huge burial tombs inspired place names linked to the dolmen-builders (Iye-Abarim, "ruins of the Travelers") and to the restless dead (Oboth, "Spirits of the Dead").

Get this: Even the place where Moses died was called the Mountain of the Travelers.

> Go up this **mountain of the Abarim**, Mount Nebo, which is in the land of Moab, opposite Jericho, and view the land of Canaan, which I am giving to the people of Israel for a possession. And

die on the mountain which you go up, and be gathered to your people, as Aaron your brother died in Mount Hor and was gathered to his people....

So Moses the servant of the LORD died there in the land of Moab, according to the word of the LORD, and he buried him in the valley in the land of Moab opposite Beth-peor; but no one knows the place of his burial to this day. (Deuteronomy 32:49–50, 34:5–6, ESV; emphasis added)

Here's a thought: Moses was buried in the Valley of the Travelers, a place where the Rephaim spirits reputedly crossed over to the land of the living. Is that why Satan, lord of the dead, thought he had a right to claim the body of Moses after his death?[283]

Another question comes to mind: Were all those dolmens up and down the Jordan Rift Valley thought to be portals to the underworld?

Here's another connection between this valley and the realm of the dead: Remember the prophecy of Balaam? After the king of Moab tried to buy a curse from the pagan prophet, Israel began drifting away from Yahweh again.

While Israel lived in Shittim, the people began to whore with the daughters of Moab. These invited the people to the sacrifices of their gods, and the people ate and bowed down to their gods. So Israel yoked himself to Baal of Peor. And the anger of the LORD was kindled against Israel. (Numbers 25:1–3, ESV)

Who was Baal of Peor? Remember, *baal* in Hebrew simply means "lord." So, the Lord of Peor was a local deity linked to a mountain near Shittim in Moab, northeast of the Dead Sea. The clue to the character of Baal-Peor is in the name.

Peor is related to the Hebrew root *pʾr*, which means "cleft" or "gap,"[284] or "open wide."[285] In this context, that definition is consistent with Isaiah's description of the entrance to the netherworld:

Therefore Sheol has enlarged its appetite and opened [*pa'ar*] its mouth beyond measure. (Isaiah 5:14, ESV)

Since we're looking at a place associated with the dead, it's worth noting that the Canaanite god of death, Mot, was described in the Ugaritic texts as a ravenous entity with a truly monstrous mouth:

He extends a lip to the earth,
a lip to the heavens,
he extends a tongue to the stars.[286]

Yeesh. But that's what's in view here: Baal-Peor was apparently lord of the entrance to the underworld.

Yes, the Canaanites believed the entrance to the underworld was at Bashan. But both Molech (or Milcom) and Chemosh, the national gods of Ammon and Moab, which controlled most of the land east of the Jordan from the Dead Sea to Mount Hermon, demanded child sacrifice. Veneration of the dead and appeasing the gods of the dead through human sacrifice appear to have been the norm in this region east of the Dead Sea.

This was also the general location of Sodom and Gomorrah. Now, I try not to put too much stock in the influence of territorial spirits. After all, God created us with free will. But you have to admit this is an awful lot of evil concentrated in a small area.

Anyway, perhaps because of the association with death and the dead, there was, shall we say, a fertility aspect to the cult of Baal-Peor.

And behold, one of the people of Israel came and brought a Midianite woman to his family, in the sight of Moses and in the sight of the whole congregation of the people of Israel, while they were weeping in the entrance of the tent of meeting. When Phinehas the son of Eleazar, son of Aaron the priest, saw it, he rose and left the congregation and took a spear in his hand and went after the man of Israel into the chamber and pierced both of them, the man of Israel and the woman through her belly. (Numbers 25:6–8, ESV)

How to put this delicately? There are only a couple of physical positions in which Phinehas could have speared both the Israelite man and Midianite woman with one thrust. If you're an adult, I don't need to draw you a picture. Emphasizing the point, the Hebrew word translated "belly," *qevah*, can refer to a woman's womb.[287] In other words, the sin here wasn't that an Israelite man brought a foreign woman home for dinner, it's that the couple performed a lewd ritual act in full view of Moses and the assembly of Israel!

Well, it's no wonder the men of Israel were tempted to follow Baal-Peor. Roughly 60 percent of the Christian pastors in America today struggle with addiction to pornography.[288] Just imagine the temptation of being surrounded by people whose god decreed that extramarital sex was a form of worship. I don't mean to be flippant, but it might take the real threat of death to keep men away from the temples! Indeed, twenty-four thousand people died in the plague that God sent as punishment for that apostasy because it wasn't just the one couple involved.

And there was even more to it than that. Not surprisingly, given the Amorite/Rephaim culture in that time and place, one of the pagan rites the Israelites adopted during their time in Moab was veneration of the dead:

Then they yoked themselves to the Baal of Peor,
and ate sacrifices offered to the dead;
they provoked the LORD to anger with their deeds,
and a plague broke out among them. (Psalm 106:28–29, ESV)

The psalmist remembered the sacrifices to the dead, which is a basic description of the Amorite *kispum* ritual. The sexual sin of the young couple (and Phinehas' violent reaction) is shocking to us today, but apparently the psalmist didn't find that worth mentioning. The *real* sin that provoked God's anger was venerating the dead, one of the "abominable practices" of the pagan nations He'd promised to drive out of the land before them.

That brings us back to the point: We've identified the area that Ezekiel called the Valley of the Travelers as the east side of the Jordan Rift Valley, specifically ancient Moab east and just northeast of the Dead Sea. And by now you're asking, "Why are we spending all of this time identifying the area and unraveling the meaning behind the word Travelers?"

Here's why: It's the link that connects the Rephaim, and thus the Titans, to Ezekiel's prophecy of Gog and Magog. How? The Rephaim texts from Ugarit specifically refer to the spirits of the Rephaim as "travelers."

[El is speaking:]

"I shall summon the [elohim] into the midst of my palace."
    To his sanctuary the [Rephaim] hurried indeed,
    to his sanctuary hurried indeed the [elohim].
    They harnessed the chariots;
    the horses they hitched.
    They mounted their chariots,
    they came on their mounts.
    They journeyed a day
    and a second.
    After sunrise on the third
    the [Rephaim] arrived at the threshing-floors,
    the [elohim] at the plantations....
    Like silver to vagabonds [travelers] were the olives,
    (like) gold to vagabonds were the dates.[289]

In the preceding text, (Ugaritic text KTU 1.22), the word chosen by the translator for the Ugaritic *'brm*, "vagabonds," is simply another word for "travelers." Klaas Spronk, whose paper, "Conceptions of Beatific Afterlife in the Ancient Near East," was an important resource for this book, renders *l'brm*, the equivalent of the Hebrew *'br* mentioned above, as "those who came over."[290] This has the same meaning. The Rephaim traveled, came over, or crossed over from one plane of existence to another; thus, the Rephaim are the Travelers.

Remember, this area east of the Jordan River is exactly where Chedorlaomer and his coalition of kings from the east defeated the Rephaim in the time of Abraham. It is exactly where the cousins of Israel, the Edomites, Moabites, and Ammonites, drove out the Rephaim between the time of Abraham and the Exodus. The last of the remnant of the Rephaim, Og of Bashan, was sent to the underworld to join his *ăbōt*, his fathers, by Moses and the host of Israel.

But the spirits of the Rephaim were believed to travel to the land of the living in that valley where Israel camped before launching its attack on Jericho. Two hundred years after the conquest of Canaan by Israel, the Amorites of Ugarit still performed rituals to summon those Travelers to banquets at the palace of El on the summit of Mount Hermon.

This is key to understanding Ezekiel's prophecy: He was shown that the hordes of Magog would be slaughtered and buried in the wilderness near Moab, east of the Dead Sea. This area is connected to the dead—and not just the dead, but dead spirits who "traveled," or "crossed over," to the land of the living. Why? Because it that's where the Travelers—i.e., the spirits of the Rephaim/Nephilim—and those who venerated them in the days of Abraham and Moses, lived when they walked the earth.

Suddenly, the location of Gog's defeat is very interesting. And I promise, it's going to get positively fascinating in a minute.

Army of Darkness

One question I try to keep in mind when I dig into this type of research is, "So what?" It's a simple question, but it's very important. So what if spirits of the Nephilim were venerated by the pagan nations around ancient Israel? What does that have to do with us today? You're probably already ahead of me here, but in the interest of clarity, let me spell it out:

It appears that Ezekiel's vision of the ultimate destruction of Gog and his horde involves an army of the dead.

First of all, let's look at the significance of Gog. Remember, his home base is *yerekah tsaphon*, Mount Zaphon. This is the place Isaiah identified as the mount of assembly of the divine rebel in Eden, Ezekiel's anointed guardian cherub, the throne guardian who schemed to overthrow his sovereign Lord. And it was known to the world as the place where the storm-god, Baal, lived in his palace of gold and silver.

Not coincidentally, it was also where the Greeks believed their storm-god, Zeus, defeated the chaos serpent Typhon, who dove under the mountain to escape the thunderbolts of Zeus and in so doing carved out the channel of the Orontes River. This is another telling of the *chaoskampf*, the name scholars give to the common ancient Near Eastern myth of a warrior god defeating chaos to create or preserve order. The Bible has the original story, of course, in which Yahweh crushed the heads of Leviathan (Psalm 74:14), but, as we've already mentioned, the story was repeated by Amorites from Babylon (Marduk vs. Tiamat) to Ugarit (Baal vs. Yamm). The story traveled north to the Hurrians and Hittites (Teshub or Tarhunz, the storm-god, vs. the chaos-dragon Illuyankas), and finally west to Greece, where it was transformed into the epic battle between Zeus and the hundred-headed serpentine monster, Typhon.

To make this point clear, in the Gospel of Matthew, Jesus specifically connected the storm-god, Baal, to Satan:

> Then a demon-oppressed man who was blind and mute was brought to him, and he healed him, so that the man spoke and saw. And all the people were amazed, and said, "Can this be the Son of David?" But when the Pharisees heard it, they said, "It is only by Beelzebul, the prince of demons, that this man casts out demons." Knowing their thoughts, he said to them, "Every kingdom divided against itself is laid waste, and no city or house divided against itself will stand. **And if Satan casts out Satan, he**

is divided against himself. How then will his kingdom stand?
(Matthew 12:22–26, ESV; emphasis added)

Beelzebul means "Baal the Prince." Jesus specifically identified the storm-god as Satan. And then, in the Revelation of John, He linked Satan to the storm-god, Zeus:

And to the angel of the church in Pergamum write: "The words of him who has the sharp two-edged sword. I know where you dwell, where Satan's throne is. Yet you hold fast my name, and you did not deny my faith even in the days of Antipas my faithful witness, who was killed among you, where Satan dwells." (Revelation 2:12–13, ESV)

Pergamum was in western Asia Minor, near the Aegean Sea. It was home to a famous and elaborate altar to Zeus, where he was hailed as a savior. Most scholars lean toward the view that Jesus had that altar in mind when He called out Satan's throne. So, in short: Zeus = Baal = Satan. Because Isaiah identified Mount Zaphon as the mount of assembly of the rebel from Eden, we can build a good case that the divine rebel was Satan/Baal/Zeus. As a servant of Satan, that's where Gog, the Antichrist, will assemble his army. The uttermost parts of the north, *yerekah tsaphon*, refers to Mount Zaphon, today called Jebel al-Aqra in Turkey.

Many of us, fascinated by the prophecy of Ezekiel, have tried for years to discern the identity of Gog by interpreting the headlines. That's pulled us in the wrong direction as we looked for a human ruler to fit the role. While a human will undoubtedly be connected to this figure, we've lost sight of the fact that we should be looking for a supernatural character.

Here's where we'll get even *more* supernatural.

Remember that we've cited several texts from the Amorite kingdom of Ugarit calling the spirits of the Rephaim "warriors of Baal." Also remember that, in the previous section, we showed you where the Rephaim spirits—demons—were called Travelers, because they traveled from one plane of existence to another.

Consider this question: When Baal's servant, Gog, leads his army to the mountains of Israel, how many of "warriors of Baal" will be marching with the troops?

By that time, I believe the church of believers in Jesus Christ will be off the earth. We're talking about Armageddon (I'll explain why in the next chapter). To ask the question another way, with the church gone and the "restrainer" Paul mentioned in 2 Thessalonians 2:6 removed to give the Antichrist free rein, how many soldiers in the army of the Antichrist will be demonically possessed? Some of them? All of them?

If, as we believe, demons are the spirits of the Rephaim, the demigod sons of the Titans who died in Noah's Flood, then the horde of Gog will essentially be an army of the living dead.

This is consistent with Second Temple Jewish beliefs about the prophesied fate of the Nephilim. The Book of Enoch tells us that God's judgment on the Nephilim will take place on "the day of the consummation of the great judgment, when the great age will be consummated."[291] That's the Day of the Lord, which is when Armageddon will be fought—and I repeat, the Gog-Magog war will end at Armageddon.

Ezekiel specifically identified the battlefield where Gog's warriors are slain as the Valley of the Travelers—the valley of the spirits of the Rephaim. Now, catch this:

> On that day I will give to Gog a place for burial in Israel, the Valley of the Travelers, east of the sea. **It will block the travelers, for there Gog and all his multitude will be buried.** (Ezekiel 39:11, ESV; emphasis added)

Block the travelers? What does *that* mean?

It could suggest that so many bodies will fall in the valley that people literally won't be able to travel along the King's Highway in Jordan. Okay, in a war of this size, especially because God intervenes and rains fire from

Heaven on Magog (notice how Yahweh uses what's supposed to be Baal's weapon, the thunderbolt), that seems plausible. But this is an army of demonically possessed soldiers—I know, it sounds weird when you say it out loud—so maybe there's something more to this than a physical obstacle created by a multitude of dead bodies.

The Hebrew word translated "block," *wəḥōsemeṯ*, is based on the root *chasam*,[292] which is only used twice in the Old Testament. The other verse is Deuteronomy 25:4: "You shall not muzzle an ox when it is treading out the grain." So, "block" means "muzzle." To muzzle an animal is to restrain it so it can't eat or bite, which is much more specific than creating an impassable obstacle. How demons are muzzled, I don't know, but I trust God has a plan for that.

Some scholars, following the KJV, take this to mean it will "stop the noses" of travelers along the King's Highway, apparently because of the stench of the decaying dead. But let's view this in the context of the necromancy rituals from Ugarit.

Their rites summoned the spirits of the Travelers, the Rephaim, to ritual meals at the house or sanctuary of El. Since Ezekiel wrote under God's direction, we can assume that he was aware of this. Then the prophecy of the destruction of the army of Gog is a reversal of those rituals. On the day of the Lord, instead of arriving at a ritual meal to be revivified by "the blessings of the name of El," they will be *muzzled*—prevented from doing whatever they did when they traveled, came over, or crossed over from the land of the dead to the realm of the living. Why? Because they'll be muzzled with extreme prejudice.

At this point, you may be thinking, "Interesting, but linking the Valley of the Travelers to a few lines in an Amorite necromancy ritual is pretty flimsy evidence to claim that spirits of the Nephilim will be the soldiers of Gog."

Fair enough. Hang tight. There's more in the next chapter.

We're building the case that Ezekiel's prophecy is of the *final* battle, Armageddon, and that the venerated dead of the Amorites, the Rephaim, play a key role. But that crossing by the Travelers, to serve as warriors of Baal in the attack on Zion, will be their last one. Ever.

HOW IT ENDS

As we've pointed out in this book, the long war by the Fallen against their Creator is ultimately for control of God's mount of assembly, Zion. That's His prize jewel, and that's why the enemy wants it:

> Great is the LORD and greatly to be praised
> in the city of our God!
>> His holy mountain, beautiful in elevation,
>> is the joy of all the earth,
>> Mount Zion, in the far north,
>> the city of the great King. (Psalm 48:1–2, ESV)

> So you shall know that I am the LORD your God,
> who dwells in Zion, my holy mountain.
> And Jerusalem shall be holy,
> and strangers shall never again pass through it. (Joel 3:17, ESV)

For the LORD has chosen Zion;
he has desired it for his dwelling place:
    "This is my resting place forever;
    here I will dwell, for I have desired it." (Psalm 132:13–14, ESV)

Plenty of other verses support this idea, but you get the point. God's holy mountain, His mount of assembly, is Zion—the Temple Mount in Jerusalem.

Yes, I know some believe Solomon's Temple was in the City of David and not on the Temple Mount. There are a number of reasons, including recent archaeological excavations in the City of David at the alternate location proposed for the Temple, that do not support this theory.[293] The most obvious bit of evidence is the testimony of first-century Jewish historian Josephus, who wrote that the platform supporting the Temple measured five hundred cubits square. That's wider than the City of David, which sits on a small, narrow hill south of the Temple Mount. Had the platform been there, it would have extended out over the Kidron Valley.[294] Bad design, to say the least.

Placing the great and terrible battle called Armageddon there makes sense from a strategic standpoint. It's the home of the prize, the mount of assembly. Besides, other apocalyptic prophecies in the Old Testament point to Jerusalem at the site of the final showdown between good and evil.

The oracle of the word of the LORD concerning Israel: Thus declares the LORD, who stretched out the heavens and founded the earth and formed the spirit of man within him: "Behold, I am about to make Jerusalem a cup of staggering to all the surrounding peoples. **The siege of Jerusalem will also be against Judah. On that day I will make Jerusalem a heavy stone for all the peoples.** All who lift it will surely hurt themselves. **And all the nations of the earth will gather against it....**

And on that day I will seek to destroy all the nations that come against Jerusalem. (Zechariah 12:1–3, 9, ESV; emphasis added)

For I will gather all the nations against Jerusalem to battle, and the city shall be taken and the houses plundered and the women raped. Half of the city shall go out into exile, but the rest of the people shall not be cut off from the city. **Then the LORD will go out and fight against those nations as when he fights on a day of battle.** On that day his feet shall stand on the Mount of Olives that lies before Jerusalem on the east, and the Mount of Olives shall be split in two from east to west by a very wide valley, so that one half of the Mount shall move northward, and the other half southward. And you shall flee to the valley of my mountains, for the valley of the mountains shall reach to Azal. And you shall flee as you fled from the earthquake in the days of Uzziah king of Judah. Then the LORD my God will come, and all the holy ones with him. (Zechariah 14:2–5, ESV; emphasis added)

For behold, in those days and at that time, when I restore the fortunes of Judah and Jerusalem, **I will gather all the nations and bring them down to the Valley of Jehoshaphat.** And I will enter into judgment with them there, on behalf of my people and my heritage Israel, because they have scattered them among the nations and have divided up my land. (Joel 3:1–2, ESV; emphasis added)

The phrase "on that day" refers to the Day of Yahweh, or Day of the Lord, the time of God's judgment against a rebellious and unbelieving world. Zechariah and Joel saw the same final battle as Ezekiel. God will personally intervene to destroy the army assembled against Israel. That's the Second Coming, the return of Messiah.

When He arrives, the Mount of Olives splits in two, creating "a very wide valley." This is probably the Valley of Jehoshaphat, a location that doesn't exist on any known map. It's not a reference to the king of Judah during the days of Ahab; Jehoshaphat's name means "Yahweh will judge,"[295] which obviously is not a coincidence in this context.

If you've studied end-times prophecy at all, you've probably read or been taught that Armageddon will be fought at Megiddo, not Jerusalem. That's understandable. It's a popular teaching, but it's based on the difficulty of transliterating from Hebrew to Greek to English. The verse in question is in Revelation 16:

> **The sixth angel poured out his bowl on the great river Euphrates, and its water was dried up, to prepare the way for the kings from the east.** And I saw, coming out of the mouth of the dragon and out of the mouth of the beast and out of the mouth of the false prophet, three unclean spirits like frogs. For they are demonic spirits, performing signs, who go abroad to the kings of the whole world, to assemble them for battle on the great day of God the Almighty. ("Behold, I am coming like a thief! Blessed is the one who stays awake, keeping his garments on, that he may not go about naked and be seen exposed!") **And they assembled them at the place that in Hebrew is called Armageddon.** (Revelation 16:12–16, ESV; emphasis added)

We've been taught that Armageddon is a compound name based on the Hebrew *har magedōn*, where the *-on* suffix indicates a place name.[296] In fact, several English translations, such as the NASB, NRSV, and ASV, render the name either "Harmagedon" or "Har-Magedon." A number of respected prophecy teachers, including Chuck Missler, Dwight Pentecost, John Walvoord, and Arnold Fruchtenbaum, identify *har magedōn* as the Mount of Megiddo, and place it near the city of Megiddo in the Valley of Jezreel.[297]

This is logical from a military standpoint. Megiddo overlooks the valley, which connects the Jordan River valley to the Mediterranean, and it guards a key pass through the Carmel mountain range. Several decisive battles were fought at or near Megiddo: In the fifteenth century B.C., probably not long before the Exodus, Pharaoh Thutmose III defeated a confederation of Canaanite city-states there. In 609 B.C., the Judean king Josiah was killed in battle at Megiddo against Pharaoh Necho, who was leading an Egyptian army north to fight with his Assyrian ally against Babylon. Apparently, Josiah and his advisers thought it was better to side with the rising power, Babylon, but things went badly for the last good king of Judah and Josiah was killed by an Egyptian archer. Despite his effort, less than twenty-five years later, Nebuchadnezzar's army marched from Babylon to sack Jerusalem and destroy the Temple. Some gratitude.

But there are problems with placing Armageddon at Megiddo. First of all, there's no mountain there. The ancient site of Megiddo is elevated above the plain, yes, but it's not a mountain, it's a tell—a mound created when people build and rebuild a settlement over centuries on the same spot. Second, it's unlikely God would descend on the Mount of Olives when the Antichrist and the armies of the world are at Megiddo, more than fifty miles away.

The problem of identification comes from the difficulty in transliterating from Hebrew to Greek. In 1938, scholar Charles C. Torrey proposed a solution: Armageddon is based not on *har magedōn*, the name of a nonexistent mountain, but on a phrase we've encountered before, *har mô'ēd* ("mount of assembly"). Remember Isaiah 14?

How you are fallen from heaven,

O Day Star, son of Dawn!
How you are cut down to the ground,
you who laid the nations low!
You said in your heart,
"I will ascend to heaven;
above the stars of God
I will set my throne on high;
I will sit on the mount of assembly [*har mô'ēd*]
in the far reaches of the north" [*yerekah tsaphon*, Mount Zaphon]. (Isaiah 14:12–13, ESV; emphasis added)

Torrey's argument was that scholars who weren't expert in both Greek and Hebrew had missed the fact that the Hebrew character *ayin*, which is transliterated in English by the character ' (a reverse apostrophe) because we don't have the sound or the letter in our alphabet, was represented in Greek by the letter *gamma*, because there is no Greek sound or letter that corresponds to *ayin*, either.[298] So, the Hebrew *mem-ayin-daleth* (M-'-D) was transliterated by John into the closest Greek approximation, *mem-gimel-daleth* (M-G-D).[299] Thus, har môʿēd became har magedōn, and the battle of Armageddon was transplanted from Mount Zion in Jerusalem to a place of no supernatural significance where no mountain exists.

Make no mistake. The spiritual war is for control of the *har môʿēd*—Armageddon. The last great battle of history will be fought at Zion, God's mount of assembly.

What Lies Below

This book was inspired by a belief that the study of end-times prophecy has been too focused on the human participants in the last great battle of the age. That's understandable; we humans see the world as though we're the main character in a movie playing inside our head. We think it's all about us. And in a sense, that's true—this war *is* all about us.

But the rebellion began with the entities created before mankind, the angels—cherubim, seraphim, malakim, Watchers, and, later, the hybrid progeny of the Watchers, the Nephilim, who were linked to the Rephaim by the Hebrews. Nations that developed writing later, such as the Greeks and Romans, called the old gods by different names, but the stories are too consistent for them not to have been passed from one culture to another over the centuries.

As a Christian, I accept the testimony of Jesus that the Old Testament is historically accurate. So, the account of this supernatural war in the Bible is the one we can trust. The prophecies of what's to come are sure as well, although we won't see the pictures clearly until the events are right on top of us, assuming the church is still here when these things come to pass.

The subject of the Nephilim/Rephaim has intrigued Christians for millennia. As we've noted, the early church fathers mainly agreed that Genesis 6:1–4 meant what it said: There were *giants* on the earth long ago, the offspring of angels and human women. Further, their spirits were the demons that plague mankind. These spirits, and their fathers now imprisoned in Tartarus, will make up the army of the Antichrist at Armageddon.

There's no question humans will be involved. Regardless of the timing of the Rapture, the "restrainer" of 2 Thessalonians 2:6 will be out of the way by the time of the showdown at Armageddon, so there will be nothing to prevent these demonic spirits from commandeering the armies of the unbelieving world. Why wouldn't the warriors of Baal volunteer for an all-out assault on Yahweh's mount of assembly? Based on the low opinion of humans they demonstrated in the Bible, they consider us expendable at best. Demons made their victims sick, blind, mute, and self-destructive, forcing their hosts to cut themselves and throw themselves into fire. If their human hosts perish in the attack, well, there are more where they came from.

Isn't it interesting that the greatest fear expressed by the demons Jesus cast out was being commanded "to depart into the abyss"?[300] That's where their supernatural parents are incarcerated. If anything, those rebel gods hate us even more than the demons do. Why? As Paul wrote, "Do you not know that we are to judge angels?"[301] Exactly how that will work, I have no idea. But Paul had inside information, so count on it. Somehow, someday, you and I will be called upon to serve in what will be the most intriguing court cases in all of history. Do you think the angels, especially powerful Watcher-class entities who acted as gods of the nations, might be just a little upset about that?

Beast from the Sea

Let's lay out a scenario here that might reflect the situation at the time of Armageddon. Some of this is necessarily speculative; remember, as Lord of Armies, God isn't going to tell you and me everything in advance because that would be telling His enemies everything in advance. But here's what we can surmise from the evidence.

An enemy from the north will arise in the last days and come against Israel. Their objective will be Zion, the *har mô 'ēd,* God's mount of assembly. North in this case is not so much geographic north as it is spiritual north.

This is consistent with the Jewish tradition of evil descending upon Israel from the north. In the physical plane, the most fearsome enemies always attacked from the north. Assyria and Babylon were the Big Two, and they entered Israel from either Lebanon or Syria because crossing the Syrian desert to the east was foolish.

Supernatural threats to Israel likewise came from the north. Bashan, the entrance to the Canaanite underworld; Mount Hermon, El's mount of assembly and the site of the Watchers' rebellion; and Mount Zaphon, the home of Baal's palace, were all located north of Israel. This is the context for viewing the war of Gog and Magog in Ezekiel 38 and 39.

As we showed you in the previous chapter, Gog is the Antichrist, the great supernatural end-times enemy of God and Israel. Speculation linking the identity of Gog to any Russian leader is misguided. First, while there may be Russians in the coalition that comes to Jerusalem for the Battle of Armageddon, Russia as a nation is not part of Ezekiel's prophecy. With all due respect to Bible teachers who hold the Russia-is-Magog view, identifying *rosh* as Russia and Meshech as Moscow is folk etymology, making connections simply because words sound the same. Language doesn't always work like that. For example, "dear" and "deer" sound the same, but you aren't going to mistake your spouse for Bambi.

More importantly, the grisly sacrificial feasts of Ezekiel 39:17–20 and Revelation 19:17–21 confirm that the war of Gog ends at Armageddon. It's the same conflict. (More on this shortly.) So, unless we create a plausible scenario that includes a Russian Antichrist, we have to let that theory go.

We can agree, however, that the Beast that emerges from the sea in Revelation 13:1 is the Antichrist figure. A couple of things about the

Beast: First, in the Bible, it's the cosmological location of the abyss. The sea represents chaos, and God subdued chaos in the first two verses of the Bible.

> In the beginning, God created the heavens and the earth. The earth was without form and void, and darkness was over the face of the deep. And the Spirit of God was hovering over the face of the waters. (Genesis 1:1–2, ESV)

As noted earlier, the Hebrew word translated "deep" is *tehom*, which is a cognate—same word, different language—to the Akkadian *têmtum*. That, in turn, is a variant of Tiamat, the Sumerian chaos monster who was subdued by a warrior god, Marduk, to bring order to creation. Similar myths were common in the ancient Near East: Baal vs. Yamm, Teshub vs. Illuyanka, Zeus vs. Typhon, and the original, Yahweh vs. Leviathan. The most obvious difference between the biblical account and the others is that the fight between God and chaos, if there *was* a fight, was over by the end of the second verse in the Bible. We see references to it later—for example, in Psalm 74:12–17—but there is no hint that God had any trouble bringing chaos to heel. Not so with the pagan stories. In every case, the warrior god needed outside help and more than one battle to subdue the sea-monster representing chaos. Chaos, being supernatural, is restrained but not dead.

Now, hang on—we're going to suggest something new.

According to the Greek poet Hesiod, Zeus threw the serpentine chaos-monster Typhon into Tartarus to share a cell block with the Titans.[302] We're reasonably sure the Titans/Watchers are in Tartarus; Hesiod and Homer agreed on that point, and Peter confirmed it (2 Peter 2:4).

Two more data points: The Greeks believed the battle between Zeus and Typhon took place at Mount Kasios, which was their name for Baal's holy mountain, Zaphon, and scholars have long noted that Typhon's name resembles Zaphon closely enough that they may be linked.[303] So, there is a clear connection between Zaphon, the mountain where the Antichrist/

Gog will marshal his forces, and the chaos-god Typhon. And while this entity is called a dragon (with a hundred heads!) by Hesiod,[304] Typhon is described elsewhere as "a hybrid between man and beast,"[305] with many wings, coils of vipers for legs, and a human head. In other words, the Greek god of chaos was a human-animal chimera, similar to the way ancient Mesopotamians described the *apkallu*, who were the Watchers/Titans.

In other words, the Greeks remembered that a monstrous deity connected to Satan/Baal's mount of assembly was buried in Tartarus—the abyss, which is represented in the Bible by the sea. In Revelation, the Beast, which is described as a chimeric entity like the chaos-monster Typhon, *emerges* from the sea—the abyss—to become the Antichrist (Gog) and lead the war against God's holy mountain, Zion:

> Then the dragon became furious with the woman and went off to make war on the rest of her offspring, on those who keep the commandments of God and hold to the testimony of Jesus. And he stood on the sand of the sea.
>
> And I saw a beast rising out of the sea, with ten horns and seven heads, with ten diadems on its horns and blasphemous names on its heads. (Revelation 12:17–13:1, ESV)

These verses suggest that the dragon is standing on the shore when the Beast, the Antichrist/Gog, rises from the abyss. Please note that Satan/Baal's mount of assembly, Zaphon, today called Jebel al-Aqra, sits on the shore of the Mediterranean Sea.

All that leads to the $64,000 question: Could the Antichrist be the spirit of chaos, Leviathan?

Yes, I think so.

Josh Peck and I briefly explored the idea of the return of chaos in our recent book *The Day the Earth Stands Still*. While the book is about the occult origins of many of the beliefs common in the UFO community, we noted in our research a strange attraction to the god of chaos in UFO circles. Occultists Kenneth Grant and Austin Osman Spare, who learned directly from the man who called himself the Great Beast 666, Aleister Crowley, developed Crowley's occult system into what Grant called the Typhonian tradition. That's been further developed into something its practitioners today call chaos magick. Ironically, chaos magick isn't anything new. Job 3:8 makes a reference to those "who are ready to rouse up Leviathan."

The key detail is that around 1955, Grant claimed he detected a "Sirius-Set current" in Crowley's teachings. That apparently convinced him and others that the chaos-god is out there near the star Sirius, in contact with Earth, and planning his big comeback.

Well, he is coming back, but not in the way the practitioners of chaos magick think.

While the chaos-god Typhon wasn't one of the original Titans, he was believed to be their half-brother and is sometimes referred to as a Titan. Interestingly, at least one of the early church fathers thought a Titan would return at the end of days. Irenaeus, a Christian theologian of the second century, offered these thoughts on John's prophecy of the Antichrist:

> Although certain as to the number of the name of Antichrist, yet we should come to no rash conclusions as to the name itself, because this number [666] is capable of being fitted to many names.... *Teitan* too, (TEITAN, the first syllable being written with the two Greek vowels ε and ι), among all the names which are found among us, is rather worthy of credit. For it has in itself the predicted number, and is composed of six letters, each syllable containing three letters; and [the word itself] is ancient, and removed from ordinary use; for among our kings we find none bearing this name Titan, nor have any of the idols which are worshipped in public among the Greeks and barbarians this appellation. Among many persons, too, this name is accounted divine, so that even the sun is termed "Titan" by those who do now possess [the rule]. This word, too, contains a certain outward appearance

of vengeance, and of one inflicting merited punishment because he (Antichrist) pretends that he vindicates the oppressed. And besides this, it is an ancient name, one worthy of credit, of royal dignity, and still further, a name belonging to a tyrant. **Inasmuch, then, as this name "Titan" has so much to recommend it, there is a strong degree of probability, that from among the many [names suggested], we infer, that perchance he who is to come shall be called "Titan."**[306] (Emphasis added)

To his credit, Irenaeus concluded that he wouldn't say absolutely that the Antichrist would be named Titan. He reasoned that if the precise name had been important, John would have revealed it instead of a number.

Still, it's intriguing, isn't it? And consider this: Jesus demonstrated His mastery over chaos to the disciples one night on the Sea of Galilee:

On that day, when evening had come, he said to them, "Let us go across to the other side." And leaving the crowd, they took him with them in the boat, just as he was. And other boats were with him. And a great windstorm arose, and the waves were breaking into the boat, so that the boat was already filling. But he was in the stern, asleep on the cushion. And they woke him and said to him, "Teacher, do you not care that we are perishing?" **And he awoke and rebuked the wind and said to the sea, "Peace! Be still!" And the wind ceased, and there was a great calm.** He said to them, "Why are you so afraid? Have you still no faith?" And they were filled with great fear and said to one another, **"Who then is this, that even the wind and the sea obey him?"** (Mark 4:35–41, ESV; emphasis added)

The storm-god, Baal/Satan, and the chaos-god, Leviathan, were no match for the Messiah. They won't do any better at Armageddon.

One last note before moving on: Typhon was identified by the Greeks as the Egyptian chaos-god, Set. Isn't it odd, then, that after decades of fascination with the return of a chaos-god to Earth, the acronym of the best-known group hunting for signs of life among the stars, SETI (Search for Extraterrestrial Intelligence), is an Egyptian word that literally means "man of Set"?

Return of the Titans

It's worth asking whether it's possible that an entity such as Typhon/Set/Leviathan—with a hundred dragon-like heads, vipers for legs, or something similar—could even *be* the Antichrist. The answer is yes. Satan is described as "a great red dragon, with seven heads and ten horns" in Revelation 12:3, and he entered into Judas Iscariot,[307] the betrayer of Jesus. Since Satan was able to possess or control Judas, then the Beast, whatever spirit it is, can and will do the same with another human host. What we perceive with our natural eyes is not the full picture. Remember, as Paul warned us, "even Satan disguises himself as an angel of light."[308]

Now, what about the Titans? Let's look at Revelation 9. When the fifth of the trumpet-blowing angels sounds his horn, a star falls from Heaven to Earth with a key to the abyss. This marks the return of the old gods.

> He opened the shaft of the bottomless pit, and from the shaft rose smoke like the smoke of a great furnace, and the sun and the air were darkened with the smoke from the shaft. Then from the smoke came locusts on the earth, and they were given power like the power of scorpions of the earth. They were told not to harm the grass of the earth or any green plant or any tree, but only those people who do not have the seal of God on their foreheads. They were allowed to torment them for five months, but not to kill them, and their torment was like the torment of a scorpion when it stings someone. And in those days people will seek death and will not find it. They will long to die, but death will flee from them.
>
> **In appearance the locusts were like horses prepared for battle: on their heads were what looked like crowns of gold; their faces**

were like human faces, their hair like women's hair, and their teeth like lions' teeth; they had breastplates like breastplates of iron, and the noise of their wings was like the noise of many chariots with horses rushing into battle. They have tails and stings like scorpions, and their power to hurt people for five months is in their tails. They have as king over them the angel of the bottomless pit. His name in Hebrew is Abaddon, and in Greek he is called Apollyon. (Revelation 9:2–11, ESV; emphasis added)

What the world knew thousands of years ago as Titans, Watchers, Anunnaki, and *apkallu* is what roars out of the abyss in Revelation 9. That's where they are now, confined until the Judgment. They'll get a short time to torment humanity, taking revenge on God's prized creation for the punishment of watching their own children, the Nephilim/Rephaim, destroyed in the Flood of Noah.

Granted, the description of the things from the pit doesn't match the Mesopotamian images of *apkallu* or Greek sculptures of the Titans. Remember, though, that those entities were sent to the bottomless pit around the time of the Great Flood. Hundreds of years, and maybe a thousand or more, had passed by the time time the Sumerians began to create images of *apkallu* on cylinder seals and clay tablets. Those descriptions captured handed-down memories of supernatural human-animal hybrids, however, and that's basically what John described. The Titans, the Watchers of the Bible, return when Apollyon opens the pit. And for humans without the seal of God on their foreheads, it will literally be Hell on Earth.

By the way, the description of the Titans/Watchers in Revelation 9 also applies to the supernatural army of locust-like beings in Joel chapter 2. It's hard to understand why, but some Christian churches today teach that being part of Joel's Army is a *good* thing, like being selected to serve as a warrior for God. Listen carefully: **Joel's Army fights for the wrong team.** What Joel saw was the army of Gog marching to the battle of Armageddon. Bad things happen to Joel's Army. Read all the way down to verse 20:

I will remove the northerner far from you,
and drive him into a parched and desolate land,
his vanguard into the eastern sea,
and his rear guard into the western sea;
the stench and foul smell of him will rise,
for he has done great things. (Joel 2:20, ESV)

Did you get that? God *destroys* Joel's Army. This verse is Yahweh's prophecy of what will happen on the Day of the Lord, the day when God judges the unbelieving nations of the world.

At the end of Joel 2, God promises Israel that He will take pity on His people and put an end to the invasion by "the northerner." The Hebrew word there, *tsephoni*, is from the same root as Zaphon. It's easy to immediately see the connection between Joel's Army and the mountain of Satan/Baal. Some English translations translate the word "northern army" or "northern horde," which is the multitude that follows Gog into battle against Israel.

Even Joel's prophecy of the destruction of "the northerner" matches Ezekiel 39. The Valley of the Travelers, in the desert east of Jordan River, is indeed "a parched and desolate land." Ezekiel calls the burial place of Gog and his army the Valley of Hamon-Gog, which means "multitude of Gog." A multitude of dead. Stench and foul smell, indeed.

One final note in this section: Because you've read the Book of Revelation, you noticed that we didn't address the four angels bound in the Euphrates who are released when the sixth trumpet sounds. That's by design. The Bible tells us nothing about them, so there isn't enough good data even for speculation. The Euphrates holds an important place in the physical and spiritual history of the world, so we can assume these entities have special significance in the spirit realm, but since we can only guess at what that is, I will leave it for others.

In whatever way this drama unfolds, we can be sure of this: Armageddon is the day the old gods return. Just as Adolf Hitler increased his efforts to exterminate the Jews within his reach in the closing days of World War

II, even as his military commanders begged for resources to hold back the advancing allied armies, the Titans/Watchers, facing their own destruction, will be driven by an unimaginably intense hatred to slaughter as many humans as possible before the end.

Sacrificial Feast in the Valley of the Travelers

Many prophecy teachers will focus on the unimaginable scale of the slaughter that takes place at Armageddon, the reason the "block the travelers" verse is taken to mean "choked with corpses," rather than the gruesome aftermath. But it's what comes after the destruction of the army of Gog that confirms that this battle is one and the same as the battle of Armageddon.

Ezekiel describes what can only be called a feast of the dead.

> As for you, son of man, thus says the Lord GOD: Speak to the birds of every sort and to all beasts of the field: "**Assemble and come, gather from all around to the sacrificial feast that I am preparing for you, a great sacrificial feast on the mountains of Israel,** and you shall eat flesh and drink blood. **You shall eat the flesh of the mighty, and drink the blood of the princes of the earth—of rams, of lambs, and of he-goats, of bulls, all of them fat beasts of Bashan.** And you shall eat fat till you are filled, and drink blood till you are drunk, at the sacrificial feast that I am preparing for you. And you shall be filled at my table with horses and charioteers, with mighty men and all kinds of warriors,' declares the Lord GOD." (Ezekiel 39:17–20, ESV; emphasis added)

Yes, this is gory, but stick with me here. There are important clues in this passage.

First, note the description of the army of Gog: "The mighty" is Hebrew *gibborim*, a word used in Genesis 6:4 to describe the Nephilim of the distant past. Nimrod, the would-be founder of the world's first empire who tried to build an artificial cosmic mountain at Babel, is described in Genesis 10:8 as "the first on earth to be a mighty man (*gibbôr*)." In his exploits, Nimrod resembles the great hero of Uruk, Gilgamesh.[309] (More on Gilgamesh and his relationship with the dead later in one of the appendices to this book.)

The imagery Ezekiel employed in his prophecy of the cataclysmic war of Gog and Magog are so intriguing that many of us have overlooked clues that the prophet salted throughout the preceding chapters. For example, if we turn back to chapter 32, we find that the prophet helpfully offered some information about just who the *gibborim* are. This is a long section, but trust me—it's worth reading.

> In the twelfth year, in the twelfth month, on the fifteenth day of the month, the word of the LORD came to me: "Son of man, wail over the multitude of Egypt, and send them down, her and the daughters of majestic nations, to the world below, to those who have gone down to the pit:
> "Whom do you surpass in beauty?
> Go down and be laid to rest with the uncircumcised."
> They shall fall amid those who are slain by the sword. Egypt is delivered to the sword; drag her away, and all her multitudes. **The mighty chiefs shall speak of them, with their helpers, out of the midst of Sheol:** "They have come down, they lie still, the uncircumcised, slain by the sword....
> **And they do not lie with the mighty, the fallen from among the uncircumcised,** who went down to Sheol with their weapons of war, whose swords were laid under their heads, and whose iniquities are upon their bones; for the terror of the mighty men was in the land of the living. (Ezekiel 32:17–21, 27, ESV; emphasis added)

The phrase translated "mighty chiefs" in verse 21 is *'ēlê gibbôrîm*, literally, "rulers of the Gibborim." The verse echoes Isaiah 14:9–11, where "the shades"—the Rephaim—were "stirred up" to welcome the rebel from Eden when he was cast down.

Verse 27 deserves special attention. The Hebrew behind the words, "the mighty, the fallen," is *gibbôrîm nōphelîm*. While it's tempting to read Nephilim for "the fallen," that doesn't quite work. The same Hebrew word appears in verse 22, in the phrase "fallen by the sword."[310] Swapping Nephilim for *nōphelîm* there yields "Nephilim by the sword," and that makes no sense.

But Ezekiel doesn't need Nephilim in that verse to make his point. Normally, I like the English Standard Version, but circumcision is not the point of this verse. A more accurate reading is, "And they do not lie with the fallen heroes (*gibbôrîm*) of ancient times."[311] The Jewish translators of the Septuagint, who produced a Greek version of the Old Testament from Hebrew texts around 200 B.C., understood the passage the same way and rendered the phrase "the giants that fell of old."

Dr. Daniel Block, an expert on the Book of Ezekiel, believes that the prophet was telling us that these rulers of the Gibborim held special status in the underworld:

> According to Ezekiel 32:21, these heroic personages speak from the midst of Sheol, which may suggest that they are located in the heart of the netherworld, perhaps a more honorable assignment than "the remotest recesses of the pit," where the uncircumcised and those who have fallen by the sword lie. The description in v. 27 indicates that these individuals have indeed been afforded noble burials. There they lie with their weapons of war, their swords laid under their heads and their shields placed upon their bones. Ancient burial customs in which personal items and symbols of status were buried with the corpses of the deceased provide the source of this image.

Ezekiel's use of the antediluvian heroic traditions at this point is shocking. How could the prophet possibly perceive these men as noble and hold them up as honorable residents of Sheol, when his own religious tradition presents them as the epitome of wickedness, corruption, and violence (Gen[esis] 6:5, 11–12)?[312]

Dr. Block may be reading into the text a more favorable depiction of these denizens of the netherworld than Ezekiel intended. I believe the prophet meant only that the Gibborim—i.e., the Rephaim/Nephilim/Travelers—were fundamentally different in substance from your run-of-the-mill dead, for the same reason the Nephilim giants in Genesis 6 were called "the mighty men who were of old, the men of renown" (*haggibbōrîm 'ăšer mē'ôlām 'anšê haš- šēm*). We remember them because of their deeds, but not because those deeds were righteous. In the same way, the Gibborim of Ezekiel 32 have status in the underworld because of what they are (spirits of human-angel hybrids), not because they're righteous. And their prophesied end in the valley that bears their name, the Valley of the Travelers, indicates that Ezekiel knew very well what those entities are like.

Back to Ezekiel 39. Did you notice in verse 18 that the rams, lambs, and he-goats representing the princes of the earth are described as "fat beasts of Bashan?" Remember, Bashan was considered an evil place, the literal entrance to the underworld. It belonged to the god Rapi'u, who, according to some scholars, was believed by the Amorites to be the founder of the Ditanu/Tidanu, the ancient tribe that produced their kings and gave its name to the old gods of the Greeks.

By linking the princes of the earth to Bashan, Ezekiel again made a theological point: The warriors fighting for Gog will be sold out to the god of Bashan, whether his name is Rapi'u, El, Dagan, Kronos, or Baal Hammon.

Remember Psalm 22 and the prophecy of the "strong bulls of Bashan" we discussed earlier? As we noted, those bulls were not cattle; they were the Gibborim of Ezekiel 32, demonic warriors of Satan/Baal. They will fall in the Valley of the Travelers when God intervenes to save His people at a battle fought on the mountains of Israel. Even the reference to horses and charioteers in Ezekiel 39:20 recalls the description of the Rephaim in the Ugaritic texts KTU 1.20–22.

Now, remember the rituals of the Amorites at Ugarit? The ones where the Rephaim are summoned to the sanctuary of El?

To his sanctuary the saviours hurried indeed,
to his sanctuary hurried indeed the divinities.

[Note: As before, "saviours" are Rephaim and "divinities" are elohim.]
They harnessed the chariots;
the horses they hitched.
They mounted their chariots,
they came on their mounts.
They journeyed a day
and a second.
After sunrise on the third
the saviours arrived at the threshing-floors,
the divinities at the plantations....
Just as Anat hurries to the chase,
(and) sets the birds of heaven wheeling in flight,
(so) he slaughtered oxen and sheep,
he felled bulls
and the fattest of rams,
year-old calves,
skipping lambs,
kids.
Like silver to vagabonds [Travelers] were the olives,
(like) gold to vagabonds were the dates.
...a table (set) with fruit of the vine,
with fruit of the vine of royal quality.[313] (Emphasis added)

You see the significance. In this Amorite religious text written about six hundred years before Ezekiel was born, the Rephaim travel until dawn of the third day to eat a sacrificial meal on Mount Hermon, the sanctuary of El, a feast of slaughtered bulls, rams, lambs, and goats. But Ezekiel prophesied a day when these warriors of Baal would *be* the bulls, rams, lambs, and goats—a sacrificial feast for creation served up by Yahweh Himself.

Now we'll link this to the New Testament.

Sacrificial Feast at Armageddon

John the Revelator studied Ezekiel. The only question is whether he studied the scrolls himself or had Ezekiel's vision imparted to him supernaturally. But there is no doubt that John's prophecy of the last great battle of human history was the same one given to Ezekiel nearly seven hundred years earlier.

Prophecy scholars still debate the timing of Armageddon and the war of Gog and Magog, whether those two are the same, and whether the second conflict with Gog of Magog after Christ's millennial reign is the same one mentioned earlier in Revelation. We're going to set all of that aside for the moment. Truth is, I don't have answers for two of those three questions, but in my defense, they haven't been settled in the two thousand years since John wrote Revelation. Expecting me to wrap it up in this book is asking a bit much.

However, we can say with confidence that John and Ezekiel were pointing to the same events. Some, involving Mystery Babylon, I will explore in a future book. The Amorites and their religion have had a much greater impact on history than we've realized.

Armageddon, however, is the topic for this book. And it's clear from the aftermath of that battle that John was shown that he and Ezekiel saw the same thing.

> The sixth angel poured out his bowl on the great river Euphrates, and its water was dried up, to prepare the way for the kings from the east. And I saw, coming out of the mouth of the dragon and out of the mouth of the beast and out of the mouth of the false

prophet, three unclean spirits like frogs. For they are demonic spirits, performing signs, who go abroad to the kings of the whole world, to assemble them for battle on the great day of God the Almighty. ("Behold, I am coming like a thief! Blessed is the one who stays awake, keeping his garments on, that he may not go about naked and be seen exposed!") **And they assembled them at the place that in Hebrew is called Armageddon....**

Then I saw an angel standing in the sun, and with a loud voice he called to all the birds that fly directly overhead, **"Come, gather for the great supper of God, to eat the flesh of kings, the flesh of captains, the flesh of mighty men, the flesh of horses and their riders, and the flesh of all men, both free and slave, both small and great."** And I saw the beast and the kings of the earth with their armies gathered to make war against him who was sitting on the horse and against his army. And the beast was captured, and with it the false prophet who in its presence had done the signs by which he deceived those who had received the mark of the beast and those who worshiped its image. These two were thrown alive into the lake of fire that burns with sulfur. And **the rest were slain by the sword that came from the mouth of him who was sitting on the horse, and all the birds were gorged with their flesh.** (Revelation 16:12–16, 19:17–21, ESV; emphasis added)

The assembly of the armies of the world at Armageddon described in Revelation 16 is followed by a description of the fall of Babylon the Great that takes up two full chapters before returning to the battle of Armageddon in chapter 19.

The invitation of the angel standing in the sun to the "great supper of God" is clearly the same as the one issued by God in Ezekiel 39. The parallels between the two are too close to be coincidental. The similarities have been noted for literally hundreds of years by Bible scholars such as Matthew Henry,[314] E. W. Bullinger,[315] Robert Jamieson, A. R. Fausset, and David Brown,[316] and others. It really isn't open to debate.

Ezekiel must have been horrified by this gruesome feast! He protested mightily when God directed him to bake his bread over a fire built from human dung:

> Then I said, "Ah, Lord GOD! Behold, I have never defiled myself. From my youth up till now I have never eaten what died of itself or was torn by beasts, nor has tainted meat come into my mouth." (Ezekiel 4:14, ESV)

But at Armageddon, Yahweh will serve the ultimate taboo, human flesh and blood, as a sacrificial feast to unclean animals, scavengers. As scholar Daniel Block notes, there is something unique about this for God to be so extreme:

> [The banquet] is designated a *zebaḥ*, which derives from a root meaning "to slaughter," and seems to have had reference to any sacrifices that were burned on an altar (*mizbēaḥ*). More than one kind of *zebaḥ* was celebrated in Israel, but it was generally assumed that this meal was eaten in the presence of Yahweh (*lipnê yhwh*), that is, as his guest.... Ezekiel's designation of this banquet as a *zebaḥ* classifies it as a ritual event. But by altering all the roles he grossly caricatures the normal image of a *zebaḥ*. In place of a human worshiper slaughtering animals in the presence of Yahweh, Yahweh slaughters humans for the sake of animals, who gather from all over the world (*missābîb*) for this gigantic celebration (*zebaḥ gādôl*) on the mountains of Israel. The battlefield has been transformed into a huge sacrificial table.
>
> Second, the invitation describes the menu. The last statement of v. 17 is thematic, calling on the participants to partake of flesh and blood, a merismic expression for carcasses as wholes. V. 18 specifies these as the flesh of heroic figures (*gibbôrîm*) and the blood of the princes of the earth (*nĕśî'ê hā'āreṣ*), which are to be devoured like fare normally served at a *zebaḥ* table: rams

(*'êlîm*), lambs (*kārîm*), male goats (*'attûdîm*), bulls (*pārîm*), and the fatlings of Bashan (*měrî'ê bāšān*). **These terms are obviously not used literally, but as animal designations for nobility.**[317] (Emphasis added)

Ezekiel probably highlighted the nobility of the Gibborim slaughtered for this gruesome ritual feast for the same reason he noted the special status of the Gibborim of the underworld: They're fundamentally different from ordinary human soldiers. They are "warriors of Baal," the Rephaim, spirits of the Nephilim destroyed in the Flood, the semi-divine sons of the Titans.

As Dr. Block notes, "The literary image sketched here must have been shocking for a person as sensitive to cultic matters as Ezekiel."[318] But the conflict the precedes this repulsive feast is not simply one more battle in a long list of the wars fought by men over the millennia. This one brings a supernaturally reinforced army led by a creature from the abyss to the foot of God's holy mountain.

John's account of the aftermath of Armageddon follows Ezekiel's description of the Gog-Magog war because they describe the same event. It will be fought at Jerusalem for Zion, God's mount of assembly, and it results in the reversal of an ancient Amorite ritual. Instead of arriving at the *har mô'ēd* for a ritual meal in their honor, the Rephaim will *become* a sacrificial feast for all of creation.

The Holy One in Israel

While it's my belief that the similarities between the gruesome ritual feasts prophesied by Ezekiel and John are evidence enough to show that the Gog-Magog war is the same conflict as Armageddon, and thus Gog is the Antichrist, it's not the only clue. Since we're already in this far, let's put all of our cards on the table. First, both battles end with a massive earthquake:[319]

But on that day, the day that Gog shall come against the land of Israel, declares the Lord GOD, my wrath will be roused in my anger. For in my jealousy and in my blazing wrath I declare, **On that day there shall be a great earthquake in the land of Israel.** The fish of the sea and the birds of the heavens and the beasts of the field and all creeping things that creep on the ground, and all the people who are on the face of the earth, shall quake at my presence. **And the mountains shall be thrown down, and the cliffs shall fall, and every wall shall tumble to the ground.** (Ezekiel 38:18–20, ESV; emphasis added)

The seventh angel poured out his bowl into the air, and a loud voice came out of the temple, from the throne, saying, "It is done!" **And there were flashes of lightning, rumblings, peals of thunder, and a great earthquake such as there had never been since man was on the earth, so great was that earthquake.** The great city was split into three parts, and the cities of the nations fell, and God remembered Babylon the great, to make her drain the cup of the wine of the fury of his wrath. (Revelation 16:17–19, ESV; emphasis added)

Our friend Joel Richardson points out in his book *Mideast Beast* that Ezekiel was telling us God Himself will be present at the Gog-Magog conflict.[320] In Ezekiel 38:19 above, the Hebrew word translated "presence" is *panim*. Elsewhere in the Bible, notably in the priestly blessing recorded in Numbers 6:23–27, *panim* literally means "face."

Trust me—the one time you do not want the Lord to lift up His *panim* upon you is when He's leading the army you're about to attack. This is what the enemy soldiers at Armageddon will see:

Then I saw heaven opened, and behold, a white horse! The one sitting on it is called Faithful and True, and in righteousness he judges and makes war. His eyes are like a flame of fire, and on his head are many diadems, and he has a name written that no one knows but himself. He is clothed in a robe dipped in blood, and the name by which he is called is The Word of God. And the armies of heaven, arrayed in fine linen, white and pure, were following him on white horses. From his mouth comes a sharp sword with which to strike down the nations, and he will rule them with a rod of iron. He will tread the winepress of the fury of the wrath of God the Almighty. On his robe and on his thigh he has a name written, King of kings and Lord of lords. (Revelation 19:11–16, ESV)

It's safe to say that Yahweh, in the form of His Messiah, will be present at Armageddon, just as Ezekiel prophesied about the war against Gog.

In the wake of the battle, Ezekiel writes that the world will recognize the greatness and holiness of Yahweh.[321] It's hard to see that happening if the Gog-Magog war is just a warm-up for all the kings of the earth assembling for the battle of Armageddon. The only way Ezekiel's prophecy makes sense is if that's the *last* battle, after which Gog, the Antichrist, is defeated and dumped into the pit for a thousand years (Revelation 20:2).

Finally, Yahweh tells Ezekiel that after Gog's defeat:

My holy name I will make known in the midst of my people Israel, and I will not let my holy name be profaned anymore. And the nations shall know that I am the Lord, the Holy One in Israel."[322]

Note that God called Himself "the Holy One *in* Israel," not the Holy One *of* Israel. This is the only place in the Bible where that phrase is used.[323] "The Holy One of Israel" appears more than two dozen times in Scripture, but only here, after the destruction of the army of Gog, does God substitute "in" Israel for "of" Israel. Again, this shows us that God is present at this battle. In other words, it is undoubtedly the Second Coming, because the war with Gog is the battle at Armageddon against the forces of Antichrist. After that, according to Revelation 20:4, Jesus will literally reign on earth for a thousand years, and He'll do it from His *har mô ʿēd*, Mount Zion.

Tyre and Babylon

We're going to go a little deeper. You may have noticed the three-chapter gap in Revelation between the armies assembling at Armageddon (Revelation 16:16) and the gruesome sacrificial feast after Armageddon (Revelation 19:17–21) that connects back to Ezekiel 39. If you did, you're probably wondering if it's significant. It is. The fall of Babylon the Great is more evidence that Ezekiel and John had the same supernatural enemies in mind.

Besides the identity of Gog, one of the great puzzles of Bible prophecy is the identity of Mystery Babylon, the Great Harlot of Revelation 17.

> Then one of the seven angels who had the seven bowls came and said to me, "Come, I will show you the judgment of the great prostitute who is seated on many waters, with whom the kings of the earth have committed sexual immorality, and with the wine of whose sexual immorality the dwellers on earth have become drunk." And he carried me away in the Spirit into a wilderness, and I saw a woman sitting on a scarlet beast that was full of blasphemous names, and it had seven heads and ten horns. The woman was arrayed in purple and scarlet, and adorned with gold and jewels and pearls, holding in her hand a golden cup full of abominations and the impurities of her sexual immorality. And on her forehead was written a name of mystery: "Babylon the great, mother of prostitutes and of earth's abominations." (Revelation 17:1–5, ESV)

The great church of the last days is called "Babylon the great," but Mystery Babylon is the name that's stuck. Isn't it intriguing that almost two thousand years after John was shown this prophecy, learned students of Bible prophecy still can't agree on who, what, or where the Babylon of the last days will be?

The imagery is fascinating. Trying to identify the seven heads and ten horns on the Beast has likewise inspired two millennia of diligent study and educated guesses, but at the end of the day, we still don't know exactly what they represent. And I'm going to cop out in this book and set that mystery aside for future study, because it's a two thousand-year-old rabbit trail we can save for another day.

John told us this much about the harlot: The Babylon of his vision is a religion and a city. Two of our friends, authors and prophecy experts Joel Richardson and Bill Salus, recently debated the identity of Babylon. Bill named Rome and the Roman Catholic Church, a popular choice since the Protestant Reformation, and Joel made a case for Mecca and Islam. Another Bible scholar I respect, Chris White, argued in his books *Mystery Babylon* and *False Christ* that the early church father Irenaeus was on the right track, pointing to Jerusalem and an Antichrist who presents himself to the world as a Jew. Others, including our friends S. Douglas Woodward, Douglas W. Krieger, and Dene McGriff, in their book, *Final Babylon*, believe the United States will fill the role of the prophesied Babylon of the Book of Revelation. After the United States invaded Iraq in 2003, some, such as Chuck Missler, suggested that Mystery Babylon might be a rebuilt Babylon, a reconstruction project that had begun under Saddam Hussein.

Let me suggest a different analysis.

It is my view that Ezekiel gave us important clues that modern prophecy scholars have missed because they haven't considered the history and religions of the people who lived in the Near East for millennia before the birth of Jesus. Further, they may not fully grasp the divine council paradigm and its implications for end-times prophecy. Put another way, if we understand what the Old Testament prophets knew about the gods of the nations around ancient Israel, and that those gods were (and still are) real, we might understand better the sections of the New Testament that draw on the writings of the prophets.

For example, Ezekiel's lament over Tyre has a clear parallel in Revelation, and it cements the connection between the visions of Ezekiel and John. And that, of course, ties together the rebellious small-*G* gods who play a key role in their prophecies. Let's turn to chapter 27 of Ezekiel, which was his lament over the Phoenician city of Tyre.

> The word of the LORD came to me: "Now you, son of man, raise a lamentation over Tyre, and say to Tyre, who dwells at the entrances to the sea, merchant of the peoples to many coastlands, thus says the Lord GOD:
>
> O Tyre, you have said,
> 'I am perfect in beauty.'
> Your borders are in the heart of the seas;
> your builders made perfect your beauty.
> **They made all your planks**
> **of fir trees from Senir;**
> **they took a cedar from Lebanon**
> **to make a mast for you.**
> **Of oaks of Bashan**
> **they made your oars;**
> they made your deck of pines
> from the coasts of Cyprus,
> inlaid with ivory." (Ezekiel 27:1–6, ESV; emphasis added)

Tyre was the preeminent commercial empire in the Mediterranean for centuries. Even after the city's influence began to fade, its colony in north Africa, Carthage, grew so powerful that it waged a long war with Rome between 218 and 201 B.C., and nearly won. But roughly three hundred fifty years earlier, in the early sixth century B.C., Ezekiel tied the strength of Tyre—the source of its wealth, its cargo ships—to Mount Hermon and Bashan.

Senir was the Amorite name for Mount Hermon. Why did Ezekiel choose to call it Senir instead of Hermon? That's a good question. The

Amorites were ancient history by Ezekiel's day. They faded from the scene after the conquest of Canaan, at least under the name "Amorites," and that was more than eight hundred years before Ezekiel. (How many places in the U.S. have the same names they did in A.D. 1200?) That said, it's a pretty good bet that the Arameans and Phoenicians were physical and spiritual descendants of the Amorites, and it's possible that the Chaldeans who restored Babylon to power in the seventh century B.C. were likewise descended from the Amorites.

While it's possible that Ezekiel identified Hermon and Bashan as the source of the lumber for the merchant ships of Tyre simply because that's where the closest trees were located, I think the prophet's intention was to link the city to the spiritual heritage of the region. His reference to Senir is the last time that name is used in the Bible, roughly four hundred years after the previous reference (Song of Solomon 4:8). Not only was Senir/Hermon the abode of El, where the Rephaim came to feast, it towered over Bashan, the entrance to the netherworld. In short, by choosing to call the mountain Senir instead of Hermon, Ezekiel deliberately linked it to people whose wickedness was legendary among Jews. The Amorites were a spiritual yardstick to measure the evil of the two most wicked kings in Jewish history, Ahab of Israel and Manasseh of Judah. Manasseh was so bad, he did "things more evil than all that the Amorites did"![324]

As noted in an earlier chapter, the Amorites founded Babylon. They were responsible for the decadent, occult religious system so notorious that it became the symbol of the Antichrist's religious system of the last days. Babylon's greatest king was an Amorite named Hammurabi, whose name meant "My Fathers are Rephaim." That name was so popular it was shared by at least five other Amorite kings down to the time of the judges in Israel, more than five hundred years after Hammurabi the Great.

But so far, we've only dealt with the link between the pagan Amorites and the city of Tyre. The link to Revelation comes in the lament over its destruction.

Your rowers have brought you out
into the high seas.
>The east wind has wrecked you
>in the heart of the seas.
>Your riches, your wares, your merchandise,
>your mariners and your pilots,
>your caulkers, your dealers in merchandise,
>and all your men of war who are in you,
>with all your crew
>that is in your midst,
>sink into the heart of the seas
>on the day of your fall.
>At the sound of the cry of your pilots
>the countryside shakes,
>and down from their ships
>come all who handle the oar.
>**The mariners and all the pilots of the sea**
>**stand on the land**
>**and shout aloud over you**
>**and cry out bitterly.**
>They cast dust on their heads
>and wallow in ashes;
>they make themselves bald for you
>and put sackcloth on their waist,
>and they weep over you in bitterness of soul,
>with bitter mourning.
>In their wailing they raise a lamentation for you
>and lament over you:
>**"Who is like Tyre,**
>**like one destroyed in the midst of the sea?**
>When your wares came from the seas,
>you satisfied many peoples;

with your abundant wealth and merchandise
you enriched the kings of the earth.
Now you are wrecked by the seas,
in the depths of the waters;
your merchandise and all your crew in your midst
have sunk with you.
All the inhabitants of the coastlands
are appalled at you,
and the hair of their kings bristles with horror;
their faces are convulsed.
The merchants among the peoples hiss at you;
you have come to a dreadful end and shall be no more forever."
(Ezekiel 27:26–36, ESV; emphasis added)

Compare that section of Ezekiel's lament over Tyre to John's prophecy of the destruction of Babylon the Great in Revelation 18.

After this I saw another angel coming down from heaven, having great authority, and the earth was made bright with his glory. And he called out with a mighty voice,
"Fallen, fallen is Babylon the great!
She has become a dwelling place for demons,
a haunt for every unclean spirit,
a haunt for every unclean bird,
a haunt for every unclean and detestable beast.…
And the kings of the earth, who committed sexual immoral-
ity and lived in luxury with her, will weep and wail over her when they see the smoke of her burning. They will stand far off, in fear of her torment, and say,
'Alas! Alas! You great city,
you mighty city, Babylon!
For in a single hour your judgment has come.'…
The merchants of these wares, who gained wealth from her,

will stand far off, in fear of her torment, weeping and mourning aloud,

'Alas, alas, for the great city
that was clothed in fine linen,
in purple and scarlet,
adorned with gold,
with jewels, and with pearls!
For in a single hour all this wealth has been laid waste.'

And all shipmasters and seafaring men, sailors and all whose trade is on the sea, stood far off and cried out as they saw the smoke of her burning,

'What city was like the great city?'

And they threw dust on their heads as they wept and mourned, crying out,

'Alas, alas, for the great city
where all who had ships at sea
grew rich by her wealth!
For in a single hour she has been laid waste.'" (Revelation 18:1–2, 9, 15–19, ESV; emphasis added)

Let's compare some key phrases from these chapters.

Tyre (Ezekiel 27)	Babylon (Revelation 18)
"enriched the kings of the earth" (Eze. 27:33)	"kings of the earth...lived in luxury with her" (Rev. 18:9)
Lamented by mariners, pilots of the sea, merchants, and kings (Eze. 27:28–36)	Lamented by kings, merchants, shipmasters, and seafaring men (Rev. 18:9–19)
"Who is like Tyre, like one destroyed in the midst of the sea? ...with your abundant wealth and merchandise you enriched the kings of the earth." (Eze. 27:32–33)	"What city was like the great city...where all who had ships at sea grew rich by her wealth!" (Rev. 18:18–19)

As with the similarities between Ezekiel 39 and Revelation 19, the parallels here have been noted by Bible scholars for generations. What I haven't seen is anyone who's connected these chapters to identify the spiritual source of this global religion—the gods of the Amorites.

When God made His covenant with Abraham in Genesis 15, He told the patriarch that his descendants would spend about four hundred years in a land that wasn't theirs because "the iniquity of the Amorites is not yet complete."[325] Wondering about the meaning of that one phrase drove me to the research that's resulted in two books (so far). There's a lot more meaning in that one line that we've been taught—that is, if we've been taught anything about it at all.

In this book, we've focused on a few members of the Amorite pantheon, specifically El (and his alternate identities, Dagan and Baal Hammon), Baal, and the Rephaim/Nephilim, and their Greek equivalents Kronos, Zeus, and the demigods/heroes like Herakles (who, remember, was most likely the *baal* of Jezebel, so he couldn't have been as nice as the Disney cartoons make him out). I've done this to show the influence of the pagan gods on the ancient world and the role they'll play in the future. The apostles and prophets knew it, but we've lost their perspective because we've been taught that those pagan gods don't exist.

When reading the Bible, we need to remember that it didn't emerge from an isolation chamber, untouched by the cultures and religious beliefs of the people who lived around ancient Israel and Judah. The prophets called by God lived in a society that was part of a greater whole. When they wrote, the cultural, political, and spiritual influences of the greater Near East were reflected in their work. That doesn't mean they turned to the gods of Mesopotamia for spiritual truth; just the opposite. What we've forgotten over the last two millennia is that those gods are real and much of what's in the Bible was written in direct response to their rebellion.

In other words, to repeat a point I made earlier, we need to check our naturalistic bias and twenty-first-century worldview at the door. The focus of end-times prophecy shouldn't be on which human political figure will lead the charge against Zion, but on a supernatural enemy with the audacity to challenge Yahweh for His throne.

Ezekiel, Isaiah, and Moses gave us the clues. They point to Mount Hermon, Bashan, and the neighbors of ancient Israel who worshiped the gods who called that region home. When we compare the surviving writings from the ancient Near East and classical Greece and Rome, we discover that the Hebrew prophets were pretty well informed.

When we compare what we know about the gods the Amorites venerated and worshiped, especially Baal, El, and the Rephaim, we discover that the gods and demigods of Greek myth were the same entities, but called Zeus, Kronos, and the heroes of the Golden Age.

And that's who's coming back to fight the Battle of Armageddon.

Who Is Mystery Babylon?

Because you've made it this far in the book, you're too sharp to let me skip to the end without addressing this question: Who, what, or where is the Babylon of Revelation 17 and 18?

I'm going to address it briefly here because I plan to write more about this in the future. The answer has more to do with the subject of my next book, which, unless plans change, will dig deeper into the gods of the Amorites. Our focus in this book is the importance of the Rephaim.

As you discerned from the last section, the connection between Mystery Babylon and the Amorites is key. Spiritual wickedness, symbolized by the kingdom of Babylon (founded by Amorites), connected to an unparalleled maritime trading empire are the two main features of prophetic Babylon.

> Then one of the seven angels who had the seven bowls came and said to me, "Come, I will show you the judgment of the great prostitute who is seated on many waters, with whom the kings of the earth have committed sexual immorality, and with the wine

of whose sexual immorality the dwellers on earth have become drunk." And he carried me away in the Spirit into a wilderness, and I saw a woman sitting on a scarlet beast that was full of blasphemous names, and it had seven heads and ten horns. The woman was arrayed in purple and scarlet, and adorned with gold and jewels and pearls, holding in her hand a golden cup full of abominations and the impurities of her sexual immorality. And on her forehead was written a name of mystery: "Babylon the great, mother of prostitutes and of earth's abominations." And I saw the woman, drunk with the blood of the saints, the blood of the martyrs of Jesus....

This calls for a mind with wisdom: the seven heads are seven mountains on which the woman is seated; they are also seven kings, five of whom have fallen, one is, the other has not yet come, and when he does come he must remain only a little while. (Revelation 17:1–6, 9–10, ESV)

As you noticed, there are other characteristics. "Sexual immorality" is a euphemism for spiritual rebellion, like the "whorings" with the gods of the pagan nations committed by Israel and Judah, against which the prophets of the Old Testament thundered.

Geography is another, but a location on seven mountains or hills is one of the easiest for potential candidates to meet. While Rome is the first name most people think of when describing a city on seven hills, it appears to be a status symbol for a city to claim that it, too, was built on seven hills. Maybe it's to encourage a comparison to Rome. Other cities ostensibly sitting on seven hills include Mecca, Jerusalem, Brussels, Tehran, Istanbul, Moscow, and dozens of others (even including Nixa, here in the beautiful Missouri Ozarks).

That's not to say that any of the aforementioned might be Mystery Babylon (especially Nixa), but there are a few that have been put forward.

After Babylon, Rome is probably the second favorite byword for spiritual wickedness in the Bible, or at least it's neck and neck with Egypt.

As mentioned, it certainly meets the seven hills requirement. As the seat of the Roman Catholic Church, prophecy scholars have ticked that box on the Mystery Babylon checklist for Rome as well, especially since the Protestant Reformation. Wealthy? Drunk with the blood of saints? Yes, especially if you consider pagan Rome's record with the early church.

But on that score, one could make a case for Jerusalem, too. It probably won't be as popular with evangelical Christians, but you can't argue that the early church was brutally persecuted by the religious authorities in Jerusalem. And to be honest, while Christian tourists are warmly welcomed today in Israel, the gospel of Jesus Christ is not.

However, the case for Jerusalem as Mystery Babylon has an issue that is difficult to overcome: Setting aside the matter of making the kings of the earth wealthy with trade, when Babylon the Great is destroyed, it's obliterated. In fact, the last verse of a chapter from Isaiah that we've studied in some detail tells us specifically what's going to happen.

> Prepare slaughter for his sons
> because of the guilt of their fathers,
> lest they rise and possess the earth,
> and fill the face of the world with [Watchers]."
>
> "I will rise up against them," declares the LORD of hosts, "and will cut off from Babylon name and remnant, descendants and posterity," declares the LORD. "And I will make it a possession of the hedgehog, and pools of water, and I will sweep it with the broom of destruction," declares the LORD of hosts. (Isaiah 14:21–23, ESV; insertion in brackets added)

While there are other prophecies of doom for Babylon in the Old Testament, especially in chapters 50 and 51 of Jeremiah, those were, generally speaking, fulfilled when the Medes and Persians overran the city in 539 B.C. At the time Isaiah lived and wrote, Assyria, not Babylon, was the dominant power in the Near East. Babylon was a vassal state that wouldn't successfully rebel against the Assyrians until nearly seventy-five years after Isaiah's death. In my view, his prophecy, which delivers the message of Babylon's destruction in the context of God's condemnation of the rebel in Eden, Helel/Lucifer/Satan/Baal (and, apparently, the Watchers and their sons, the Nephilim/Rephaim), is directed at a spiritual Babylon in the far-distant future.

That would rule out Jerusalem. Jesus sets up His millennial kingdom there, and He won't be ruling from a city that God says will be reduced to a wasteland forever.

Joel Richardson and Walid Shoebat have put forward an interesting theory in recent years that has appeal. Mecca, as we pointed out, is, also seated on seven hills. It, too, is the home of a major religion that has taken the lives of many saints over the last 1,400 years. (We use the biblical definition of "saint"—anyone who's accepted Jesus Christ as Lord.) And since the OPEC oil embargo of 1973, there isn't another nation in the world that compares with the Saudis for the ability to "enrich the kings of the earth."

In my next book, I intend to show that the religion of Mecca, Islam, is the spiritual equivalent of a corporate merger. I believe the old gods of Mesopotamia have banded together in their rebellion against the Creator. But going deeper is beyond our scope here.

Where I disagree with Richardson and Shoebat is on the nature of the Antichrist. He will not be a Muslim. There is no reality in which a Muslim at the head of an army is welcomed into Jerusalem by the people of Israel,[326] whether they believe in end-times prophecy or not. I believe the Antichrist will present himself to the world as a Jew, which is a view held by several early church fathers, such as Irenaeus and Hippolytus.

I'm not saying he'll *be* a Jew, just that he will *claim* to be. Interestingly, since Irenaeus was a disciple of Polycarp, who in turn was a disciple of the Apostle John, who wrote the Book of Revelation, it's possible that the idea was transmitted to Irenaeus through Polycarp from John himself.

Proponents of Rome as end-times Babylon have pointed out that the oil wealth of the Saudis and their Sunni allies around the Persian Gulf may not last much longer. Financial experts cite the exploding debt of the Saudi kingdom after oil prices collapsed in 2015 as a sign that its hold on Western economies isn't as firm as most of us think. The truth is the United States has enough untapped oil to make dependence on Middle Eastern sources voluntary. So, it's argued, the Saudis aren't likely to be Mystery Babylon because their days are numbered.

That may actually support the Mecca-as-Babylon theory. Any nation that has a complete stranglehold on the global economy isn't likely to be thrown under the bus. The fact that the Antichrist and his minions turn on Mystery Babylon in the greatest double-cross in history means that she's expendable. As I wrote in *The Great Inception*:

> To put it bluntly, the best use the Enemy has for Muslims is cannon fodder. They will be a bloody sacrifice to lure Jews and Christians into worshipping the Beast, whom they will mistakenly see as a literal godsend. The destruction of a Muslim coalition would be the point in the prophetic timeline for the cosmic double-cross of Revelation 17:16–17, when the Beast and the kings of the earth betray the woman and destroy her. That would mark the transfer of the spiritual power of Islam to the Beast, and from Mecca to Jerusalem. Not by suddenly converting the world's Muslims; under the scenario we envision, the destruction of Mecca as part of a war to save Israel would be the Antichrist's means of establishing his bona fides as Messiah to the world's Christians and Jews.[327]

While the scarlet woman of Revelation 17 has "dominion over the kings of the earth,"[328] she's resented by those kings, or at least by the ten principal kings represented by the ten horns on the beast. They and the beast "hate" her, so they "devour her flesh and burn her up with fire."[329]

Think about the irony of that for a moment. Regardless of whether the prostitute turns out to be Rome, Mecca, Jerusalem, New York City, or somewhere else, the ultimate end of Mystery Babylon is to be slaughtered and served up as a sacrifice for the Beast from the Abyss—just like the thousands upon thousands of children who were passed through the fire and buried in the tophets of the ancient world.

Conclusion

When you look through a magnifying glass at a picture in a newspaper, especially one from the era before the Internet when the resolution on wire service images wasn't very high, you mainly see a lot of blobs of black and white. They may look like recognizable shapes and they may not. Not until you pull back and look at images from a distance do you see the pictures for what they are. At a distance, the pixels seem to blend together to form cohesive shapes.

That's a good analogy for the study of the religions of the ancient world. When we focus on the beliefs of a particular people, what we see may be confusing until we draw back and fit those shapes into a larger picture. The winged bull-creatures outside the palaces of Assyrian kings, for example, seem like the product of a hyperactive imagination until you pull back, look around, and discover that other cultures in the region also knew about them. And since they're in the Bible, too, the Assyrians based their sculptures on the memory of something that a few people in history have actually seen, like the prophet Ezekiel.

On the other side of the coin, we may keep ourselves from a deeper understanding of the Bible by stubbornly insisting that we've got the whole picture from the shape of a few blobs in one corner.

I am not suggesting that we can only properly understand the Bible by viewing it through the surrounding cultures. That's something a skeptic would say. The Bible is the true Word of God, inerrant in the original languages. But events and customs described in the Bible make more sense when they're considered in the context of the beliefs and practices of the pagan neighbors of ancient Israel and Judah. After all, those beliefs and practices prompted God to inspire the the prophets and apostles to write the words between the covers of your Bible.

In our modern age, we've forgotten to view the natural world as a small part of a much larger whole, one that includes God, of course, but also His supernatural enemies. Where most American Christians miss the mark is by failing to recognize the reality of the enemy. We're so convinced that our close-up, scientist view of one small corner of reality is actually the *whole* picture that we no longer recognize intelligent evil when it manifests right in front of us.

If you pay attention to the news at all, it won't surprise you that the Roman Catholic Church has reported a surge in demand for exorcisms all over the world in recent years. The Vatican launched an annual seminar to train priests and lay people in 2004, and with the shift in its membership to the global south, the Catholic Church is developing a new awareness of the reality of witchcraft and the power of these small-*G* gods.[330]

See, we here in the northern hemisphere are too educated to believe in such superstitions. But the apostles knew they were real. And since they learned directly from Jesus, I submit that their theological training was better than yours and mine.

Patterns

So, when looking down from thirty thousand feet at the religions of the ancient world, what picture do we see? It's a lot more cohesive than we think. There are patterns that repeat from culture to culture over the centuries. In those patterns, we see the outlines of the history that's recorded in the Bible—but spun from the viewpoint of the Fallen, of course.

First, we have the conflict between the Creator and chaos. In the Bible, it's over quickly. God subdues *tehom*, or Tiamat (Leviathan), by the second verse of Genesis 1. It's almost as though Yahweh simply said, "Stay!" to a very large, dangerous dog—one that, thankfully, is bound to obey His commands. The pagan gods, on the other hand, had a lot more trouble dealing with their chaos monsters. Although Marduk, Baal, and Zeus defeated their enemies, it was difficult and usually required the help of other gods.

Then there is the transfer of power from one generation to the next.

From Sumer to Greece, each culture had a memory of a time when the old gods ruled. Over time, either by violent rebellion, as in the conflicts between Anu, Kumarbi, and Teshub or Ouranos, Kronos, and Zeus, or by decree, as with the transfer of kingship from Anu to Enlil to Marduk in Babylon, the people of the Near East and the Mediterranean believed that there had been times in history when the gods, and the people who served them, were not as they are now.

This reflects several periods of history in the Bible, but of course the stories have been twisted. In God's original design, humans walked in His garden among the divine assembly. We were part of the family, as it were, with our older siblings, the small-*G* gods (or angels, if you prefer). Because of the rebellion in Eden, both on the part of the "anointed guardian cherub" and our human ancestors, the divine rebel and humanity were ejected from Eden. I believe the stories of the first transfer of power, from the first-generation sky-god (Anu or Ouranos) to the second-generation (Enlil / El / Dagan / Kumarbi / Kronos), are a retelling of the true story of humanity's banishment from the mountain of God. We no longer had access to Yahweh directly, and so to the pagans, the first-generation "god of heaven" was distant, remote, inaccessible, and uncaring.

The rebellion at Mount Hermon resulted in the imprisonment of the Watchers in Tartarus until the judgment. Ancient pagans remembered the story as the overthrow of the second-generation gods, the Titans or Anunnaki, who, like the Watchers, were locked away in the underworld and had strong links to Mount Hermon. Of course, the rebel gods who were still free twisted the story to explain away what Yahweh had done by claiming credit for punishing the bad old Titans.

Was the fallen angel who called himself the storm-god, Baal/Zeus, whom Jesus identified as Satan, waiting in the wings for the Watchers to overreach and incur the wrath of God? Maybe. Or maybe Baal and the other gods of the Amorites, such as Sîn, Ishtar, Shamash, Resheph, and the rest just tried to make the best of a bad situation. Maybe they're faithful to the old gods in Tartarus, staying in touch with their colleagues who are chained up in the dark and waiting for the abyss to open so they can put the old gang back together and literally raise some hell.

We just don't know. Any scenario we put forward to explain how and why the pagans came to believe what they did about their gods is sheer speculation. What we do know is that the Amorites and their descendants, the Canaanites and Phoenicians, not only served the gods of their pantheons, they believed the spirits of their ancestors played an active role in the world of the living, especially the spirits of their dead kings.

This is where our Venn diagram circles representing Canaanite religion, Greek mythology, and Bible prophecy begin to overlap.

Hercules at Armageddon

We can't assume that the visions John recorded in the Book of Revelation follow a chronological order, events following one another in a neat line, moving from front to back as we read through the chapters. Scholars are divided on that, and since those debates are about two thousand years old we're not going to settle them here. However, we can say with confidence that the fifth angel blows his trumpet and the bottomless pit opens before the battle of Armageddon takes place, because the things that fly out have five months to torment the world and they won't be active after Armageddon.

So, what are those things? In my view, they can only be what the Bible tells us is confined to the abyss, the angels who sinned and "left their proper dwelling"—the Watchers, otherwise known as the Titans. Kronos and his colleagues will have a short window of time to wreak vengeance on mankind for the long millennia of their imprisonment, but they won't be able to touch those with the seal of God on their foreheads. One can imagine that will only make the Watchers that much angrier and the torment of the unbelievers that much more excruciating.

At some point after the release of the Watchers/Titans from the abyss, the armies of the world will gather for their date with destiny at Armageddon. Presumably, the released Watchers will be among the enemy horde.

We can infer from Ezekiel 39 that another group of spirits eager for payback will be on the march with the army of Gog.

Around the time of the Judges, and presumably for some time before the Exodus, the Amorite neighbors of the ancient Israelites practiced rituals that summoned the spirits of their venerated dead kings, the Rephaim, to sacrificial meals at the sanctuary of El. This was on Mount Hermon, El's mount of assembly, where he held court with his seventy sons. Some scholars believe the purpose of that ritual gathering was the restore the Rephaim to life.

The Rephaim were the heroes of the Golden Age ruled by Kronos, the *meropes anthropoi* of the Greek poets Homer and Hesiod. Since we've identified the Titans as the Watchers of the Bible, the demigods of Greek mythology like Herakles and Theseus, were, by definition, Nephilim.

The ancient Greeks, Jews, and early Christians agreed on what happened to the spirits of the Rephaim/Nephilim/*meropes anthropoi* when they died: They became demons. Although the Greeks believed the *daimones* were kindly and helpful, Jews and early Christians had another view. According to 1 Enoch, God forbid the spirits of the Nephilim to enter the usual places reserved for the mortal dead, so they were doomed to wander the earth causing trouble until the final judgment. Significantly, these spirits were described as "warriors of Baal" in the Rephaim texts from Ugarit.

The parallels between Ezekiel 39 and Revelation 19, and between Ezekiel 27 and Revelation 18, identify the war of Gog and Magog as the battle of Armageddon. They are the same event. By comparing Isaiah 14 to Ezekiel 38 and 39, we see that the rallying point for the army of Gog is *yerekah tsaphon*, Mount Zaphon, the home of Baal's palace. The mountain was also connected to the Hurrian, Hittite, and Greek storm-gods, and to the Greek god of chaos, Typhon. The conflict between Zeus and Typhon is clearly a parallel to the battle for divine kingship between Baal and Yamm, which in turn reflected the biblical conflict between Yahweh and the spirit of primordial chaos, Leviathan.

Zaphon is today's Jebel al-Aqra, an imposing mountain in Turkey on the Mediterranean coast just north of the border with Syria. This was also the mountain where the rebel from Eden, Helel ben Shachar (i.e., Lucifer), wanted to establish his mount of assembly to make himself "like the Most High." Since Jesus specifically identified the storm-god Baal/Zeus as Satan,[331] it's logical to assume that this entity is the one who rebelled in Eden. Thus, the divine rebel from Eden was Baal, Zeus, and Satan. Thus we can identify Gog, the Antichrist of Revelation, as a servant of the storm-god/Satan. He will come from the "uttermost parts of the north," which is Mount Zaphon.

When Satan/Baal, the dragon of Revelation, sends Gog/Antichrist to war, his army will be comprised of demonic "warriors of Baal," the spirits of the Rephaim/Nephilim. How do we know this? Because the Canaanite texts also refer to the Rephaim spirits as Travelers. In context, the term means travel between one plane of existence and another—specifically, between the realm of the dead and the land of the living. That's what makes Ezekiel 39 so fascinating: It is in the Valley of the Travelers that the army of Gog will fall.

That place, the valley in the desert east of the Dead Sea, was known in the ancient world as a land of the dead. Several of the places the Israelites stopped during the Exodus had names associated with the underworld— Oboth ("Spirits of the Dead") and Iye-Abarim ("Ruins of the Travelers"). While in this valley, the Israelites were lured into worshiping Baal-Peor ("Lord of the Opening [to the Underworld]") and ate sacrifices to the dead.[332]

Think about that for a moment. Gog will lead a demonic horde from the north against Israel. This will literally be an army of the dead—the ultimate zombie apocalypse.

The defeat of Gog will be total. The slaughter will *block* the Travelers, and the word rendered "block" was translated "muzzle" the only other time it was used in the entire Bible. A muzzle prevents an animal from biting or feeding. Interpretations of Ezekiel 39:11 must have that sense of the word in mind. This isn't a physical barrier to travel caused by the multitude of corpses (although there will no doubt be an astonishing number of dead), it's a *spiritual* barrier that prevents the spirits of the Nephilim—the warriors of Baal, and the demigods and heroes of Greek mythology—from "biting" ever again.

Summary

At the risk of putting too fine a point on the thesis of this book, let's summarize it one more time. I've been studying deities and demigods for the better part of the last two years, but you most likely haven't. It's entirely possible that I haven't connected these names, dates, and places with enough skill to make the picture clear.

The Greeks and Romans inherited much of their religion from older societies to the east. Scholars don't know the exact order or routes of transmission, but by comparing the stories of their gods, and the type of worship and sacrifices they demanded, it's clear that the the accounts of creation, flood, and former gods now confined to the underworld moved over the centuries from Sumer and Syria toward the north and west, where they eventually reached Greece, Rome, and the rest of the Mediterranean world. Names changed, but the broad outlines of their stories remained the same.

This was a public relations effort by the Fallen to get out ahead of the Truth. The false religions of the rebel gods were ancient before Moses came down from Sinai with the Law. Several consistent themes emerged: The old gods, while confined to the netherworld, still had power to affect the living; spirits of the ancestors had to be appeased; and dead kings of old, the "men of renown," could be summoned through rituals to bless current rulers. Sometimes, as with the cults of Molech, Kronos, and Baal Hammon, the sacrifice of children was required to satisfy the old gods.

There were locations in and around the Holy Land connected to the dead, places where the spirits of the dead were believed to cross over, or travel, between the netherworld and the land of the living. The prophets, apostles, and Jesus Himself knew about this, which explains certain Bible verses related to the wilderness of Moab and Mount Hermon.

In the time of the end, entities that we've been taught are imaginary are coming back to wage war against our Creator. The Greeks called them Titans, gods, demigods, and heroes; the Amorites, neighbors of the ancient Israelites, summoned them, sacrificed to them, and believed their kings were descended from them. The Bible calls them angels, Watchers, Nephilim, Rephaim, devils, and demons.

Our children and grandchildren are being taught that these entities are awesome characters in movies, graphic novels, and young adult fiction. Schools assign homework to ask students, "Could you be a demigod?"[333] and to write essays explaining which immortal parent they'd choose if they could.[334]

Our society has been so convinced that the supernatural realm is unreal that most teachers and parents see no harm in this, even in Christian homes. We are called to be the firewall between this pagan propaganda and our families, but we've been told for so long that these entities are nonexistent, and their stories nothing more than classical literature, that we fail to see it for what is is—the greatest marketing campaign in history.

That lie will explode in the last days. God has seen the end from the beginning, and we recognize now in the prophecies of the Bible that He has not only planned the defeat of these rebels, but He will do it in a way that shows to one and all the futility of their schemes.

> He who sits in the heavens laughs;
> the Lord holds them in derision.
>> Then he will speak to them in his wrath,
>> and terrify them in his fury, saying,
>> "As for me, I have set my King
>> on Zion, my holy hill." (Psalm 2:4–6, ESV)

The Watchers are in Tartarus now, but they are loosed for five months at the end. With their demonic offspring and the rest of the rebel gods who still walk the earth, the angels who sinned will draw the kings of the earth into the greatest, most terrible battle the world has ever known: Armageddon, the Last Clash of the Titans.

THE FIGHT THAT SHOWS NO PITY

Christian Transhumanists and the Quest of Gilgamesh

For mankind, whatever life it has, be not sick at heart,
be not in despair, be not heart-stricken!
> The bane of mankind is thus come, I have told you,
> what was fixed when your navel-cord was cut is thus come,
> I have told you.
> The darkest day of mortal man has caught up with you,
> the solitary place of mortal man has caught up with you,
> the flood-wave that cannot be breasted has caught up with you,
> the battle that cannot be fled has caught up with you,
> the combat that cannot be matched has caught up with you,
> the fight that shows no pity has caught up with you!
—*Epic of Gilgamesh*

More than five thousand years ago, the legendary Sumerian king Gilgamesh embarked on a single-minded quest to procure the secret of immortality. According to the story, he was so distressed by the death of his best friend, Enkidu, and obsessed with overcoming his own mortality, that he tracked down the Sumerian Noah, Utnapishtim the Far-away, for advice.

A thousand years or so after Gilgamesh succumbed to the fate that awaits us all, around 2000 B.C., Amorites overwhelmed the native Sumerian and Akkadian rulers of the Fertile Crescent. By 1900 B.C., the time of Abraham, Amorite dynasties controlled nearly every kingdom and city-state from the Persian Gulf to the Levant—modern Iraq, Syria, Jordan, Lebanon, and Israel. By the time of Jacob, Amorites had moved south and taken over northern Egypt, too.

To the pre-Flood magical and religious practices of the Sumerians, the Amorites added ancestor worship, but with a twist. From the evidence, some of which has only been found within the last hundred years and translated within the last forty, it appears that the kings of the Amorites believed they descended from the gods who ruled before the Flood—the ones who, in Babylonian, Hittite, and Greek cosmology (as well as the Bible),[335] were locked away in an underworld prison reserved for supernatural threats to the divine order.

Further, the Amorites, at least during the second millennium B.C., performed rituals to summon the spirits of those gods to bless their kings.

Now, flash forward four thousand years to today: In the West, we've been so indoctrinated by positivism (a philosophy that teaches science is the only reliable tool for finding truth) that we're more likely to believe the old gods were alien astronauts than supernatural beings. But the quest to unlock the secret of immortality continues. The modern transhumanist movement holds out the same promise offered to Adam and Eve in Eden: To paraphrase, "Ye shall not surely die; your eyes shall be opened, and ye shall be as gods."

As Christians, we reject positivism. That's not to say we're anti-science, but admittance to our club requires believing (among other things) that an invisible, all-powerful deity spoke everything into existence; that He manifested as a fully human man in a dusty, backwater province of the Roman empire about two thousand years ago; that He died for our sins; and then, three days later, literally rose from the dead. There is no way to syncretize Christian faith with a philosophy that rejects theology and the metaphysical. And yet that's exactly what transhumanists are trying to do—even if most of them don't realize it or won't admit it.

Transhumanism is a growing movement that wants to fundamentally transform human physiology through cutting-edge technology, with the goal of achieving eternal life through science. In other words, transhumanists are trying to weld together two diametrically opposed worldviews—one based on the supernatural and the other that denies its existence.

Of all people, then, it's surprising to find that some Christians are making common cause with transhumanists. By so doing, these Christians are unwittingly summoning those old gods and offering them one last shot at knocking God off His mount of assembly.

That's why The Milieu is speaking up.

⸺

Two generations before Gilgamesh, a Sumerian king named Enmerkar ruled the ancient Near East. Both men ruled from the city of Uruk in what is today southeastern Iraq—which, you might have noticed, is just a different spelling of the city's name. In the Bible, it's spelled a third way—Erech, which, along with Babel, was "the beginning of [Nimrod's] kingdom." From there, the legendary kings of Uruk ruled nearly the entire Fertile Crescent, the land between the Euphrates and Tigris rivers in what is now Iraq, Syria, and southern Turkey. Scholars call this the Uruk Expansion, a period between about 4000 B.C. and 3100 B.C. Logically, Nimrod and Gilgamesh would fit somewhere in that time frame.

Like Nimrod, Enmerkar was the second generation after the Flood. In my book *The Great Inception*, I show why Babel is not to be confused with Babylon, which wasn't founded until at least a thousand years after the tower's construction was interrupted, and make the case that Enmerkar and Nimrod were one and the same. Babel was most probably at the ancient city of Eridu, and the tower was a ziggurat, the largest and oldest ever found in Mesopotamia, built as a temple to the Sumerian god Enki, the lord of the abyss.

According to a poem from the time of Abraham, Enmerkar/Nimrod hoped to build up the temple of Enki into a "holy mountain," and to "make the great abode, the abode of the gods, famous for me."[336] An abode of the gods directly above the *abzu*, the abyss? No wonder YHWH decided to personally intervene!

The Sumerian King List names Lugalbanda as Enmerkar's successor as king of Uruk, and he was succeeded in turn by Gilgamesh. We don't know whether Gilgamesh was Enmerkar/Nimrod's grandson, but scholars generally consider him a historical character. A team of German archaeologists mapped Uruk in 2001 and 2002 using cesium magnetometry, and among their discoveries was a building under what was the bed of the Euphrates River in the 3rd millennium B.C. that might be the burial crypt of the legendary king.[337]

We don't know whether Gilgamesh was Nimrod's grandson, but he had his predecessor's ambition and then some. Where Nimrod tried to conquer the known world and build a home for the gods in his kingdom, Gilgamesh set his sights on becoming immortal.

Evidence suggests that the king may have resorted to bringing back knowledge that had been lost beneath the waters of the Great Flood. According to the Book of Enoch, a group of angelic beings, called Watchers by the Hebrews, descended to the summit of Mount Hermon in the days of the patriarch Jared.[338] As Dr. Michael Heiser noted in *Reversing Hermon*, there was more to the visit of the Watchers than producing monstrous offspring; the rebellious angels brought with them information mankind was not meant to possess: Sorcery, charms, the cutting of roots and plants (probably for mixing potions), metalworking and the making of weapons, makeup (and presumably the art of seduction), and reading fortunes in the movement of the stars. In short, the Watchers lured humanity into evil, and "all the earth was filled with the godlessness and violence that had befallen it."[339]

Gilgamesh was referred to on a Mesopotamian cylinder seal "master of the apkallu,"[340] and by the time of Hammurabi the Great, who was probably a contemporary of Isaac and Jacob, Gilgamesh was viewed as the one who had returned to mankind the pre-Flood knowledge of the *apkal-lus*—the Mesopotamian name for the Watchers.[341] In fact, it appears the sages and priests of Babylon believed it was precisely that arcane knowledge which (to borrow a phrase) Made Babylon Great Again.

Interestingly, the Old Babylonian text of the Gilgamesh epic establishes another link between Gilgamesh and the Watchers. To make a name for himself, Gilgamesh and his drinking buddy Enkidu decided to kill Huwawa (or Humbaba), the monster who guarded the Cedar Forest. In a sense, the pair aimed for a sort of immortality by performing a great deed.

> Hear me, O elders of Uruk-the-Town-Square!
> I would tread the path to ferocious Huwawa,
> I would see the god, of whom men talk,
> whose name the lands do constantly repeat.
> I will conquer him in the Forest of Cedar:
> let the land learn Uruk's offshoot is mighty!
> Let me start out, I will cut down the cedar,
> I will establish forever a name eternal![342]

The Old Babylonian text of the epic locates the cedar forest on the peaks of "Hermon and Lebanon."[343] After killing Huwawa, the two friends "penetrated into the forest, opened the secret dwelling of the Anunnaki."[344]

This is significant for a couple of reasons. First, the mission of Gilgamesh and Enkidu may have been far darker than it appears on the surface. The late Dr. David Livingston, founder of Associates for Biblical Research, pointed out that "Huwawa" may have sounded a lot like "Yahweh" in ancient tongues. If Livingston was right, then the real mission of Gilgamesh was to achieve immortal fame and glory by killing the guardian of the secret home of the gods—Yahweh.[345]

Secondly, the Anunnaki, who were originally the great gods of

Mesopotamia, had become the gods of the underworld by the time of Abraham.[346] Marduk, after defeating the chaos dragon Tiamat, decreed that the Anunnaki, or at least half of them, should relocate permanently to the nether realm.[347] The Hittites, who lived north of Mesopotamia in what is now Turkey, identified the Anunnaki as primordial deities of the underworld, possibly "an earlier generation of gods who had retired or were banished by the younger gods now in charge."[348]

This is relevant because Gilgamesh, despite his desperate effort to avoid "the bane of mankind," died anyway—and upon his death, according to the legend, was made ruler of the dead.

> Gilgamesh, in the form of his ghost, dead in the underworld, shall be the governor of the Netherworld, chief of the shades![349]

This has special significance because of the importance of the ancestor cult among the Amorites, who founded the old kingdom of Babylon. For more than a thousand years, Amorites in the ancient Near East (modern Iraq, Syria, Lebanon, Jordan, Israel, Saudi Arabia, and northern Egypt) venerated their dead, especially the dead ancestors of their kings.[350] Although Gilgamesh was a Sumerian king who had departed this world a millennium before the great kings of Babylon, it seems he epitomized the venerated royal dead, and he played an important role in the ancestor cult and magical healing rituals of Babylon.[351]

In *The Great Inception*, I quote Canaanite (western Amorite) texts that describe rituals to summon the Rephaim—the spirits of the Nephilim (note that the Hebrew word rapha is sometimes rendered "shades" in the Bible)—and something called the Council of the Didanu, which was apparently an underworld assembly of the old gods.

Now, get this: Didanu was the name of an ancient Amorite tribe from which the kings of Babylon, old Assyria, and Canaan claimed descent, and—here's the good part—it was the word from which the Greeks got the name of their former gods, the Titans.[352]

Pause for that to sink in. Kings of the Amorites, neighbors of the ancient Hebrews from the time of Abraham through the time of the Judges, apparently believed they descended from gods later known to the Greeks as the Titans—the elder generation of deities who were overthrown by Zeus and the Olympians and banished to Tartarus.

Let's take a moment to stop and summarize here. This is starting to make my head spin, and I'm the one writing.

- Gilgamesh, a legendary (but probably historical) post-Flood king of Uruk in the fourth millennium B.C., was obsessed with finding the key to immortality.
- He died anyway sometime around 3000 B.C., give or take a few centuries.
- Amorites more than a thousand years later linked Gilgamesh with the "shades" (the Rephaim?), the *apkallu* (the Watchers/Titans), and the Anunnaki, the gods of the underworld.
- If the Hittites were correct in identifying the Anunnaki as "former gods" who'd been overthrown and banished to the netherworld, then they, too, can be identified as the Hebrew Watchers and Greek Titans.
- The Anunnaki and the Watchers (and thus the Titans) were linked to Mount Hermon. Mount Hermon is also where Gilgamesh and Enkidu killed the monstrous Huwawa.
- By comparing their stories with the Bible, we can identify the Titans, the Anunnaki, and the *apkallu* as the Watchers of Genesis 6, "the angels who did not stay within their own position of authority" who are "kept in eternal chains under gloomy darkness until the judgment of the great day."[353]

All well and good, you might say, but what does any of that ancient history have to do with modern transhumanism, and especially with Christians who call themselves transhumanists? Glad you asked.

Without realizing it, today's transhumanists are replicating the quest of Gilgamesh for the secret of immortality. Most transhumanists are atheists, which makes their mission easier to understand. (Although Gilgamesh wasn't an atheist, the Mesopotamian afterlife couldn't have been much fun if he was driven to such lengths to find a way to avoid it.)

Christian transhumanists, on the other hand, are more like Adam and Eve, or those who lived during the time of the Watchers' descent—people who should have known better (Adam lived another 470 years after the birth of Jared), but who willingly traded away their lives for secrets that would make them like gods. Or so they thought.

First things first: Your view of end-times prophecy has a powerful effect on how you live out your Christian faith. For example, if you believe that Jesus won't return until the end of the millennial reign prophesied in Revelation 20, or that the thousand-year reign is symbolic rather than literal, then it's understandable that you might believe a Christian's duty is to work toward the creation of Heaven on Earth.

Amillennialism, which teaches the latter view, is the majority view among the world's Christians. It is the official position of the largest Christian denominations—Roman Catholicism, the Eastern and Oriental Orthodox churches, and some of the mainline Protestant denominations. While many of the believers in the Catholic and Orthodox churches hold a supernatural worldview, it's no surprise that the combination of a scientistic culture and an eschatology that foresees the world getting better and better until Jesus returns would produce a subset of Christians who accept, at least in part, the philosophy of the transhumanists.

What is transhumanism, exactly? According to leading bioethicist Wesley J. Smith, it is "an emerging social movement that promotes the technological enhancement of human capacities toward the end of creating a utopian era in which 'post humans' will enjoy absolute morphological freedom and live for thousands of years."[354]

Transhumanists themselves are more direct in describing their goals and the means of attaining them:

> Biology mandates not only very limited durability, death and poor memory retention, but also limited speed of communication, transportation, learning, interaction and evolution…transhumanists everywhere must support the revolutionary movement against death and the existing biological order of things.[355]

In short, transhumanists believe God's design is inherently flawed, so we humans must get busy "speeding up evolution and becoming true masters of our destiny."[356]

Zoltan Istvan, who ran for president in 2016 as a candidate for the Transhumanist Party (which he founded), distilled the objectives of transhumanism into a philosophy he calls Teleological Egocentric Functionalism. Istvan summarized those ideas with his Three Laws of Transhumanism:

A transhumanist must safeguard one's own existence above all else.

A transhumanist must strive to achieve omnipotence as expediently as possible—so long as one's actions do not conflict with the First Law.

A transhumanist must safeguard value in the universe—so long as one's actions do not conflict with the First and Second Laws.[357]

You probably noticed that the first of Istvan's laws runs head first into Jesus' description of true love: "Greater love hath no man than this, that a man lay down his life for his friends."[358]

It shouldn't surprise you that Istvan is an atheist. His three laws make perfect sense to those who believe there's no God and no existence whatsoever after death. Even the actions of Jethro Knights, the protagonist of Istvan's novel *The Transhumanist Wager*, are understandable, if chilling. To rid the world of the corrosive superstition of religion (as Istvan sees it), Knights and his team of super geniuses form a new, independent nation called Transhumania, and then they proceed to destroy the Vatican, the

Kaaba in Mecca, and the Wailing Wall in Jerusalem, among other iconic religious and cultural sites around the world.

Knights has no problem with adopting a eugenics program that would have made Hitler proud:

> We need to divert the resources to the genuinely gifted and qualified. To the achievers of society—the ones who pay your bills by their innovation, genius, and hard work. They will find the best way to the future. Not the losers of the world, or the mediocre, or the downtrodden, or the fearful. They will only drag us down, like they already have.[359]

To be fair, even other transhumanists are put off by *The Transhumanist Wager*.

> *The Transhumanist Wager* has only one idea—a fascistic interpretation of the meaning of transhumanism in which the complexity of every other current of human thinking, including transhumanism itself, is reduced to a cartoon.[360]

I bring this up because it's important to understand that transhumanism means different things to different people, and not all transhumanists are ready to exterminate the "unfit."

Obviously, whether one believes in God is a key factor in whether one thinks living forever through technology is a good idea. But theists (like Christians) can have very different views of transhumanism ranging from acceptance to, well, The Milieu.

For example, there is a very active Mormon Transhumanist Association. This isn't entirely unexpected, since Mormon theology is about apotheosis (at least for men)—literally becoming gods.[361] But while it's a shorter leap to transhumanism from the doctrines of the Church of Latter Day Saints than from the New Testament, there are, as noted above, a small, but growing, Christian Transhumanist Association.

It is difficult to see how any Christian who holds a futurist view of prophecy can embrace transhumanism. That said, not all Christian transhumanists are working toward virtual immortality and "absolute morphological freedom"—changing one's body shape, physical abilities, and gender at will. Many of them appear to be concerned with just improving the quality of life for the poor and downtrodden, seeing this as a mission that follows in the footsteps of Jesus.

Yet well-meaning Christians who ally themselves with the transhumanist movement, because they believe advances in genetics, robotics, artificial intelligence, and nanotechnology will yield better tools for fulfilling this mission, are giving tacit approval to an alternate religion that promises salvation through technology. By promising to make us more than human, transhumanists and their Christian allies declare that God's design is imperfect and must be improved.

By us. Sure. Because we're smarter and have better technology than God.

In other words, in their effort to make humanity into H+, they will, ironically, downgrade the species to H-. And there is no guarantee that if they succeed to any degree, Humanity 2.0 will still be "human" in any meaningful way.

———

Christian transhumanists have good intentions. The Christian Transhumanist Association describes its mission as follows:

As Christian Transhumanists, we seek to use science & technology to participate in God's redemptive purposes, to cultivate life and renew creation.

1. We believe that God's mission involves the transformation and renewal of creation including humanity, and that we are called by Christ to participate in that mission: working against illness, hunger, oppression, injustice, and death.

2. We seek growth and progress along every dimension of our humanity: spiritual, physical, emotional, mental—and at all levels: individual, community, society, world.

3. We recognize science and technology as tangible expressions of our God-given impulse to explore and discover and as a natural outgrowth of being created in the image of God.

4. We are guided by Jesus' greatest commands to "Love the Lord your God with all your heart, soul, mind, and strength…and love your neighbor as yourself."

5. We believe that the intentional use of technology, coupled with following Christ, will empower us to become more human across the scope of what it means to be creatures in the image of God.[362]

Analyzing the CTA's affirmation runs the risk of setting up a series of straw men, and we don't have any intention of doing that if we can help it. How we respond to their five points depends on how we define our terms.

The opening statement sounds harmless enough, but what exactly is meant by participating in "God's redemptive purposes"? If we accept the definition of the word "redemptive" as "acting to save someone from error or evil," then transhumanism, properly directed, is a means toward that end. Who can look on a child suffering from, say, a debilitating injury or genetic defect of any type without thinking it an error or evil? Wouldn't any of us use whatever was in our power to correct such a wrong?

But how do we define "error" or "evil"? If we interpret God's redemptive purpose according to the straightforward gospel that Paul gave to the church at Corinth "as of first importance"—that "Christ died for our sins in accordance with the Scriptures, that he was buried, that he was raised on the third day in accordance with the Scriptures"[363]—then the evil from which we are redeemed is spiritual, even if the physical, emotional, and mental imperfections that plague our world are sometimes side effects of that evil. In other words, what the Christian Transhumanist Association calls "the transformation and renewal of creation" needs sharper definition before we can sign on to that mission.

And we are certainly sympathetic to "working against illness, hunger, oppression, injustice, and death." Jesus healed the sick and fed the hungry, and the Bible is clear about a Christian's duty to help the poor, orphans, and widows. But Jesus also came "to destroy the works of the devil."[364] He cast out a lot of demons, and his choice of Mount Hermon for the Transfiguration was deliberate.[365] We are in the middle of a very long spiritual war, and God isn't called Lord of Hosts—i.e., Lord of Armies—for nothing.

Jesus didn't say, "The poor you always have with you," because there aren't enough charities, but because evil is the default setting of the human heart. There will always be men and women who enrich themselves at the expense of others.

That is the evil from which the world must be redeemed. And Christ is the Redeemer—not you and me.

That's the heart of the matter. What are Christian transhumanists trying to accomplish? While they embrace science, technology, and the full engagement of our minds in the service of our Lord, they recognize the danger in going too far. Scientists and tech entrepreneurs like Stephen Hawking and Elon Musk have likewise sounded warnings about the dangers of runaway science; in fact, Musk described the development of artificial intelligence, "our biggest existential threat," as "summoning the demon."[366]

The Rev. Dr. Christopher J. Benek, founding chair of the Christian Transhumanist Association, acknowledges that "the practical outcomes of escapist concepts in science and technology are just as bad as they are in theology."[367] But, like Hawking and Musk, he argues that we must push forward anyway:

> Christians are called to help in Christ's redemptive purposes on earth as we seek to actualize Christ's great prayer "on Earth as it is in Heaven."

The reality of humanity is that humans are called to be CoCreators with God and one another. We have a divine appointment
to explore possibilities and discern what constitutes proper choices
in order to appropriately steward science and technology.[368]

Well, we can agree in part. Yes, we Christians have a duty to appropriately steward science and technology. That's why I'm proud to be called a part
of The Milieu, and why I'm writing this instead of watching Doctor Who.

But "CoCreators with God"?

Whoa, there. That's where we run into trouble. That's where hubris
can lead to spectacular mistakes. While I don't think for a minute that
Christian transhumanists are likely to do anything close to what secular
transhumanists propose (like merging human biology with machinery to
acquire godlike abilities), just describing the mission as co-creation with
God moves humanity up a step in the cosmic order without His express
written consent.

Frankly, the concept of co-creation moves uncomfortably close to territory occupied by Dominionists, a group within charismatic Christian-
ity that believes we Christians must literally take over the world before
Jesus can return. They, too, would describe their mission as participating
in "Christ's redemptive purposes on earth." They believe we're called to
defeat God's enemies and make them a footstool beneath Christ's feet.
What could be more redemptive than that?

Christian transhumanists don't share that view. My concern is that
their emphasis is on the wrong end of the rope. As noble as their motives
are, they're pulling in the same direction as the rest of the transhumanists; which is to say, Luciferian transhumanists—an accurate description,
whether they recognize it or not.

I don't mean that non-Christian transhumanists worship Satan.
Most of them wouldn't even acknowledge the existence of Satan.[369] By
"Luciferian," I mean they're committed to the goal of creating Heaven on
Earth—what scholars would call "anthropocentric soteriology," or salva-
tion by our own works.

Being Christians, I am confident that the Rev. Dr. Benek and his colleagues deny that their hope for salvation is in anything other than the atoning death of Jesus Christ. But then that begs the question: Why work for the "transformation and renewal of creation"? Dr. Benek rationalizes it thus:

> When Christ sent people out—to effectively do what seems miraculous from [a] given perspective in time—he was calling them to imagine a better way of looking at the world and then challenging them to believe that better way into existence with action. Now that technology is expanding the possibilities of our imaginations, we are faced with new opportunities to virtuously live into the wonder of these possibilities.[370]

But those weren't our marching orders. In the beginning, we were told to "be fruitful and multiply and fill the earth and subdue it."[371] Later, Jesus commanded His disciples to "go therefore and make disciples of all nations, baptizing them in the name of the Father and of the Son and of the Holy Spirit."[372] There was nothing in there about transforming and renewing. That's what the military calls mission creep.

And it can be dangerous. First, it puts our focus on this world instead of the next. Christians have an absolute duty to demonstrate sacrificial love to those around us—but we should never, ever forget that the whole point of doing so is to open doors so that we can share the gospel of Jesus Christ.

Second, we're on the verge of being able to permanently change what it means to be human at the genetic level. We are nearing a day when we can create an autonomous intelligence capable of thinking millions, if not billions, of times faster than us. It is misguided to join forces with those who not only want to put that kind of power into human hands, they want to redesign and fundamentally transform God's ultimate creation, humankind.

That is ironic. As Christians, we are all transhumanists by definition. To paraphrase what Paul wrote to the Corinthians, we won't all die but we will all be changed.[373] At His return, Jesus will grant all who have accepted Him as Lord the immortality we were originally created to enjoy.

Now, it's understandable that non-Christian transhumanists would reject that in favor of a Manhattan Project-scale effort to unlock the key to eternal life. By why on God's green earth would a Christian trade that God's promise for an offer of artificial immortality?

———

A few final thoughts and some speculation from a prophetic perspective. If advances in genetics, robotics, artificial intelligence, and nanotechnology ever succeed in bringing virtually unlimited lifespans to humanity, it's not going to create the Heaven on Earth transhumanists are looking for.

As with every breakthrough in medicine, science, and technology, it will be reserved for the military or the wealthy, at least at first. Lt. Col. Robert Maginnis and journalist Annie Jacobsen have explored the potential military uses of cutting edge tech in their books *Future War* and *The Pentagon's Brain*. If there are perceived advantages to restricting radical life extension technologies for the military, you can bet civilians won't see them.

If and when the private sector does get access to medical miracles, the wealthy will be the beneficiaries. You might ask why I'm so skeptical. Fair enough. Consider education: Isn't it in the best interests of society to provide the highest quality education for every child? In fact, wouldn't society be better off if the lowest economic classes were given priority access to the best schools?

Of course it would. So, why do the wealthy send their children to expensive, top-notch learning academies that are out of reach for the poor and middle class?

Because they can. Be honest—if you could do that for your kids and grandkids, wouldn't you?

Now, ask a transhumanist: Why do they think physical and mental upgrades that offer godlike power and near-immortality will be available for everybody?

Next question: Who gets to upgrade? Refer back to the attitude of Zoltan Istvan's fictional transhumanist hero, Jethro Knights:

Not the losers of the world, or the mediocre, or the downtrodden, or the fearful. They will only drag us down, like they already have.[374]

Obvious follow-up: Who decides who's a loser, or mediocre, or downtrodden? Transhumanism's promise of immortality could easily bring back the eugenics programs of the last century, which sought to improve mankind by removing the unfit from the gene pool.

It is a sad legacy of the United States that the eugenics program adopted by Hitler's Germany was modeled in part on the one in California.[375] Indiana was the first state in the Union to adopt a compulsory sterilization law (1909), but even though eugenics lost public support after World War II because of the horror of the Nazis' implementation, women were still being sterilized in some states until the 1970s.[376]

Although the United States Congress recently repealed the individual health insurance mandate, American progressives will keep fighting for a single-payer system. If they get their wish, how long before the right to have children is restricted for people with a family history of poor health to keep health care costs down for everyone else? And then how long before government requires genetic "improvements" to ensure all babies are healthy? And for a small up-charge, parents can specify height, minimum IQ, gender, eye color, and sexual preference. (Think that's an exaggeration? A National Academy of Sciences panel has already endorsed the concept of "designer babies," at least in limited circumstances.)[377]

We won't even bring up death panels for the elderly. I will, however, point out that a global push to legalize euthanasia is growing. In Belgium, a child who isn't terminally ill may be put to death if a doctor deems them mature enough to make that decision. In the Netherlands, where infanticide is still illegal, doctors admit that killing sick and disabled babies goes on anyway.[378]

Already, transhumanists—unwittingly, I'm guessing, because I can't believe they'd do this on purpose—have adopted the motto of the International Eugenics Congresses held in 1912, 1921, and 1932: "Self-directed evolution."[379]

How quickly we forget.

Next question: Assuming that science somehow overcomes the problems of death and distribution and rolls out the miracle of immortality to everyone on earth, does that really look like Heaven?

Here's why I ask: Imagine a world where most of the people, who do *not* subscribe to a biblical standard of morality, are immortal, and therefore no longer restrained from doing things that might have gotten them killed previously. Put another way, imagine a world in which Adolf Hitler, Josef Stalin, and Charles Manson could never die—and where others, who might have been too afraid of dying to live out their vile fantasies, no longer have that check on their behavior.

I don't know about you, but that sounds more like Hell than Heaven to me.

Last question: How can Christians with a true understanding of what's at stake call themselves transhumanists?

———

Now the speculation: For several years now, we've considered the possibility that an autonomous artificial intelligence might be used by the Antichrist to give life to the image of the Beast. While this sounds like science fiction, it's not a new idea.

More than a hundred years ago, theologian E. W. Bullinger put forward the very same idea in his commentary on the Book of Revelation:

Nikola Tesla, the Hungarian-American electrician, boldly declares (in The Century magazine for June, 1900), that he has a plan for the construction of an automaton which shall have its "own mind," and be able, "independent of any operator, to perform a great variety of acts and operations as if it had intelligence." He speaks of it, not as a miracle, of course, but only as an invention which he "has now perfected."

But again we say we care not how it is going to be done. God's word declares that it will be done, and we believe it.... We already hear of talking machines; with "a little" Satanic power thrown in, it will be a miracle very easily worked.[380]

Bullinger was not without controversial beliefs. He was an ultradispensationalist,[381] a believer in the cessation of the soul between death and resurrection,[382] and a member of the Universal Zetetic Society—a flat-earther.[383] Regardless, Bullinger's 1903 observation about the potential prophetic application of Tesla's research was profoundly insightful and relevant to our discussion of the transhumanist movement.

The human body in general, and the brain especially, is a bio-electrical machine. An electroencephalogram measures electrical activity in the brain to diagnose disorders such as epilepsy.[384] As Christians, we know (or we should) that this bio-electrical device can be overwhelmed and controlled by an external entity—it's what we call "demonic possession." Is it possible, then, that an autonomous, electrical superintelligence could provide a substrate for "the image of the Beast"?

Speculative, yes. Has this phenomenon ever observed? The abomination that was Windows ME notwithstanding, no, not as far as we know. But then, there wouldn't be any advantage for the Enemy to disclose this ability. To quote the famous line by Baudelaire (paraphrased in the popular 1995 film *The Usual Suspects*), "The finest trick of the devil is to persuade you that he does not exist."

This is precisely the type of blind spot to which Christian transhumanists have fallen victim. They're not alone, of course; about 60 percent of American Christians believe Satan "is not a living being but is a symbol of evil."[385] In my forthcoming book, *Last Clash of the Titans*, I'll make the case that the horde of Magog in Ezekiel 38 and 39, which is the army that comes against Jerusalem at Armageddon, is linked to the "shades"—the Rephaim, which, I argue, the ancient Amorites believed were the spirits of the Nephilim.

We can't say with certainty that artificial intelligence will produce the false miracle that is the resurrected Beast or an army of demonically possessed supersoldiers, but it is a fact that leading transhumanists see their goal as transcendence—rising above the limits of our flawed (they think) biology. Inventor Ray Kurzweil, Google's Director of Engineering, foresees what he calls the Singularity, "a future period during which the pace of technological change will be so rapid, its impact so deep, that human life will be irreversibly transformed."[386]

Kurzweil and his followers mean that literally. They foresee what Dr. Kurzweil calls the Sixth Epoch of Evolution. In his view, we're now in the final stages of Epoch 4 (humans working with technology) and about to enter Epoch 5, where biology and technology merge to create higher forms of life. Epoch 6 is when "the Universe wakes up," and virtually immortal human-machine hybrids go forth into the universe, presumably to be fruitful and multiply.[387]

Seriously.

As speculative as it sounds, this, like a demonically possessed AI, is not a new idea. The French Jesuit Pierre Teilhard de Chardin, a paleontologist by training and philosopher by nature, believed in the reverse entropy of Darwinian evolution. In his 1959 book, *The Phenomenon of Man*, Teilhard theorized that creation was evolving to ever-higher levels of complexity toward something he called he called the Omega Point. At some future date, he believed, a sphere of sentient thought surrounding the earth he called the noosphere joins with itself, human thought unifies, and "our ancient itch to flee this woeful orb will finally be satisfied as the immense expanse of cosmic matter collapses like some mathematician's hypercube into absolute spirit."[388]

In other words, mind merges with matter and the universe wakes up. Teilhard's Omega Point and Kurzweil's Singularity are the same thing.

Although Teilhard's writings were cited with a warning by the Vatican in 1962, the Pontifical Council for Culture recently approved a petition asking Pope Francis to remove it. The council expressed its desire for the pope to "acknowledge the genuine effort of the pious Jesuit to reconcile the scientific vision of the universe with Christian eschatology."[389] The problem is that any such reconciliation of science and the Bible is neither scientific nor biblical. There is no evidence to support Teilhard's theory of a noosphere as a "living thinking machine with enormous physical powers,"[390] and believing in his Omega Point (and likewise the transhumanist Singularity) requires throwing out the Book of Revelation, for a start, and then deleting every other end-times prophecy in the rest of the Bible.

But transhumanists have begun to recognize that appealing to Teilhard's work can help them win over skeptical Christians by providing christianized language to describe their vision of the future.[391] Christians should see through this ruse. Trading God's promise of a resurrected, incorruptible body for the transhumanists' promise of eternal life for you in a cosmic mainframe is like Esau trading his inheritance to Jacob for a bowl of beans.

—◦—

Transhumanists believe the Singularity will be humanity's crowning achievement, our great evolutionary leap forward to finally exceed the limits of our biology—in other words, apotheosis; finally realizing the promise from the garden to "be as gods."

This is a sad delusion. Transhumanism is nothing more than the ill-fated quest of Gilgamesh with a sci-fi veneer.

Now, the search will unquestionably yield benefits. We in The Milieu are not technophobes.[392] Medical advances are a good thing, but they are *restoration*, not *transformation*. Christians should never confuse the two. An artificial knee is not the first installment in a full-body immortality upgrade.

According to the epic, when Gilgamesh died, he was laid to rest in a tomb of stone in the bed of the Euphrates River. There is evidence that Gilgamesh didn't go to his eternal rest alone:

His beloved wife, his beloved children, his beloved favorite and junior wife, his beloved musician, cup-bearer and ......, his beloved barber, his beloved ......, his beloved palace retainers and servants and his beloved objects were laid down in their places as if ...... in the purified (?) palace in the middle of Uruk.[393]

Scholars have debated the meaning of that text for the last hundred years, but tombs of the wealthy at the Sumerian city of Ur, dated at least five hundred years after the probable time of Gilgamesh, included as many as sixty-five servants and retainers.[394] It's possible that this was a tradition that extended back to the kingdom of Uruk ruled by Gilgamesh, and by Nimrod before him.

Sadly, Christian transhumanists are following in the footsteps of Gilgamesh. While we take them at their word that they have accepted Christ as Lord, and are thus ensured of eternity in our Father's house, they, like the king of old, may be leading their beloved spouses, children, friends, and colleagues into death by signaling that Kurzweil is an acceptable substitute for Jesus Christ.

And the journey of unsaved transhumanists will not end inside an earthly tomb. If their trust is in science instead of Christ—in hoping to find their names written in lines of incorruptible computer code rather than in the Book of Life—then their final destination is the second death and a place in the Lake of Fire.

APPENDIX

II

GENERATIONS OF THE GODS

Trying to draw precise, one-to-one connections between the gods of ancient cultures is a good way to drive yourself crazy. First of all, we don't have all of the ancient texts. Some have been destroyed. Papyrus and clay don't last forever. Other documents are undiscovered, still hidden under sand, soil, and sea. Apparent contradictions in the stories may have embedded themselves in the stories as they were repeated, changing and twisting as cultures and languages evolved over the centuries.

We must also remember that since the pagan gods rebelled against the Creator, there is a high probability that the stories they told their followers were half-truths at best.

The best we can do is offer some basic connections to show that the gods of the ancient Near East were the source of the myths and religions of the Western world, and they were well known to the Hebrew prophets and the apostles of the early Christian church.

Generation 1: The Sky-god

Anu (Mesopotamia/Anatolia) – Patron god of the city of Uruk until about the middle of the fourth millennium B.C. Based on the epic poem *Enmerkar and the Lord of Aratta*, it appears Anu was replaced by Inanna (Ishtar), the goddess of sex and war, during the reign of Enmerkar, the second king of Uruk after the Flood. Anu was the father of Enlil and Enki, the other main gods of the Sumerian pantheon. Enlil had already replaced Anu as the chief god of Mesopotamia by the time of the first written records in Sumer, around 3000 B.C. Anu occupied the same slot in the pantheon of the Hurrians and Hittites, who occupied the area from northern Iraq west through most of Turkey from about 2100 B.C. until about 1200 B.C.

Ouranos (Greeks) – Sky-god of the Greek pantheon and father, with Gaia (Earth), of the Titans. According to myth, Ouranos kept his children imprisoned inside Gaia, which caused her great distress. Eventually, Gaia convinced her children to rebel against their father. Taking the lead, the youngest, Kronos, castrated Ouranos with an adamantine sickle and assumed his place at the head of the pantheon.

Caelus (Roman) – Roman manifestation of Ouranos. His name comes from the Latin *caelum* ("sky" or "heavens"), from which we get the English word "celestial." Interestingly, one of the groups of "extraterrestrials" purportedly known to the UFO community is referred to as Celestials. Josh Peck and I discuss them in our book *The Day the Earth Stands Still.* According to the now-deceased NASA astronaut Dr. Edgar Mitchell, Celestials are warlike ETIs kept in check by peaceful ETIs from a "contiguous universe" who are loyal to God. (If this sounds like a crock, you're right. As noted above, the rebel gods lie.)

We believe Anu/Ouranos/Caelus is a false identity given by the rebel gods to the Creator, Yahweh. Note that this god is depicted as distant, uncaring, and powerless. In most of the myths—Hurrian, Hittite, Greek, and Roman—he was castrated by his son and successor, which is the ultimate indignity.

Generation 2: The Wind-god or Grain-god

Enlil (Sumer and Akkad) – Enlil, "lord of the wind," was the king of the gods in Sumer and Akkad (modern Iraq) from about 3000 B.C. until the rise of Babylon around 1800 B.C., when he was replaced by the city god of Babylon, Marduk. Enlil conveyed kingship on human rulers but was also the god who wanted to annihilate the human race with a global flood because our noise kept him from sleeping. Unlike the later Hittite, Hurrian, Greek, and Roman stories, Enlil seems to have taken the top spot of the pantheon from Anu without any kind of coup or violence.

Dagan (Middle Euphrates region) – A grain-god who occupied the pantheon "slot" and role of Enlil in along the Euphrates River in what is modern Syria. He's attested in that region as far back as 2500 B.C. As Dagon, he was the chief god of the Philistines during the time of the judges in the Bible, although changes in language modified the spelling and pronunciation of his name. Little is known about Dagan and his precise connections to the underworld, although texts have been found documenting his epithet "Lord of the Corpse." Contrary to an old and popular misconception, there is no evidence whatsoever from the ancient world that Dagan/Dagon was ever considered a fish-god.

El (Canaan) – Creator god of the Canaanites (i.e., the western Amorites). Texts from the ancient kingdom of Ugarit, dated to the time of the judges, place the tabernacle or sanctuary of El at Mount Hermon. He was depicted as an ancient deity, bearded and gray, but still lusty—which may explain the common epithet "Bull El." He appointed the storm-god Baal (Hadad) king of the gods, but only after first passing the kingship to Yam, the sea-god, who was defeated by Hadad in combat. Interestingly, we don't have any record of El replacing an older god, which may have been by design. Due to the close proximity of the Canaanites to the Israelites, the rebel gods may have changed the story to conflate El and Yahweh in the minds of the Hebrews. And it's a fact that many scholars today believe Yahweh and El are one and the same.

Kumarbi (Hurrians and Hittites) – A grain-god worshiped by the people who lived in northern Mesopotamia and Anatolia (modern Turkey). According to the Hurrian myth, Kumarbi fought his father Anu for the kingship and succeeded by castrating Anu—with his teeth.

Kronos (Greeks) – Youngest son of Ouranos and Gaia who became king of the gods when he castrated his father with an adamantine sickle. His parents later prophesied that Kronos would be deposed by his children, so the Titan swallowed his children as soon as his wife, Rhea, gave birth. His use of a sickle as a weapon not only suggests that Kronos was a grain-god, it points to his origin in Anatolia where the Hittites used sickle-swords in combat. Attested in Greek literature beginning around the seventh century B.C.

Saturn (Romans) – Roman equivalent of Kronos. The main difference in their mythologies is that the Romans believed Saturn had escaped the netherworld after being overthrown by Jupiter, arriving in Italy in ancient times as a fugitive. His worship is attested from the third century B.C. on.

Baal Hammon (Phoenicians) – Chief god of Carthage, the Phoenician colony in north Africa established by Tyre around 800 B.C. Specifically identified as Saturn and Kronos by Greek historians of the classical era. He emerged as the chief god of Carthage after the city broke relations with Tyre around 480 B.C. Child sacrifice was an element of the worship of Baal Hammon; some twenty thousand burial urns containing the charred remains of newborns and infants were found at the Tophet in Carthage.

We believe these gods are various identities of the fallen angel we identify as the leader of the rebellious Watchers, called Shemihazah in the Book of 1 Enoch. The Watchers were the angels who sinned referred to in 2 Peter 2:4.

Generation 3: The Storm-god

Marduk (Mesopotamia) – Marduk replaced Enlil as king of the gods when Babylon emerged as the dominant political power in the ancient

Near East in the eighteenth century B.C., about the time of Isaac and Jacob. Little is known about Marduk before Babylon's rise; it appears he was simply the patron god of Babylon which, until the time of Abraham, had been an unimportant village surrounded by more powerful city-states. Marduk wasn't a storm-god *per se*, but had aspects of the storm-god (called Ishkur in Sumer) attributed to him.

**Addu/Hadad/Ba`al (Syria/Canaan)** – This is the Baal of the Bible. Ba`al simply means "lord," but it became a personal name over time. He ascended to the kingship by defeating El's first choice, Yam the sea-god, and surviving a challenge from Mot, the god of death, who was called (surprisingly) the "beloved of El."

Baal's holy mountain, Zaphon (Jebel al-Aqra on the Mediterranean coast of Turkey), was so important to his Canaanite worshipers that *tsaphon* became the Hebrew word for the compass point "north." While Baal didn't fight El for the kingship, the fact that he had to fight two of El's preferred choices for the throne suggests that their relationship was pretty dysfunctional.

Teshub/Tarhunz (Hurrians/Hittites) – Essentially Hadad by a different name. Worshiped by the Hurrian and Hittite people who lived in what is today Turkey and northern Syria and Iraq. Teshub avenged the indignity done to his grandfather, Anu, by defeating Kumarbi in battle and banishing him to the underworld.

Zeus (Greeks) – According to the Greek myth, Zeus was spared being eaten by Kronos when Rhea substituted a stone wrapped in swaddling clothes for the baby storm-god. Zeus was raised in secret on Crete, and when he reached maturity, he slipped Kronos a mickey that caused his father to cough up his siblings. After a terrible war called the Titanomachy, Zeus and the Olympians sent Kronos and the Titans to Tartarus. The tension between Zeus and his brothers, Poseidon the sea-god and Hades the death-god, echoes the conflict between the Canaanite gods Baal, Yam, and Mot, which is more evidence that the origin of the Greek myths was in the religion of Mesopotamia, and specifically the Amorites.

Jupiter (Romans) – Essentially the same god under a different name. Interestingly, classical historians noted that while Jupiter was the head of Rome's imperial religion, the common people still worshiped Saturn (Kronos/Baal Hammon), especially in north Africa where Phoenician influence was apparently still strong.

It is not a coincidence that the storm-god emerges as king of the gods in nearly every culture linked to the ancient Near East. This is the entity Isaiah linked to the divine rebel in Eden and was identified by Jesus as Satan.

The Venerated Dead

Nephilim – Offspring of the "sons of God" and "daughters of man," as recorded in Genesis 6:1–4. Upon death, their spirits became the demons that still plague the earth to this day.

Rephaim – Another name for the Nephilim and their descendants. They were known to the Israelites as the tribes inhabiting the Transjordan from Mount Hermon to the Dead Sea, the lands of Bashan, Ammon, Moab, and Edom from north to south. They were also called Emim, Zamzummim, Horim, and Anakim. The Anakim lived in the hill country of Judah and Israel and were the primary target of the war of Joshua.

The Rephaim were also known to the Amorites, as suggested by the popular name of Amorite kings, Ammurapi/Hammurabi ("My kinsmen are Rephaim"). As in the Bible, they seem to have been considered mighty kings of old and accorded special status in the afterlife. They were also summoned in rituals found at the Amorite kingdom of Ugarit in which they were called "warriors of Baal" and "travelers," in the sense that they traveled, or crossed over, from one plane of existence to another.

Heroes – A concept very different to ancient Greeks than to us in the twenty-first century. They were, to borrow a biblical phrase, the mighty men who were of old, demigods and kings to which supernatural events were attributed after their deaths. They were worshiped, and scholar Amar Annus has shown that the term used by the poet Hesiod to describe the heroes of the Golden Age ruled by Kronos is based on the same Semitic root from which we get the name Rephaim. In other words, demigods and heroes like Herakles/Hercules, Theseus, and Bellerophon were, by definition, Rephaim, and thus Nephilim.

Summary

There are many other gods in all these cultures, of course, but in this book, we're concerned with deities who convinced the pagan world that they once ruled supreme. They are variously called Titans, Anunnaki, and "former gods," but the story originates with the Watchers—angels who rebelled against God and were punished by confinement in the nether-world until the Day of the Lord.

APPENDIX

III

THE TIMELINE

This is, of course, only my best estimate of the important dates in ancient history. Scholars and lay people alike will disagree with some or all of these dates.

~4000 B.C.	The great Flood of Noah
~3500 B.C.	Nimrod (Sumerian king Enmerkar) builds Babel at city of Eridu
3200 B.C.	Bronze Age begins
~3000 B.C.	Oldest known writing in Sumer
~2500 B.C.	Amorites mentioned in tablets at Ebla (northern Syria)
2004 B.C.	Last Sumerian kingdom in Mesopotamia collapses
1894 B.C.	Amorite kingdom of Babylon founded
1876 B.C.	Abraham arrives in Canaan
1851 B.C.	Isaac born
1792 B.C.	Hammurabi crowned king of Babylon
1791 B.C.	Jacob and Esau born
1776 B.C.	Abraham dies
~1750 B.C.	Amorites (the Hyksos) take over Lower (northern) Egypt

1661 B.C.	Jacob arrives in Egypt
1595 B.C.	Amorite dynasty of Babylon falls to Kassites, who rename city Karanduniash
~1550 B.C.	Hyksos driven out of Egypt
1446 B.C.	Moses leads the Exodus
1406 B.C.	Joshua begins the conquest of Canaan
~1250 B.C.	Trojan War
~1200 B.C.	Last Amorite king of Ugarit, Ammurapi III, crowned with necromancy ritual
1200-1150 BC	Sea Peoples overrun most of eastern Mediterranean, the "Bronze Age Collapse"
1155 B.C.	Kassite Babylon falls to Assyria
~1007 B.C.	David crowned king of Judah
~1000 B.C.	David crowned king of all Israel
971 B.C.	Solomon becomes king of Israel
722 B.C.	Samaria conquered by Assyria; northern tribes deported
600s B.C.	Greek poet Hesiod writes *Theogony* and *Works and Days*
605 B.C.	Nabopolassar makes Babylon great again
582 B.C.	Jerusalem sacked by Nebuchadnezzar; Jews exiled to Babylon
532 B.C.	Cyrus allows Jews to return to Jerusalem
332 B.C.	Alexander the Great conquers the Levant
200 B.C.	Antiochus III the Great takes Judea from Ptolemy V Epiphanes of Egypt
167 B.C.	Antiochus IV Epiphanes erects altar to Zeus in the Temple; Maccabees lead revolt
165 B.C.	Temple liberated and rededicated; Hasmonean dynasty rules Judea
63 B.C.	Romans invade and make Judea a client state
40 B.C.	Parthians invade Judea
37 B.C.	Herod the Great drives out Parthians with Roman help
4 B.C.	Jesus born in Bethlehem

NOTES

1. Barna Group (2009). "Most American Christians Do Not Believe that Satan or the Holy Spirit Exist," https://www.barna.com/research/most-american-christians-do-not-believe-that-satan-or-the-holy-spirit-exist/, retrieved 4/29/18.
2. Hosea 4:6.
3. See Psalm 82.
4. Pritchard, James B., editor. 1958. *The Ancient Near East: Volume I, An Anthology of Texts and Pictures*, (Princeton, NJ: Princeton University Press) p. 225.
5. Homer. *Iliad Book VIII*, A.T. Murray translation. http://www.perseus.tufts.edu/hopper/text?doc=urn:cts:greekLit:tlg0012.tlg001.perseus-eng1:8.1-8.40, retrieved 11/12/17.
6. Hesiod. *Theogony*. Hugh G. Evelyn-White translation. http://www.perseus.tufts.edu/hopper/text?doc=Perseus%3Atext%3A1999.01.0130%3Acard%3D687, retrieved 11/12/17.
7. Lipinski, E. (1971). "El's Abode: Mythological Traditions Related to Mount Hermon and to the Mountains of Armenia" (p. 69). *Orientalia Lovaniensa Periodica* II.
8. Ugaritic text KTU 1.4, vi, 46.
9. Whiting, Robert M. "Amorite Tribes and Nations of Second-Millennium Western Asia," in J. M. Sasson, ed., *Civilizations of the Ancient Near East*, vol. 2 (New York: Charles Scribners Sons, 1995), p. 1234.

10. Silver, Minna. "The Earliest State Formation of the Amorites: Archaeological Perspectives from Jebel Bishri," in *Aram* 26: 1 & 2 (Oxford: Aram Publishing, 2014), p. 244.

11. Whiting, op. cit.

12. Chiera, Edward & Kramer, Samuel Noah & University of Pennsylvania. University Museum. Babylonian Section. *Sumerian Epics and Myths* (Chicago: The University of Chicago Press, 1934), plate nos. 58 and 112.

13. There is good scriptural evidence for this. See Joshua 24:2–3, where Joshua recalls that Abraham came from "beyond the Euphrates." Ur in Sumer is on the west bank of the river, meaning one does not cross it to travel to Canaan. Harran, on the other hand, is on the opposite side of the Euphrates from Canaan (and it's known from a Hittite text that a town named Ura was close by). See Gordon, Cyrus H. "Abraham and the Merchants of Ura," *Journal of Near Eastern Studies* 17:1 (1958), pp. 28–31.

14. Bodi, Daniel. "Is There a Connection Between the Amorites and the Arameans?", *Aram* 26:1 & 2 (Oxford: Aram Publishing, 2014), p. 385.

15. Spronk, K. (1999). "Dedan," in Karel van der Toorn, Bob Becking, Pieter Willem van der Horst, eds., *Dictionary of Deities and Demons in the Bible.* (Leiden: Brill), p. 232.

16. Silver, Minna. "Climate Change, the Mardu Wall, and the Fall of Ur," in: Olga Drewnowska and Malgorzata Sandowicz, eds., *Fortune and Misfortune in the Ancient Near East: Proceedings of the 60th Rencontre Assyriologique Internationale Warsaw, 21–25 July 2014* (Winona Lake, IN: Eisenbrauns, 2016), p. 277.

17. Ibid., p. 276.

18. Ibid., p. 277.

19. Jacobsen, Thorkild. *Cuneiform Texts in the National Museum, Copenhagen, Chiefly of Economical Contents* (Leiden: Brill, 1939), p. 7.

20. Sallaberger, Walther. "From Urban Culture to Nomadism: A History of Upper Mesopotamia in the Late Third Millennium," in: Catherine Kuzucuoğlu and Catherine Marro, eds., *Sociétés humaines et changement climatique à la fin du troisième millénaire: une crise a-t-elle eu lieu en Haute Mésopotamie?, Actes du Colloque de Lyon (5-8 décembre 2005)* (Istanbul: Institut Français d'Études Anatoliennes-Georges Dumézil, 2007), pp. 444–445.

21. Whiting, op. cit., p. 1235.

22. Genesis 10:10.

23. Gilbert, D. (2017). *The Great Inception: Satan's PSYOPs from Eden to Armageddon* (p. 22). Crane, Mo.: Defender.

24. Wall-Romana, C. (1990). "An Areal Location of Agade" (pp. 205–245). *Journal of Near Eastern Studies*, Vol. 49, No. 3.

25. Albright, W. (1944) "The End of 'Calneh in Shinar'" (pp. 254–255). *Journal of Near Eastern Studies* 3, no. 4.

26. Genesis 10:11–12.

27. Jarus, O. (2010) "New Discoveries Hint at 5,500 Year Old Fratricide at Hamoukar, Syria." *The Independent* (Sept. 24, 2010). http://www.independent.co.uk/life-style/history/new-discoveries-hint-at-5500-year-old-fratricide-at-hamoukar-syria-2088467.html, retrieved 11/19/17.

28. Roux, G. (1992). *Ancient Iraq: Third Edition.* (London: Penguin Books). https://erenow.com/ancient/ancient-iraq-third-edition/13.html, retrieved 11/19/17.

29. Gilbert, D. (2017). "Babel, the Abyss, and the Gate of the Gods." *The Great Inception.* http://thegreatinception.com/2017/02/12/the-great-inception-part-3-babel-the-abyss-and-the-gate-of-the-gods/, retrieved 11/19/17.

30. 1 Samuel 5:4.

31. Annus, Amar. "On the Origin of the Watchers: A Comparative Study of the Antediluvian Wisdom in Mesopotamian and Jewish Traditions." *Journal for the Study of the Pseudepigrapha.* 19 (2010), pp. 277–320.

32. This formula was reached by the Phoenician historian Philo of Byblos in the second century A.D.

33. Emanuel, J. (2015). "King Taita and His 'Palistin': Philistine State or Neo-Hittite Kingdom?" *Antiguo Oriente*, volume 13, 2015, pp. 11–40.

34. Ibid.

35. Heiser, M. (2004). "The Divine Council in Late Canonical and Non-canonical Second Temple Jewish Literature" (pp. 47–48). Doctoral dissertation, Univ. of Wisconsin-Madison.

36. Cross, F.M. (1973). *Canaanite Myth and Hebrew Epic: Essays in the History of the Religion of Israel* (London; Cambridge: Harvard University Press) 40, 115.

37. Herrmann, W. (1999). El. In K. van der Toorn, B. Becking, & P. W. van der Horst Eds., (Leiden; Boston; Köln; Grand Rapids, MI; Cambridge: Brill; Eerdmans) *Dictionary of Deities and Demons in the Bible* (2nd extensively rev. ed.) p. 275.

38. Cross (1973), op. cit., p. 15.

39. Day, J. (2000). *Yahweh and the Gods and Goddesses of Canaan* (London; New York: Sheffield Academic Press) p. 34.

40. Wyatt, N. (2002). *Religious Texts from Ugarit* (2nd ed.) (London; New York: Sheffield Academic Press) pp. 409–412.

41. Ibid., p. 131.

42. Probably the proper name of a peak in the Hermon range. See Lipinski (1991), op. cit., p. 40 (note 133).

43. Lipinski (1991), op. cit., p. 41.

44. Peterson, J. (2011). "Nanna/Suen Convenes in the Divine Assembly as King" (p. 279). *Aula Orientalis* 29

45. "Inana and Ishme-Dagan," http://etcsl.orinst.ox.ac.uk/section2/tr25411.htm, retrieved 11/26/17.

46. 2 Kings 23:7.

47. Matthew 19:4.

48. Scurlock, J. (1995). "Death and the Afterlife in Ancient Mesopotamian Thought." In: Sasson, J. (Ed.), *Civilizations of the Ancient Near East* (New York: Simon and Schuster Macmillan) p, 1889.

49. Ibid.

50. Ibid.

51. MacDougal, R. (2014). "Remembrance and the Dead in Second Millennium BC Mesopotamia" (p. 59). Doctoral thesis (University of Leicester).

52. Ibid, p. 52.

53. Ibid., p. 55.

54. Scurlock (1995), op. cit., p. 1885.

55. John 11:31.

56. Ibid.

57. MacDougal (2014), op. cit., p. 23.

58. Ibid., pp. 24–25.

59. 1 Samuel 28:7–20

60. Matthew 14:26; Mark 6:49.

61. Bennett, R. (2013). *I Am Not Afraid: Demon Possession and Spiritual Warfare* (Saint Louis: Concordia Publishing).

62. Ibid., p. 26.

63. Schmidt, B. (1991). "Israel's Beneficent Dead: The Origin and Character of Israelite Ancestor Cults and Necromancy" (pp. 158–159). Doctoral thesis (University of Oxford).

64. MacDougal (2014), op. cit., p. 31.

65. Spronk, K. (1986). *Beatific Afterlife in Aancient Israel and in the Ancient Near East* (Kevelaer: Butzon & Bercker) p. 151.
66. Heider, G. (1985). "The Cult of Molek: A Reassessment" (p. 96). *Journal for the Study of the Old Testament: Supplement Series 43.* (Sheffield: University of Sheffield.)
67. Ibid., p. 129.
68. Ibid., p. 115.
69. Wyatt, N. (2002). *Religious Texts from Ugarit* (2nd ed.) (London; New York: Sheffield Academic Press) p. 395.
70. Deut. 3:1; Joshua 12:4, 13:12.
71. 1 Kings 11:7.
72. 2 Kings 23:10.
73. Diodorus Siculus. Library XX, xiv.
74. Cross (1973), op. cit., pp. 24–25.
75. Ibid., p. 19.
76. Ibid., pp. 26–27.
77. Ribichini, S. (2001). "Beliefs and Religious Life." In: Moscati, S. (Ed.), *The Phoenicians* (London; New York: I.B. Tauris) p. 132.
78. Cross (1973), op. cit., p. 29.
79. Day, J. (1986). "Asherah in the Hebrew Bible and Northwest Semitic Literature" (p. 396). In *Journal of Biblical Literature*, Vol. 105, No. 3.
80. Cross (1973), op. cit., p. 32.
81. Ibid.
82. Ibid., p. 19.
83. Wyatt, N. (1999). Asherah. In K. van der Toorn, B. Becking, & P. W. van der Horst (Eds.), *Dictionary of Deities and Demons in the Bible* (2nd extensively rev. ed.) (Leiden; Boston; Köln; Grand Rapids, MI; Cambridge: Brill; Eerdmans), p. 100.
84. Day (1986), op. cit., p. 389.
85. Diodorus Siculus, *The Library of History*, XX:14. http://penelope.uchicago.edu/Thayer/E/Roman/Texts/Diodorus_Siculus/20A*.html, retrieved 4/14/18.
86. Ibid.
87. Plutarch, *On Superstition*. http://penelope.uchicago.edu/Thayer/E/Roman/Texts/Plutarch/Moralia/De_superstitione*.html, retrieved 4/14/18.
88. Garnand, B., Stager, L., & Greene, J. (2013). "Infants as Offerings: Palaeodemographic Patterns and Tophet Burial" (p. 194), *Studi Epigrafici e Linguistici* 29-30, 2012–13.

89.   Ibid., p. 215.

90.   Cross (1973), op. cit., p. 25.

91.   Rundin, J. (2004). "Pozo Moro, Child Sacrifice, and the Greek Literary Tradition" (p. 426). *Journal of Biblical Literature*, Vol. 123, No. 3.

92.   Orsingher, A. (2018). "Understanding *Tophets*: A Short Introduction. *The Ancient Near East Today.*" http://www.asor.org/anetoday/2018/02/Understanding-Tophets-Short, retrieved 4/14/18.

93.   Aubet, M.E. (1987). *The Phoenicians and the West* (Cambridge: Cambridge University Press). p. 252.

94.   Smith, P., Avishai, G., Greene, J., & Stager, L. (2011). "Aging Cremated Infants: The Problem of Sacrifice at the Tophet of Carthage. *Antiquity*, 85(329), 859–874. doi:10.1017/S0003598X00068368.

95.   Nickelsburg, G.W.E.. *1 Enoch: The Hermeneia Translation* (Fortress Press. Kindle Edition), p. 29.

96.   Jews and early Christians believed that demons were the spirits of the Nephilim who died in the Flood, condemned to wander the earth until the Judgment. Similarly, the Greeks believed that *daimones* were the spirits of the heroes of the Golden Age, although they believed the *daimones* were helpful spirits.

97.   With apologies to Dr. Michael Heiser, author of the highly recommended book *Reversing Hermon*.

98.   Spronk (1986), op. cit., p. 162.

99.   Deuteronomy 4:47, 31:4.

100.   Deuteronomy 3:11.

101.   However, archaeologist and Bible scholar Kenneth A. Kitchen has argued against Larsa being Ellasar, noting that "Larsa" lacks the initial *aleph* and transposes the *r* and *s*. See Kitchen's *On the Reliability of the Old Testament* (Grand Rapids; Cambridge: 2003), p. 568.

102.   Deuteronomy 2:10–20.

103.   Gordon, C. (1958). "Abraham and the Merchants of Ura" (pp.28–31). *Journal of Near Eastern Studies* 17:1.

104.   Gllbert, D. (2017). "The Great Inception Part 5: Abraham Was Not from Ur". *The Great Inception*, http://www.thegreatinception.com/long-war/the-great-inception-part-5-abraham-was-not-from-ur/, retrieved 2/25/18.

105.   Schmidt (1991), op. cit., pp. 158–159.

106.   Wyatt, N. (2002). *Religious Texts from Ugarit* (2nd ed.) (London; New York: Sheffield Academic Press), p. 314.

107. KTU 1.20 i 1–3, ii 2–3. From Wyatt, op. cit, pp. 315–316.

108. Ibid.

109. See also Lipinski, E. (1971). "El's Abode: Mythological Traditions Related to Mount Hermon and to the Mountains of Armenia" (pp. 13–69). *Orientalia Lovaniensa Periodica* II.

110. Spronk, K. (1986), op. cit., p. 171.

111. See Leviticus 19:31, 20:6, 20:27 and Deuteronomy 18:11.

112. MacDougal, R., op cit., pp. 22–23.

113. Deuteronomy 4:19–20.

114. Lipinski, op. cit., p. 69.

115. Ugaritic text KTU 1.4 v 49–57. In Wyatt, N. (2002). *Religious Texts from Ugarit* (2nd ed.) (London; New York: Sheffield Academic Press), p. 104.

116. Ugaritic text KTU 1.101 R 1–3. Ibid., pp. 388–389.

117. See Psalm 74:14. The victory of a warrior god over Chaos is a common theme in ancient Near Eastern religion: Zeus vs. Typhon; Baal vs. Yamm (or Tiamat); Tarhunz vs. Illuyanka; Marduk (or Enlil, or Enki) vs. Tiamat, etc. Although scholars would disagree, it is my view that these accounts are derivative of what actually happened, as described in Psalm 74.

118. Talshir, D. (2003). "The Relativity of Geographic Terms: A Re-investigation of the Problem of Upper and Lower Aram" (pp. 264–265). *Journal of Semitic Studies* XLVIII/2.

119. Hays, C. (2012). An Egyptian Loanword in the Book of Isaiah and the Deir ʾAlla Inscription: Heb. *nṣr*, Aram. *nqr*, and Eg. *nṯr* as "[Divinized] Corpse" (p. 17). *Journal of Ancient Egyptian Interconnections* Vol. 4:2.

120. Mariottini, C. (2014). "The Seal of Hezekiah." https://claudemariottini. com/2014/08/05/the-seal-of-hezekiah/, retrieved 4/16/18.

121. Hays (2012), op. cit., p. 18.

122. Heiser, M. The Nephilim. *Sitchin Is Wrong.com*, http://www.sitchiniswrong. com/nephilim/nephilim.htm, retrieved 4/16/18.

123. Ibid.

124. Ibid.

125. Münger, S. (1999). Ariel. In K. van der Toorn, B. Becking, & P. W. van der Horst (Eds.), *Dictionary of Deities and Demons in the Bible* (2nd extensively rev. ed.) (Leiden; Boston; Köln; Grand Rapids, MI; Cambridge: Brill; Eerdmans), p. 89.

126. 2 Samuel 21:16, 18, 20, 22; also 1 Chronicles 16.

127. Mulder, M. J. (1999). Carmel. In K. van der Toorn, B. Becking, & P. W.

van der Horst (Eds.), *Dictionary of Deities and Demons in the Bible* (2nd extensively rev. ed.) (Leiden; Boston; Köln; Grand Rapids, MI; Cambridge: Brill; Eerdmans), pp. 182–183.

128.   Barry, J. D., Mangum, D., Brown, D. R., Heiser, M. S., Custis, M., Ritzema, E., ... Bomar, D. (2012, 2016). *Faithlife Study Bible* (Ge 3:14) (Bellingham, WA: Lexham Press).

129.   Annus, A. (2010). "On the Origin of Watchers: A Comparative Study of the Antediluvian Wisdom in Mesopotamian and Jewish Traditions." *Journal for the Study of the Pseudepigrapha*, 19(4), 277–320. doi:10.1177/0951820710373978.

130.   Dagan (the final "a" shifted to an "o" over the centuries) was a grain god, not a fish god, worshiped in Syria 1,500 years before the Philistines set up his temple in Ashdod.

131.   *The Erra Epic*, lines 132, 133, 147. Translation by Benjamin R. Foster, *Before the Muses: An Anthology of Akkadian Literature* (Bethesda: CDL Press, 3rd ed).

132.   Hesiod. (1914). *The Homeric Hymns and Homerica with an English Translation by Hugh G. Evelyn-White*. Theogony. (Medford, MA: Cambridge, MA., Harvard University Press; London, William Heinemann Ltd.)

133.   Suriano, M. (2009). Dynasty Building at Ugarit (p. 118). *Aula Orientalis* 27.

134.   Suriano, M. (2009). "Dynasty Building at Ugarit: The Ritual and Political Context of KTU 1.161," *Aula Orientalis* 27, p. 107.

135.   Wyatt, N. (2002). *Religious Texts from Ugarit* (2nd ed.). (London; New York: Sheffield Academic Press), p. 210.

136.   Vidal, J. (2006). "The Origins of the Last Ugaritic Dynasty." *Altorientalishce Forschungen* 33, p. 169.

137.   Annus, A. (1999). "Are There Greek Rephaim? On the Etymology of Greek *Meropes* and *Titanes*." *Ugarit-Forschungen* 31, pp. 13–30.

138.   Hesiod, *Works and Days*, l. 109.

139.   Ibid., 117ff.

140.   1 Enoch 15:8–16:1. Nickelsburg, George W. E.. 1 *Enoch: The Hermeneia Translation* (Fortress Press. Kindle Edition), p. 37.

141.   Graf, F. (1999). "Heros." In K. van der Toorn, B. Becking, & P. W. van der Horst (Eds.), *Dictionary of Deities and Demons in the Bible* (2nd extensively rev. ed.). (Leiden; Boston; Köln; Grand Rapids, MI; Cambridge: Brill; Eerdmans), p.413.

142. Ibid.

143. Ibid., p. 414.

144. Ibid.

145. Annus, op. cit., p. 22.

146. Kerenyi, K. (1959). *The Heroes of the Greeks* (London: Thames and Hudson), p. 75.

147. Wyatt, op. cit., p. 594.

148. We could really go down a rabbit trail here, but we won't. The Greeks believed that Glaucus, who was Bellerophon's mortal father (or stepfather, if Poseidon was the true father), was the son of Merope, one of the seven Pleiades star-nymphs born to the Titan Atlas. As we've already shown, Merope is likely derived from the Semitic root *rp'*, from which we also get the Hebrew word "Rephaim."

149. "Bellerophon (Bellerophontes)". *Theoi Project*, http://www.theoi.com/Heros/Bellerophontes.html, retrieved 2/24/18.

150. Bremmer, J. (2004). "Remember the Titans!" In *The Fall of the Angels*, Auffarth, A. and Stuckenbruck, L. eds. (Leiden: Brill), p. 42.

151. Bremmer, J. (2004), op. cit, p. 42.

152. Ibid., p. 42.

153. The sickle sword was used as a weapon by the Hittites. See Bremmer, op. cit., p. 39.

154. Keen, A. G. (n.d.). *Dynastic Lycia* (p. 207). Leiden, The Netherlands: BRILL.

155. Porphyry. *On Abstinence from Killing Animals*. Translated by Gillian Clark (2000). (London: Bloomsbury), p. 76.

156. Ibid., p. 77.

157. Sophocles, fragment 126.

158. Bremmer (2004), op. cit., p. 46.

159. Ibid.

160. Brisch, N. (2016), "Anunna (Anunnaku, Anunnaki) (a Group of Gods)", *Ancient Mesopotamian Gods and Goddesses*, University of Pennsylvania Museum, http://oracc.museum.upenn.edu/amgg/listofdeities/anunna/, retrieved 4/7/18.

161. Wyatt, N. (2010). "À la Recherche des Rephaïm Perdus" (p. 56). *The Archaeology of Myth: Papers on Old Testament Tradition*. (Sheffield: Taylor and Francis).

162. Lipinski, E. (1971), op. cit, p 69.

163. Wyatt, N. (2007). "A la recherche des Rephaïm perdus," in J. M. Michaud (ed.) *Le royaume d'Ougarit de la Crète à l'Euphrate: Nouveaux axes de recherche* (Proche-Orient et Littérature Ougaritique II, Sherbrooke, QC: Éditions GGC), pp. 597–598.

164. Wyatt, N. (1999). Calf. In K. van der Toorn, B. Becking, & P. W. van der Horst (Eds.), *Dictionary of Deities and Demons in the Bible* (2nd extensively rev. ed.). (Leiden; Boston; Köln; Grand Rapids, MI; Cambridge: Brill; Eerdmans), p. 181.

165. Ibid.

166. Wyatt, S. and Wyatt, N. (2013). "The *longue durée* in the Beef Business. In: O. Loretz, S. Ribichini, W. G. E. Watson, & J. Zamora (Eds.), *Ritual, Religion and Reason*. (Münster: Ugarit-Verlag), p. 346.

167. KTU 1.4, vi, 46.

168. Exodus 24:9.

169. Luke 10:1.

170. Deuteronomy 4:19.

171. Matthew 22:30; Mark 12:25; Luke 20:35–36.

172. John 8:44.

173. Miller, R. (2014). Baals of Bashan. https://repository.up.ac.za/handle/2263/45173, retrieved 4/1/18.

174. Exodus 34:22–23.

175. Cohen, M. (1993). *The Cultic Calendars of the Ancient Near East*. (Bethesda, MD: CDL Press), p. 401.

176. Ibid.

177. Ibid., p. 403.

178. Black, J. & Green, A. (1992). *Gods, Demons and Symbols of Ancient Mesopotamia: An Illustrated Dictionary*. (London: The British Museum Press), p. 136.

179. Numbers 28:16–25.

180. 1 Kings 8:65; Ezekiel 45:25;

181. Ayali-Darshan, N. (2015). "The Seventy Bulls Sacrificed at Sukkot (Num 29:12–34) in Light of a Ritual Text from Emar (Emar 6, 373)." *Vetus Testamentum* 65:1, pgs. 9–19.

182. Ibid.

183. Bremmer, J. (2004), op. cit., p. 48.

184. Yuhong, W., and Dalley, S. (1990). "The Origins of the Manana Dynasty at Kish, and the Assyrian King List." *Iraq* 52, pp.159–65.

185. Jacobsen, T. (1976). *The Treasures of Darkness: A History of Mesopotamian Religion*. (New Haven, CT: Yale University Press), p. 124.

186. See the entries for "Sinai" in the *International Standard Bible Encyclopedia*, *Easton's Bible Dictionary*, and the *Jewish Encyclopedia*.

187. Annus, A. (2002). *The God Ninurta in the Mythology and Royal Ideology of Ancient Mesopotamia* (pp. 111–12). State Archives of Assyria Studies, Volume XIV. Helsinki: The Neo-Assyrian Text Corpus Project.

188. Annus (1999), op. cit., p.

189. Heiser, M. "The Nachash and His Seed: Some Explanatory Notes on Why the 'Serpent' in Genesis 3 Wasn't a Serpent." http://www.pidradio.com/wp-content/uploads/2007/02/nachashnotes.pdf, retrieved 4/7/18.

190. Deuteronomy 8:15.

191. This should be of interest to ufologists in light of the accounts of reptilians by "alien" abductees.

192. See Numbers 7:89; 1 Samuel 4:4; 2 Samuel 6:2: Psalms 80:1 and 99:1; and Isaiah 37:16.

193. Mettinger, T. N. D. (1999). Cherubim. In K. van der Toorn, B. Becking, & P. W. van der Horst (Eds.), *Dictionary of Deities and Demons in the Bible* (2nd extensively rev. ed.) (Leiden; Boston; Köln; Grand Rapids, MI; Cambridge: Brill; Eerdmans) p. 190.

194. Bodi, D. (1991). *The Book of Ezekiel and the Poem of Erra*. (Freiburg: Universitätsverlag) p. 263.

195. Genesis 3:24, ESV.

196. Ritter, N. (2010). "Human-headed Winged Bull ("Aladlammu")" in: Eggler J./Uehlinger Ch., eds., *Iconography of Deities and Demons in the Ancient Near East*, http://www.religionswissenschaft.uzh.ch/idd/prepublications/e_idd_human_headed_winged_bull.pdf, accessed 4/9/18.

197. Ibid.

198. Annus, A. (2012). "The Antediluvian Origin of Evil in the Mesopotamian and Jewish Traditions" in: Dietrich M./Loretz O., eds., *Ideas of Man in the Conceptions of the Religions*. (Münster: Ugarit-Verlag), p. 25.

199. Ibid., p. 32.

200. Ibid.

201. Ibid., p. 33.

202. Ezekiel 1:7 (ESV).

203. Ezekiel 10:14 (ESV).

204. Heiser, M. (2015). *The Unseen Realm: Recovering the Supernatural Worldview of the Bible* (Bellingham, WA: Lexham Press), p. 190.

205. Schmitz, B. (2010). "Holofernes's Canopy in the Septuagint." In Kevin R.
      Brine, Elena Ciletti and Henrike Lähnemann. *The Sword of Judith: Judith
      Studies across the Disciplines.* (Open Book Publishers.)

206. KTU 1.108:1–3. Translation by Wyatt, N. (2002). *Religious Texts from
      Ugarit* (2nd ed.) (London; New York: Sheffield Academic Press), p. 395.

207. Pardee, D., & Lewis, T. J. (2002). *Ritual and Cult at Ugarit* (Vol. 10).
      (Atlanta, GA: Society of Biblical Literature), p. 193.

208. RS 24:244:40–41. Translation by Pardee and Lewis, op. cit., p. 177.
      Ugaritic text RS 24:251:42 likewise places the god *Milku* in Ashtaroth.

209. Deuteronomy 32:17.

210. Veijola, T. (2003).. "King Og's Iron Bed (Deut 3:11): Once Again," *Studies
      in the Hebrew Bible, Qumran, and the Septuagint* (ed. Peter W. Flint et al.;
      VTSup 101; Leiden/Boston: Brill), p. 63.

211. Gilbert, D. (2017). "The Great Inception Part 7: Iniquity of the
      Amorites—Babylon, Og, and the Angels Who Sinned." *The Great
      Inception.* http://www.thegreatinception.com/long-war/the-great-inception-
      part-7-iniquity-of-the-amorites-babylon-og-and-the-angels-who-sinned/,
      retrieved 2/26/18.

212. For example, Egyptologist Kim Ryholt points out that the name of the best-
      attested Hyksos king, Khayan, "has generally been interpreted as Amorite
      'Hayanu' (reading *h-ya-a-n*) which the Egyptian form represents perfectly."
      Hayanu is also attested in a list of ancestors for a powerful eighteenth-
      century century B.C. Amorite king, Shamsi-Adad.
          See Ryholt, K (1997). *The Political Situation in Egypt During the Second
      Intermediate Period c.1800–1550 B.C.* (Museum Tuscalanum Press), p.128.

213. Bietak, M. (1996). *Avaris: The Capital of the Hyksos.* (London: British
      Museum Press), p. 29.

214. We know this because Ramesses the Great set up a stela to commemorate
      four hundred years of Set's rule in northern Egypt. The stela featured an
      image of Ramesses' father, Seti I, whose name literally means "man of Set."

215. Pritchard, J. B. (2005). *Ancient Near Eastern Texts: Relating to the Old
      Testament* (Ann Arbor, Mich: Pro Quest), p. 329.

216. Ibid.

217. Annus, A. (1999). Op. cit., p. 18.

218. Most Bible commentaries place the land of Uz near Edom.

219. Ibid.

220. Heltzer, M., & Arbeli-Raveh, S. (1981). *The Suteans.* Naples: Istituto
      universitario orientale. Cited in Annus, A. (1999), op. cit., p. 19.

221. "Biblical Archaeology: Evidence of the Exodus from Egypt." *Institute for Biblical and Scientific Studies.* https://www.bibleandscience.com/archaeology/exodus.htm, retrieved 3/3/18.

222. Wilson, J. (1927). "The Texts of the Battle of Kadesh," *The American Journal of Semitic Languages and Literatures*, Vol. 34, no. 4, p.278.

223. Ibid.

224. Sullivan, R. (2015). "Egyptian War Correspondents and the Biblical Giants," *Associates for Biblical Research.* http://www.biblearchaeology.org/post/2015/02/27/Egyptian-War- Correspondents-and-the-Biblical-Giants.aspx, retrieved 12/17/16.

225. Shahine, A. (2008). "Ancient Egyptians Did It Tough." *ABC Science.* http://www.abc.net.au/science/articles/2008/03/31/2203404.htm, retrieved 3/3/18.

226. Ewen, M. (2015). "How Tall Were Ancient Egyptians?" *Researchers in Museums.* https://blogs.ucl.ac.uk/researchers-in-museums/2015/01/21/question-of-the-week-how-tall-were-ancient-egyptians/, retrieved 3/3/18.

227. Malul, M. (1999). Taboo. In K. van der Toorn, B. Becking, & P. W. van der Horst (Eds.), *Dictionary of Deities and Demons in the Bible* (2nd extensively rev. ed.), (Leiden; Boston; Köln; Grand Rapids, MI; Cambridge: Brill; Eerdmans), p. 826.

228. See Joshua 7:10–26.

229. Deuteronomy 32:17.

230. Heiser, M. (2012). "Deuteronomy 32:8–9 and the Old Testament Worldview," *Faithlife Study Bible*, John D. Barry, Michael R. Grigoni, et al. (Bellingham, WA: Logos Bible Software), p. 3.

231. Heiser, M. (2015), op. cit., p. 291.

232. Matthew 20:28.

233. Sasson, J. M. (1984). "Thoughts of Zimri-Lim," *Biblical Archaeologist*, June 1984, pp. 118–119.

234. Lipinski, op. cit., p. 69.

235. In these translations by respected Ugaritic scholar Nicolas Wyatt, I have substituted "Rephaim" (Ugaritic *rpum*) for Wyatt's choice, "saviours," and "elohim" (Ugaritic *ilnym*) for Wyatt's preferred word, "divinities."

236. KTU 1.20:ii:2–7. Wyatt, N. (2002). *Religious Texts from Ugarit*, 2nd ed. (London; New York: Sheffield Academic Press), pp. 316–317.

237. KTU 1.21:ii:1-7. Ibid., p. 319.

238. KTU 1.22:ii:21-25. Ibid., p. 320.

239. KTU 1.22:i.5–7. Spronk, K. (1986). Op. cit., p. 171.

240. Lewis, T. (1996). "Toward a Literary Translation of the Rapiuma Texts," in *Ugarit, Religion, and Culture: Proceedings of the International Colloquium on Ugarit, Religion, and Culture, Edinburgh, July 1994. Essays presented in honour of John C. L. Gibson.* Ugaritisch-Biblische Literatur 12 (ed. N. Wyatt, W.G.E. Watson, and J.B. Lloyd); (Münster: Ugarit-Verlag), p. 130.

241. Mangum, D. (2012, 2016). "Interpreting First Peter 3:18–22." In *Faithlife Study Bible.* (Bellingham, WA: Lexham Press).

242. Anyone living in the Near East in Ezekiel's day would have recognized what he described as a royal throne. Existing artwork from that time and place makes it clear that Ezekiel did *not* see an alien spacecraft.

243. Colavito, J. (2012). "The Secret History of Ancient Astronauts: Ancient Astronauts and the Cthulhu Mythos in Fiction and Fact," http://www.jasoncolavito.com/secret-history-of-ancient-astronauts.html, retrieved 3/10/18.

244. Richardson, J. "Rosh: Russia or Chief?" https://joelstrumpet.com/rosh-russia-or-chief/, retrieved 3/10/18.

245. Ibid.

246. Scofield, C. I. (1917). "Ezekiel 38:2." *Scofield Reference Notes (1917 Edition).* https://www.biblestudytools.com/commentaries/scofield-reference-notes/ezekiel/ezekiel-38.html, retrieved 3/10/18.

247. Block, D. (1998). *The New International Commentary on the Old Testament on Ezekiel,* cited by Richardson, op. cit.

248. Block, D. I. (1997–). *The Book of Ezekiel, Chapters 25–48* (Grand Rapids, MI: Wm. B. Eerdmans Publishing Co.), p. 434.

249. Alexander, R. (1986). Ezekiel. In: *Expositor's Bible Commentary* (ed. F.E. Gaebelein) (Grand Rapids: Zondervan).

250. Cunliffe, B., editor (1994). *The Oxford History of Prehistoric Europe* (Oxford University Press), pp. 381–382.

251. Bryce, T. (2012). *The World of the Neo-Hittite Kingdoms: A Political and Military History* (Oxford; New York: Oxford University Press), p. 44.

252. Block, D. I. (1997). *The Book of Ezekiel, Chapters 25–48* (Grand Rapids, MI: Wm. B. Eerdmans Publishing Co.), p. 74).

253. Burney, C. (2004). *Historical Dictionary of the Hittites* (Lanham, MD; Toronto; Oxford: Scarecrow Press), p. 268.

254. Block, D. I. (1997–), op. cit., pp. 72–73.

255. Diakonoff, I. (1984). *The Pre-History of the Armenian People* (New York: Caravan Books) pp. 115–119.

256. Bryce, T. (2012), op. cit., p. 198.

257. Ibid., pp. 44–45.

258. Oren, E. D. (2013). *The Sea Peoples and Their World: A Reassessment* (Philadelphia: University of Pennsylvania Press), p. 76.

259. Wolf, H. J. (1995). Tiras. *International Standard Bible Encyclopedia*. http://www.internationalstandardbible.com/T/tiras.html, retrieved 4/28/18.

260. Josephus, *Antiquities of the Jews* 1.123.

261. Heiser, M. (2015). op. cit., p. 372.

262. Gilbert, D. (2016). *I Predict! What 12 Global Experts Believe You Will See Before 2025*. (Crane, MO: Defender).

263. Furnish, T. (2018). "Talking Turkey about the Mahdi," *Occidental Jihadist*, https://occidentaljihadist.com/2018/03/12/talking-turkey-about-the-mahdi/, retrieved 3/17/18.

264. Dillinger, J. (2018). "29 Largest Armies in the World." *World Atlas*, https://www.worldatlas.com/articles/29-largest-armies-in-the-world.html, retrieved 3/18/17.

265. "MBS: Palestinians Should 'Accept Trump Proposals or Shut Up,'" *Al Jazeera*, April 30, 2018. https://www.aljazeera.com/news/2018/04/mbs-palestinians-accept-trump-proposals-shut-180430065228281.html, retrieved 5/2/18.

266. Heiser, *The Unseen Realm*, pp. 364–365.

267. Kohler, K. (1906). "Eschatology." *The Jewish Encyclopedia*, http://www.jewishencyclopedia.com/articles/5849-eschatology, retrieved 3/30/19.

268. Kohler, K., and Ginzburg, L. (1906). "Armilus." *The Jewish Encyclopedia*, http://www.jewishencyclopedia.com/articles/1789-armilus, retrieved 3/30/18.

269. Spronk, K. (1999). "Travellers." In K. van der Toorn, B. Becking, & P. W. van der Horst (Eds.), *Dictionary of Deities and Demons in the Bible* (2nd extensively rev. ed.) (Leiden; Boston; Köln; Grand Rapids, MI; Cambridge: Brill; Eerdmans), p. 876.

270. Tropper, J. (1999). "Spirit of the Dead." In K. van der Toorn, B. Becking, & P. W. van der Horst (Eds.), *Dictionary of Deities and Demons in the Bible* (2nd extensively rev. ed.) (Leiden; Boston; Köln; Grand Rapids, MI; Cambridge: Brill; Eerdmans), p. 806.

271. Spronk (1986), op. cit., p. 229.

272. Major Contributors and Editors. (2016). "Iye-Abarim." In J. D. Barry, D. Bomar, D. R. Brown, R. Klippenstein, D. Mangum, C. Sinclair Wolcott,

... W. Widder (Eds.), *The Lexham Bible Dictionary* (Bellingham, WA: Lexham Press).

273. Schuster, R. (2017). "Monumental Carved Dolmen More Than 4,000 Years Old Found in Golan Rewrites History of Civilization." *Haaretz* (March 6, 2017), https://www.haaretz.com/archaeology/huge-dolmen-found-in-golan-rewrites-history-of-civilization-1.5444970, retrieved 3/26/18.

274. Yassine, K. (1985). "The Dolmens: Construction and Dating Reconsidered." *Bulletin of the American Schools of Oriental Research*, No. 259 (Summer, 1985), pp. 63–69.

275. Sharon G, Barash A, Eisenberg-Degen D, Grosman L, Oron M, et al. (2017) "Monumental Megalithic Burial and Rock Art Tell a New Story about the Levant Intermediate Bronze 'Dark Ages.'" *PLOS ONE* 12(3): e0172969. https://doi.org/10.1371/journal.pone.0172969, retrieved 3/28/18.

276. Savage, S. (2010). "Jordan's Stonehenge: The Endangered Chalcolithic/ Early Bronze Age Site at al-Murayghât–Hajr al-Mansûb," *Near Eastern Archaeology* 73:1, p. 32.

277. Spronk, K. (1986). Op. cit., p. 228.

278. Yassine, K. (1985), op. cit.

279. Ibid., p. 66.

280. Sharon G., et al (2017). Op. cit., p. 1.

281. Ibid., p. 10.

282. Ibid., p. 17.

283. See Jude 1:9.

284. Strong's Concordance #H6465, http://lexiconcordance.com/hebrew/6465.html, retrieved 3/27/18.

285. Spronk, K. (1999). "Baal of Peor." In K. van der Toorn, B. Becking, & P. W. van der Horst (Eds.), *Dictionary of Deities and Demons in the Bible* (2nd extensively rev. ed.) (Leiden; Boston; Köln; Grand Rapids, MI; Cambridge: Brill; Eerdmans), p. 147.

286. KTU 1.5, ii, 1. In Wyatt, N. (2002). *Religious Texts from Ugarit* (2nd ed.) (London; New York: Sheffield Academic Press), p. 120.

287. Barry, J. D., Mangum, D., Brown, D. R., Heiser, M. S., Custis, M., Ritzema, E., ... Bomar, D. (2012, 2016). *Faithlife Study Bible* (Nu 25:8), (Bellingham, WA: Lexham Press).

288. Torres, H. (2016). "57% Percent of Pastors, 64% of Youth Pastors in U.S.

Struggle with Porn Addiction, Survey Shows." *Christian Today*, January 30, 2016. https://www.christiantoday.com/article/57-percent-of-pastors-and-64-of-youth-pastors-in-u-s-struggle-with-porn-addiction-survey-shows/78178.htm, retrieved 3/27/18.

289. KTU 1.22 ii, 20-27; I, 15. In Wyatt, N. (2002). *Religious Texts from Ugarit* (2nd ed.), (London; New York: Sheffield Academic Press), p. 322.

290. Spronk, K. (1986), op. cit., p. 172.

291. Nickelsburg, George W.E.. *1 Enoch: The Hermeneia Translation* (Fortress Press. Kindle Edition), p. 37.

292. Strong's H2629.

293. See, for example, www.TempleMountLocation.com.

294. Franz, G. (2015). "Eight Reasons Why the Temples of King Solomon and Herod the Great Were NOT Over the Gihon Spring in the City of David." *Life and Land Seminars*, http://www.lifeandland.org/2015/11/cornuke-temple/, retrieved 3/30/18.

295. Barry, J. D., Mangum, D., Brown, D. R., Heiser, M. S., Custis, M., Ritzema, E., ... Bomar, D. (2012, 2016). *Faithlife Study Bible* (Joe 3:2). (Bellingham, WA: Lexham Press).

296. Kline, M. (1996). "Har Magedon: The End of the Millennium." *Journal of the Evangelical Theological Society* 39, 2.I, p. 208.

297. Putnam, C. (2011). "Armageddon OT Background to the Battle for the Cosmic Mountain." http://www.logosapologia.org/armageddon-ot-background-to-the-battle-for-the-cosmic-mountain-2/, retrieved 3/31/18.

298. Heiser, M. (2015). Op. cit., p. 371.

299. Ibid.

300. Luke 8:31.

301. 1 Corinthians 6:3.

302. Hesiod. (1914). *The Homeric Hymns and Homerica with an English Translation by Hugh G. Evelyn-White. Theogony.* (Medford, MA: Cambridge, MA, Harvard University Press; London, William Heinemann Ltd.)

303. Van Henten, J. W. (1999). Typhon. In K. van der Toorn, B. Becking, & P. W. van der Horst (Eds.), *Dictionary of Deities and Demons in the Bible* (2nd extensively rev. ed.), (Leiden; Boston; Köln; Grand Rapids, MI; Cambridge: Brill; Eerdmans), p.879.

304. Hesiod (1914), op. cit.

305. Apollodorus. (1921). *Library and Epitome (English)*. (J. G. Frazer, Ed.) (Medford, MA: Perseus Digital Library), Vol. 1, p. 47.

306. Irenaeus. *Against Heresies*, Book V, Chapter 30.

307. Luke 22:3.

308. 2 Corinthians 11:4.

309. Coxon, P. W. (1999). Gibborim. In K. van der Toorn, B. Becking, & P. W. van der Horst (Eds.), *Dictionary of Deities and Demons in the Bible* (2nd extensively rev. ed.), (Leiden; Boston; Köln; Grand Rapids, MI; Cambridge: Brill; Eerdmans), p. 345.

310. Heiser, M. (2009). "Sheol: The OT Bad Place?" http://drmsh.com/sheol-the-ot-bad-place/, retrieved 4/1/18.

311. The technical explanation of the underlying Hebrew boils down to this: It appears the Masoretic text, on which most English translations are based, substitutes (or miscopied) *m 'a re lîm* ("uncircumcised") for the original *me 'ôla m* ("ancient times"). See Block, D. (1992). "Beyond the Grave: Ezekiel's Vision of Death and Afterlife," *Bulletin for Biblical Research* 2, p. 125.

312. Ibid.

313. KTU 1.22 ii 21–27, i 15–16. In Wyatt, N. (2002). Op. cit., pp. 320–322.

314. Henry, M. *Matthew Henry Commentary on the Whole Bible*. https://www.biblestudytools.com/commentaries/matthew-henry-complete/ezekiel/39.html, retrieved 4/3/18.

315. Bullinger, E. W. (1909). *Commentary on Revelation*. http://www.ccel.org/ccel/bullinger/apocalypse.xix.html?highlight=xxxix#highlight, retrieved 4/3/18.

316. Jamieson, R.; Fausset, A. R.; and Brown, D. (1871). *Commentary Critical and Explanatory on the Whole Bible*. https://www.blueletterbible.org/Comm/jfb/Eze/Eze_039.cfm?a=841017, retrieved 4/3/18.

317. Block, D. I. (1997–). *The Book of Ezekiel, Chapters 25–48* (Grand Rapids, MI: Wm. B. Eerdmans Publishing Co.), pp. 475–476.

318. Ibid., p. 477.

319. This section summarized from the article "Is Gog of Magog the Antichrist?" by Matt McClellan at *Christian Worldview Press*. http://christianworldviewpress.com/gog-magog-antichrist/, retrieved 4/4/18.

320. Richardson, J. (2012). *Mideast Beast* (Washington D.C.: WND Books), p. 175.

321. Ezekiel 38:28, 39:6–7; also Isaiah 11:9 and Psalm 22:27.

322. Ezekiel 39:7 (ESV).

323. Richardson (2012). Op. cit., p. 176.

324. 2 Kings 21:11.

325. Genesis 15:16.

326. Daniel 11:45.

327. Gilbert, D. (2017). *The Great Inception: Satan's PSYOPs from Eden to Armageddon* (Crane, MO: Defender), pp. 280–281.

328. Revelation 17:18.

329. Revelation 17:16.

330. Allen, J. (2018). "Focus on Witchcraft at Exorcists' Summit Signifies a Paradigm Shift." *Crux*, https://cruxnow.com/news-analysis/2018/04/18/focus-on-witchcraft-at-exorcists-summit-signifies-a-paradigm-shift/, retrieved 4/19/18.

331. Matthew 12:22–27; Revelation 2:13.

332. Psalm 106:28.

333. http://rickriordan.com/content/uploads/2016/04/GreekGods_EventKit.pdf, retrieved 4/20/18.

334. http://rickriordan.com/content/uploads/2016/04/lightning-thief-complete-unit.pdf, retrieved 4/20/18.

335. "God did not spare angels when they sinned, but cast them into hell and committed them to chains of gloomy darkness to be kept until the judgment" (2 Peter 2:4, ESV). The only place in the Bible where we are told of angels sinning is Genesis 6:1–4 (the Watchers/*apkallu* who took human wives and produced the Nephilim). The Greek verb translated "cast them into hell" is *tartaroo*, which literally means "thrust down to Tartarus." In Greek cosmology, Tartarus was a special place of punishment located as far below Hades (Hell) as Earth was below Heaven. Since Peter wrote under the guidance of the Holy Spirit, we assume he knew the difference between Tartarus and Hades. It is the only place in the Bible where that word is used.

336. "Enmerkar and the Lord of Aratta: Translation." *The Electronic Corpus of Sumerian Literature.* http://etcsl.orinst.ox.ac.uk/section1/tr1823.htm, retrieved 12/27/17.

337. Becker, Helmut and Fassbinder, Jörg W.E. (2003), "Magnetometry at Uruk (Iraq): The City of King Gilgamesh," *Archaeologia Polona, 41*, pp. 122–124.

338. 1 Enoch 6:6. Although the scholar Edward Lipinski suggested in his 1971 paper "El's Abode" that "days of Jared" should read "days of the *yarid*," which was a ritual libation—a drink offering for the gods. As Lipinski

noted, the summit of Mount Hermon is scooped out, and earlier scholars, such as Charles Clermont-Ganneau in 1903, speculated that this may have been where worshipers poured their liquid offerings.

339. Nickelsburg, George W. E. *1 Enoch: The Hermeneia Translation.* (Fortress Press. Kindle Edition,) p. 26.

340. Greenfield, J. C. (1999). "Apkallu," *Dictionary of Deities and Demons in the Bible.* Van der Toorn, K., Becking, B., & Van der Horst, P. W. (Eds.). Brill, p. 73.

341. Annus, Amar (2010). "On the Origin of Watchers: A Comparative Study of the Antediluvian Wisdom in Mesopotamian and Jewish Traditions." *Journal for the Study of the Pseudepigrapha,* Vol 19, Issue 4, pp. 277–320.

342. George, Andrew (1999). *The Epic of Gilgamesh* (London: Penguin Books), pp. 111–112.

343. Lipi ski, Edward (1971). "El's Abode: Mythological Traditions Related to Mount Hermon and to the Mountains of Armenia," *Orientalia Lovaniensa Periodica II,* p. 19.

344. Ibid.

345. Livingston, David (2003). "Who Was Nimrod?" http://davelivingston.com/nimrod.htm, retrieved 12/27/17.

346. "Anunna." *Ancient Mesopotamian Gods and Goddesses.* http://oracc.museum.upenn.edu/amgg/listofdeities/anunna/index.html, retrieved 12/27/17.

347. Pritchard, James B., ed. (2010). *The Ancient Near East: An Anthology of Texts and Pictures* (Princeton University Press), p. 34.

348. Lieck, Gwendolyn (1998). *A Dictionary of Ancient Near Eastern Mythology* (New York City, New York: Routledge), p. 141.

349. George, *op. cit.,* p. 199.

350. This is well established, but see, for example: Spronk, Klaas (1986). *Beatific Afterlife in Ancient Israel and in the Ancient Near East.* (Kevelaer: Butzon & Bercker, Neukirchen-Vluyn).

351. Frölich, Ida (2014). "Mesopotamian Elements and the Watchers Traditions," in *The Watchers in Jewish and Christian Traditions* (ed. Angela Kim Hawkins, Kelley Coblentz Bautch, and John Endres), (Minneapolis: Fortress), p. 23.

352. Annus, Amar (2000). "Are There Greek Rephaim? On the Etymology of Greek *Meropes* and *Titanes,*" *Ugarit Forschungen* 31 (1999), pp. 13–30.

353. Jude 6.

354. Smith, Wesley J. "The Trouble with Transhumanism," *Christian Life*

Resources, http://www.christianliferesources.com/article/the-trouble-with-transhumanism-1191, retrieved 12/24/17.

355. Danaylov, Nikola. "A Transhumanist Manifesto (Redux)." *Singularity Weblog*, March 11, 2016. https://www.singularityweblog.com/a-transhumanist-manifesto/, retrieved 12/24/17.

356. Ibid.

357. http://www.zoltanistvan.com/TranshumanistWager.html, retrieved 12/24/17.

358. John 15:13.

359. Istvan, Zoltan. *The Transhumanist Wager*. (Futurity Imagine Media LLC, 2013), pp. 127–128.

360. Searle, Rick. "Betting Against The Transhumanist Wager." Institute for Ethics and Emerging Technologies, September 16, 2013. https://ieet.org/index.php/IEET2/more/searle20130916, retrieved 12/25/17.

361. Which is just one of several key points of LDS doctrine that disqualifies Mormonism as a Christian denomination.

362. https://www.christiantranshumanism.org, retrieved 12/28/17.

363. 1 Corinthians 15:3–4 (ESV).

364. 1 John 3:8.

365. See Matthew 16:13–17:13. Jesus led Peter, James, and John "up a high mountain" in the vicinity of Caesarea Philippi, which can only be Hermon.

366. Kumparak, Greg (2014). "Elon Musk Compares Building Artificial Intelligence to 'Summoning the Demon'," *TechCrunch*, October 26, 2014. https://techcrunch.com/2014/10/26/elon-musk-compares-building-artificial-intelligence-to-summoning-the-demon/, retrieved 12/31/17.

367. Benek, Christopher J. "How to Prevent an Artificial Intelligence God," *The Christian Post*, October 20, 2017. https://www.christianpost.com/news/how-to-prevent-an-artificial-intelligence-god-203458/, retrieved 12/28/17.

368. Ibid.

369. Sadly, most American Christians don't, either.

370. Benek, *op. cit.*

371. Genesis 1:28.

372. Matthew 28:19.

373. See 1 Corinthians 15:35–58.

374. Istvan, Zoltan. *The Transhumanist Wager*. (Futurity Imagine Media LLC, 2013), pp. 127–128.

375. Murphy, Timothy F., and Marc A. Lappé (1994). *Justice and the Human Genome Project*. (Berkeley: University of California Press), p. 18.

376. Ko, Lisa. "Unwanted Sterilization and Eugenics Programs in the United States," *Independent Lens*, January 29, 2016. http://www.pbs.org/independentlens/blog/unwanted-sterilization-and-eugenics-programs-in-the-united-states/, retrieved 12/28/17.

377. Regalado, Antionio (2017). "U.S. Panel Endorses Designer Babies to Avoid Serious Disease," *MIT Technology Review*, February 14, 2017. https://www.technologyreview.com/s/603633/us-panel-endorses-designer-babies-to-avoid-serious-disease/, retrieved 12/31/17.

378. Smith, Wesley J. "Netherlands Push to Euthanize Children," *National Review Online*, April 28, 2016. http://www.nationalreview.com/corner/434712/netherlands-push-euthanize-children, retrieved 12/28/16.

379. For example, Vita-More, Natasha. "Transhuman: A Brief History." http://www.natasha.cc/quiz.htm#Transhuman%20History, retrieved 12/28/17.

380. Bullinger, E. W. (1903). *The Apocalypse or "The Day of the Lord."* (London: Eyre & Spottiswoode).

381. He believed that the Church Age started at Acts 28:28 rather than Pentecost, and that Paul's authoritative teaching began after the conclusion of the Book of Acts.

382. Bullinger, E. W. (1902). *The Rich Man and Lazarus or "The Intermediate State,"* (London: Eyrie & Spottiswoode).

383. Schadewald, Robert J. (2000). *The Plane Truth: A History of the Flat Earth Movement.* http://www.cantab.net/users/michael.behrend/ebooks/PlaneTruth/pages/Chapter_04.html, retrieved 12/30/17.

384. Mayo Clinic (2014). "EEG Definition," https://www.mayoclinic.org/tests-procedures/eeg/basics/definition/prc-20014093, retrieved 12/30/17.

385. "Most American Christians Do Not Believe that Satan or the Holy Spirit Exist," https://www.barna.com/research/most-american-christians-do-not-believe-that-satan-or-the-holy-spirit-exist/, retrieved 12/31/17.

386. Kurzweil, Raymond (2005). *The Singularity is Near: When Humans Transcend Biology.* (New York: Penguin Books), p. 7.

387. Honan, Daniel. "Ray Kurzweil: The Six Epochs of Technology Evolution," *Big Think.* http://bigthink.com/the-nantucket-project/ray-kurzweil-the-six-epochs-of-technology-evolution, retrieved 12/30/17.

388. Draper, Lucy (2015). "Could Artificial Intelligence Kill Us Off?" *Newsweek*, June 24, 2015. http://www.newsweek.com/artificial-intelligenceomega-pointai-603286, retrieved 12/30/17.

389. O'Connell, Gerard (2017). "Will Pope Francis Remove the Vatican's

'warning' from Teilhard de Chardin's Writings?" *America: The Jesuit Review*, November 21, 2017. https://www.americamagazine.org/faith/2017/11/21/will-pope-francis-remove-vaticans-warning-teilhard-de-chardins-writings, retrieved 12/30/17.

390. Steinhart, Eric (2008). "Teilhard de Chardin and Transhumanism," *Journal of Evolution and Technology*, Vol. 20, Issue 1, 1–22. http://jetpress.org/v20/steinhart.htm, retrieved 12/31/17.

391. Ibid.

392. For example, as I write this from my living room couch, there are six Internet-connected devices in view, three more in the next room, and seven more in our office on the other side of the wall.

393. "The Death of Gilgamesh: Translation." *The Electronic Text Corpus of Sumerian Literature*, http://etcsl.orinst.ox.ac.uk/section1/tr1813.htm, retrieved 12/31/17.

394. Marchesi, Gianni (2004). "Who Was Buried in the Royal Tombs of Ur? The Epigraphic and Textual Data," Orientalia, NOVA SERIES, Vol. 73, No. 2, p. 154.